Conversations About Visiting and Managing the National Parks

Crowdsourcing America's Best Idea

———————————————

Conversations About Visiting and Managing the National Parks

Crowdsourcing America's Best Idea

––––––––––––––––––

Robert E. Manning

University of Vermont, Burlington, Vermont, USA

Elizabeth E. Perry

Michigan State University, East Lansing, Michigan, USA

CABI

CABI is a trading name of CAB International

CABI	CABI
Nosworthy Way	200 Portland Street
Wallingford	Boston
Oxfordshire OX10 8DE	MA 02114
UK	USA
Tel: +44 (0)1491 832111	T: +1 (617)682-9015
E-mail: info@cabi.org	E-mail: cabi-nao@cabi.org
Website: www.cabi.org	

The views expressed in this publication are those of the author(s) and do not necessarily represent those of, and should not be attributed to, CAB International (CABI). Any images, figures and tables not otherwise attributed are the author(s)' own. References to internet websites (URLs) were accurate at the time of writing.

CAB International and, where different, the copyright owner shall not be liable for technical or other errors or omissions contained herein. The information is supplied without obligation and on the understanding that any person who acts upon it, or otherwise changes their position in reliance thereon, does so entirely at their own risk. Information supplied is neither intended nor implied to be a substitute for professional advice. The reader/user accepts all risks and responsibility for losses, damages, costs and other consequences resulting directly or indirectly from using this information.

CABI's Terms and Conditions, including its full disclaimer, may be found at https://www.cabidigitallibrary.org/terms-and-conditions.

A catalogue record for this book is available from the British Library, London, UK.

ISBN-13: 9781836993315 (paperback)
9781800626744 (hardback)
9781800626751 (ePDF)
9781800626768 (ePub)

DOI: 10.1079/9781800626768.0000

Commissioning Editor: Claire Parfitt
Editorial Assistant: Helen Elliott
Production Editor: James Bishop

Typeset by Exeter Premedia Services Pvt Ltd, Chennai, India
Printed in the USA

Contents

Acknowledgements

This book draws on the experiences of visitors to the national parks and related public opinion as expressed in a variety of crowdsourcing platforms. We incorporate short postings—both text and photographs—in the book from the following 17 crowdsourcing platforms: Reddit, Tripadvisor, Google Reviews, Wikimedia Commons, X, Facebook, Yelp, LinkedIn, YouTube, *National Parks Traveler*, *New York Times*, Amazon Reviews, Flickr, Instagram, AllTrails, Letterboxd, and Recreation.gov. We appreciate the ways in which these platforms contribute to public expression about the national parks, and the ways in which these postings allowed us to identify issues important to the public and to begin our series of 100 authentic "conversations" about the diversity of the National Park System, how to visit the national parks in ways that contribute to the enjoyment and appreciation of these places and that also protect the parks, and the range of issues associated with managing the national parks. We are especially grateful to the people who took the time to contribute the postings we have incorporated into the book. We are also grateful for the many students in the Department of Community Sustainability at Michigan State University who assisted in the search for crowdsourcing postings. Of particular note are Josh Doyle, an undergraduate research assistant in the Park Connections Lab, and the spring 2024 class of Sustaining Our National Parks and Recreation Lands. Thanks also to the staff at CABI Publishing, particularly Claire Parfitt, Commissioning Editor, Lucy Pritchard, Managing Editor, and Helen Elliott, Editorial Assistant, for all their help throughout the publication process.

Introduction to the Book

_____

Crowdsourcing the National Parks

This book is about the US national parks, with special emphasis on visiting and managing the parks. There are more than 400 diverse national parks in the US that help tell so many of the important stories of the nation's natural and cultural history. All of these parks are managed by the National Park Service (NPS), an agency of the federal government. Many of these parks are well known and heavily visited—parks such as Yellowstone, Yosemite, and Grand Canyon—while others are not widely known and sparsely visited. But all of these parks must be managed carefully to protect their natural and cultural integrity and to help visitors enjoy and appreciate them. It is also important that visitors are informed about these parks and associated management issues, so they can get the most out of their visits and help protect the parks in the process.

The book takes an innovative approach to all this by using a sample of crowdsourcing postings—comments and photographs by park visitors posted on more than a dozen crowdsourcing platforms (e.g. Yelp, Reddit, Facebook, LinkedIn) to start a series of "conversations" about the national parks. For example, visitors often post comments or photos about what they liked (and sometimes didn't like) about the parks they've visited and how they're managed. We then respond to these postings to complete the conversations in a substantive and informed manner. We've given each conversation a short descriptive title as listed in the Contents and organized the conversations in three broad categories: (i) the types and diversity of the national parks; (ii) how to successfully plan and conduct visits to the parks; and (iii) issues associated with national park management. We encourage you to read some or all of these conversations to develop a greater sense and appreciation of the national parks, how to get the most out of your park visits, and how to be an informed and responsible national park visitor.

National Parks

National parks are "America's best idea", author and conservationist Wallace Stegner famously wrote (Stegner, 1999, p. 137). He noted that America was the first nation to preserve large areas

© Robert Manning and Elizabeth Perry 2024. *Conversations About Visiting and Managing the National Parks* (R.E. Manning & E.E Perry)
DOI: 10.1079/9781800626768.intr

of its land for the benefit of all, not just a privileged elite; in this important way, national parks are a foundational expression of American democracy. Our national parks are also called "America's crown jewels" because they represent the very best of our natural and cultural history—the underlying geology, biology, and ecology that have shaped our remarkable landscapes, and the history, values, and issues that have helped define our society. It's no wonder our National Park System attracts hundreds of millions of visits each year, from our own citizenry and from around the world.

The first national park—Yellowstone—was established in 1872, but this was preceded by a nascent conservation movement. In 1832, ethnographer and painter George Catlin saw America's Great Plains and western frontier rapidly disappearing as a result of the nation's westward expansion and called for a "nation's Park" to protect the landscape that supported great herds of bison and the Indigenous peoples that depended on them (Catlin, 1876, p. 262). In a similar vein, writer and philosopher Henry David Thoreau "wished to speak a word for nature" in his 1862 essay, *Walking*, and later asked "Why should not ... we have our national preserves?" (Thoreau, 1862). Just 2 years later, President Abraham Lincoln signed legislation granting Yosemite Valley and the Mariposa Grove of giant sequoias to the State of California to be protected for the benefit of the nation, "inalienable for all time" (Senate Bill 203, 13 Statute 325, June 30, 1864, cited in National Park Service, 2024). Expounding on this idea, Frederick Law Olmstead, America's great 19th-century landscape architect and park pioneer, asserted that "establishment by government of great public grounds ... for the free enjoyment of the people" (Olmstead, 1865) is an essential responsibility of a democracy. John Muir, unofficial father of the national parks, rebelled against the rampant growth of materialism in 19th-century American society, writing that "Everybody needs beauty as well as bread, places to play in and pray in" (Muir, 1912).

World-famous Old Faithful Geyser erupts in Yellowstone National Park; this was the first national park in the US and the world and is a celebration of the democratic character of national parks.

In response to this social movement, Congress established Yellowstone National Park in 1872, more than two million acres in what would become the states of Wyoming, Montana, and

Idaho. Over the next several decades, thanks to conservationists such as Muir, President Theodore Roosevelt, and many others, more of the great western parks—Glacier, Yosemite, Mount Rainier, Rocky Mountain, and Sequoia—were established. These are celebrations of America's grandest and most sublime landscapes: tall mountains, ancient forests, expansive glaciers, wild rivers, lush valleys, and iconic wildlife. These were great swathes of wilderness that our ancestral European countries had lost long ago. These are the places that helped define our nation and many of the values to which we subscribe.

Many national parks were established to protect and appreciate the geology, biology, and ecology of our national landscape (Grand Canyon National Park).

Shortly after the turn of the 20th century, the country became more conscious of its remarkable prehistory and associated antiquities, especially Indigenous sites in the Southwest and elsewhere. To protect these areas from looting and vandalism, Congress passed the Antiquities Act in 1906, allowing presidents to create "national monuments" as a way to safeguard the archeological, scientific, and other features of these places. President Theodore Roosevelt swiftly set aside several national monuments, including the Grand Canyon and Mesa Verde; these and many other national monuments were eventually designated as national parks by Congress. American presidents continue to create national monuments, and many are eventually designated national parks by Congress.

Given the growing list of national parks and monuments, Congress created the National Park Service (NPS) in 1916 to manage these areas. Prior to this time, the US Cavalry kept order in the national parks, protecting them from unauthorized uses and related denigration. The Buffalo Soldiers, regiments of the Army staffed by African Americans, were instrumental in protecting the parks prior to establishment of the NPS. (Indigenous people who fought in the Indian Wars bestowed the name, "Buffalo Soldiers", possibly referring to the soldiers' characteristic curly black hair, the bison coats they wore in winter, or their fierce fighting ability; nevertheless, the term became a source of pride among the soldiers.) The 1916 Organic Act creating the NPS eloquently and presciently stated the mission of the agency: "to conserve the scenery and the natural and historic objects and the wildlife

The Antiquities Act of 1906 authorized the president to establish national monuments, many of which were eventually designated national parks by Congress. Acadia National Park was originally established as Sieur de Monts National Monument in 1916, but was designated Acadia National Park in 1929.

therein and to provide for the enjoyment of the same in such manner and by such means as will leave them unimpaired for the enjoyment of future generations" (United States Government, 2019, p. 1). Striking a balance between conservation of these areas and their use for recreation is a foundational issue that the NPS has wrestled with ever since, and this conundrum has become more urgent as the National Park System now accommodates more than 300 million visits/year. (See Conversations 3, 73, and 74 for more about this vital issue.)

The first director of the NPS was Stephen Mather, an entrepreneur who worked with the railroad and automobile industries to promote access to the parks as a way to build a constituency for them. During the Great Depression, President Franklin Roosevelt orchestrated creation of the Civilian Conservation Corps to engage unemployed men in great public works projects, a large number of them in the national parks. Many of the resulting artfully designed and crafted facilities—roads, trails, picnic shelters, and campgrounds—are still in use.

In 1933, President Franklin Roosevelt transferred the War Department's historic military sites to the National Park System, places such as the Civil War battlefield at Gettysburg, along with monuments in Washington, DC, such as the Thomas Jefferson Memorial, substantially enlarging the National Park System and adding a strong historical and cultural component. As a part of Roosevelt's New Deal program, the NPS conducted comprehensive nationwide surveys of scenic road corridors and coastlines, recommending that the most prominent among them be incorporated into the National Park System, further expanding the collection of national parks; Blue Ridge Parkway and Cape Hatteras National Seashore are early examples.

In 1947, the National Park System was further extended by the addition of Everglades National Park. While most of the early national parks were established for their remarkable scenery, Everglades was designated primarily for its ecological significance. Given the wetland character of much of

This monument at the Gettysburg National Military Park honors the fallen soldiers who rest here.

An alligator protects its nest in Everglades National Park. This was the first park established (in 1947) explicitly to protect its ecological values.

the park, it was not widely considered as inherently beautiful as other parks, but it featured a rare and remarkably complex and productive ecosystem that warranted protection, and environmental protection of the national parks became a more important priority for the NPS.

After World War II, the National Park System began to expand more rapidly. Dramatic growth in US population, economic well-being, leisure time, and transportation led to steep increases in visits to the national parks that threatened to overwhelm park facilities and services, and the National Park System expanded and improved its visitor-based infrastructure accordingly. In 1956 the NPS received funding from Congress to institute its Mission 66 program, a 10-year effort (1956–1966) to expand and upgrade visitor facilities and services throughout the national parks. The program was designed to help commemorate the 50th anniversary of the establishment of the NPS (in 1916), and many of these improvements are still enjoyed by park visitors today.

Recent decades have seen the National Park System continue to expand in size and diversity. The Environmental Movement of the 1960s stimulated establishment of more national parks based on their scenic landscapes, ecological significance, and opportunities for outdoor recreation. As cities became larger and more crowded, resulting societal issues such as lack of open space and recreation opportunities led to more units of the National Park System established in and around urban areas; prominent examples include Gateway National Recreation Area in New York City and New Jersey and Golden Gate National Recreation Area in the San Francisco Bay area, both established in 1972. The Civil Rights Movement of the 1960s also resulted in a substantial expansion of the National Park System to commemorate related sites and explore these and associated issues: examples included Brown v. Board of Education National Historical Park, Freedom Riders National Monument, Tuskegee Airmen National Historical Park, Cesar E. Chavez National Monument, and Women's Rights National Historical Park.

Golden Gate National Recreation Area protects more than 80,000 acres of land, historic sites, and recreation opportunities in the San Francisco Bay area. This urban national park is the most heavily visited area in the National Park System.

Women's Rights National Historical Park commemorates the First Women's Rights Convention in 1848; the Declaration of Sentiments was signed by convention participants.

The largest expansion of the National Park System occurred in 1980 when the longstanding national debate over the status of the vast public lands in Alaska was finally settled. Congress passed the Alaska National Interest Lands Conservation Act that year, transferring 47 million acres of public land in Alaska into the National Park System, more than doubling its size. Some of the new and previously created national parks received the title "National Park and Preserve", the word "Preserve" formally acknowledging the subsistence rights of Alaskan Natives to hunt, fish, and gather in these parks as vital elements of their traditional way of life.

Since then, the National Park System has continued to expand and evolve, and more than 400 national parks can now be found—in all 50 states and even some US territories. (When this book went to press, there were 431 national parks in the National Park System, but more continue to be added.) Expansion of the system is sure to continue as the national parks are a reflection of our evolving natural and human history as well as the changing values of American society. For example, many national parks celebrate the history and accomplishments of traditionally underrepresented racial and ethnic groups, provide for the inclusion of more diverse ecosystems and historical periods, and help address the need for more open space and recreation opportunities throughout the nation. Still more parks address the value of science in the National Park System, the role of national parks in public education, the provision of vital ecological services in the parks (such as clean air and water and carbon sequestration), and partnerships with local communities.

Expansion of the National Park System has led to a great diversity of parks that have been given a wide variety of names or titles. "National parks", "national monuments", "national historic sites", "national historical parks", "national seashores", "national lakeshores", "national recreation areas" are just some of the many types of units of the National Park System, and this can be confusing to the public. For the purposes of this book, we simplify this complexity by referring to all of the more than 400 units of the National Park System as "national parks" (see more about this in Conversation 1).

The Alaska National Interest Lands Conservation Act of 1980 more than doubled the size of the National Park System; Denali National Park and Preserve includes the highest peak in North America and the surrounding six million acres of wilderness.

Many national parks celebrate the history of the US; this photo shows the Assembly Room of Independence Hall (part of Independence National Historical Park) where the Continental Congress declared independence in 1776 and the US Constitution was debated and signed in 1787.

Crowdsourcing

Crowdsourcing is generally defined as information voluntarily derived from a large group of dispersed individuals. Initial forms of crowdsourcing can be traced back hundreds of years, but contemporary forms involve the Internet and digital platforms, and have proliferated exponentially over the past two decades. The term "crowdsourcing" was coined in 2006 by Jeff Howe in *Wired* and is derived from a combination of the words "crowd" and "outsourcing", meaning that collection of desired data/information is outsourced (transferred to others) to the crowd (members of the public). There are many crowdsourcing platforms, some of them especially well known and widely used, including Yelp, Google Reviews, Angie's, Tripadvisor, X (formerly Twitter), Facebook, TikTok, LinkedIn, Flickr, Google Reviews, and Wikimedia Commons. Some contemporary crowdsourcing platforms are business oriented, focusing on reviews of restaurants, hotels, and other enterprises. But many are designed for discussion of social and political issues and have public policy implications, sometimes helping to inform governmental decision making. In this latter application, crowdsourcing can contribute to democracy by inviting and facilitating public involvement and helping to put power into the hands of citizens (or "netizens" in this case). Crowdsourcing is sometimes thought of as a form of citizen science, constituting a type of creative consciousness, and representing an expression of monitorial citizenship.

Park planning, management, and research have begun to use information derived from various forms of crowdsourcing due to its relatively low cost compared to direct observations of park visitors and field-based surveys. Many of these uses of crowdsourcing information/data have recently been reported in the scientific and professional literature. For example, an increasingly common approach has been to use geo-referenced photographs taken by park visitors and posted to crowdsourcing platforms such as Flickr and Wikimedia Commons. These geo-referenced photos provide useful information on the number of visits to parks and their spatial and temporal distribution. An extension of these studies has used such data to estimate the preferences of visitors for various types of landscapes and other park features and the public health and social benefits derived from park visits. However, use of text-based crowdsourcing postings is less common.

We use crowdsourcing in this book to access information from and about national park visits and visitors; examples of such information include what visitors liked most and least about their park visits, questions they ask about national park-related issues, and their thoughts about national parks and how they should be managed. We use mostly text-based postings, but also use photos as appropriate. We then respond to these comments by offering: (i) information about the national parks; (ii) how the quality of visits can be enhanced through better information; (iii) how and when to best plan a national park visit; (iv) how and why the national parks are managed as they are; and (v) how a better understanding of all this can contribute to the enjoyment of park visits and ultimately lead to a greater appreciation of the national parks and public support for their protection.

Conversations

As noted above, this book primarily comprises a series of "conversations" about the national parks, including visiting and managing them. These conversations are started by visitors to the parks through their crowdsourcing postings and are completed by our informed and considered responses. These conversations are "authentic" in that they use crowdsourcing postings to draw directly on the experiences of visitors to these parks—aspects of their visits they particularly enjoyed or found displeasing, things they didn't expect or understand, questions they had about the parks, and issues they wished they'd understood beforehand. Our responses to these postings are also as "authentic" and authoritative as possible; they're based on our careers as university professors who teach the history, philosophy, and management of national parks and related areas, and conduct long-term programs of research for the NPS and associated agencies. We also have extensive personal and professional experience in the parks, visiting them often, having prior careers in the NPS, and even living in some parks for a year at a time while on sabbatical leave and working with NPS staff.

While we draw on our academic and research backgrounds, we're careful to ensure that our responses are as readable as possible. We take a conversational tone, avoid technical language (or explain the meaning of technical terms when needed), and keep our responses short and as plain-spoken as possible; "snappy" is our goal. These conversations remind us of the "teachable moments" we enjoy so much in our classes, when students make comments or ask questions and we have the opportunity to respond in respectful and informed ways. We think this represents an interactive form of education at its best—for both students (and in this case, the public as well) and us.

With the help of several of our student researchers (acknowledged at the beginning of the book), we've combed through thousands of postings about the national parks on nearly 20 crowd-sourcing platforms. Many of these postings didn't surprise us, but some certainly did (as do some of the comments and questions we get in class!). Formulating responses to some postings was pretty straightforward, but others required research and deliberation on our part. We've been appropriately respectful in responding to all these postings, just as we strive to do with our students, and we always maintain the anonymity of those who make these posts.

The diversity of topics raised in the postings we examined was even more pronounced than we expected. To bring order to this, we've categorized the conversations into three groups as referenced in the Contents: (i) Part 1: The National Parks (sample issues include urban national parks, wilderness in the national parks, national parks as models of sustainability); (ii) Part 2: Visiting the National Parks (sample issues include visitor safety in the national parks, public transit in the national parks, national park museums); and (iii) Part 3: Managing the National Parks (sample issues include entrance fees and passes in the national parks, wildfires in the national parks, and how to become a friend of the national parks). In the Contents, we've given each of the conversations a number and a short descriptive title (sort of like "Frequently Asked Questions" on many Internet sites) to lead readers to those that are of most interest. We have done a lot of cross-referencing in the conversations; for example, in the conversation in Part 1 on the growing number of visits to the national parks (Conversation 3), we've noted the number of the conversation in Part 2 on how to avoid crowding in the parks (Conversation 55).

Park Visitors, Managers, and Students

We've prepared this book for three audiences. The first is visitors to the national parks, from prospective to experienced. It's vital that visitors prepare themselves for their time in the national parks, as this will result in more informed and enjoyable experiences in our remarkable National Park System and help protect the parks as well. The second audience is park managers. Our experiences working with NPS staff suggest that managers are hungry for information on, about, and from park visitors—their primary clientele—and this book offers interesting and helpful insights into this large and diverse group. The third audience is students of the national parks and related areas. More college students are finding that careers with the NPS, and other park and outdoor recreation-related agencies and organizations, can be especially rewarding. This book is intended to help inform students about issues associated with the national parks and related areas, and by doing this in a more authentic and engaging format than conventional textbooks.

But most of all, we've prepared the book to enhance public enjoyment, appreciation, and support of the national parks and the challenging management issues they face. A wise observer of the national parks, Freeman Tilden, noted that appreciation of the parks ultimately leads to their protection (Tilden, 2008, p. 38).

How the Book is Organized

The book is organized into four parts, the first of which is the Introduction that you are currently reading. This includes a discussion of the history of the US National Park System and its present form. This is followed by an introduction to the contemporary concept and practice of "crowdsourcing" and how we've used crowdsourcing postings to prepare a series of conversations about the national parks, and the intended audiences for whom the book was written.

The heart of the book is a series of 100 "conversations" about the national parks as described above. These conversations are organized into the three primary parts of the book. Part 1 addresses the national parks themselves, including their diverse titles, topics, and themes, and a variety of related information. Readers should gain a better understanding and appreciation of the large and diverse National Park System. Part 2 addresses visiting the national parks, including how to plan visits to the parks, the variety of activities that can be pursued, what and how visitors can learn in the parks, logistical considerations, and a number of tips for planning park visits and getting the most out of them. We hope this will help visitors develop a greater appreciation of the parks and lead to protection of the parks in the process. Part 3 addresses managing the national parks and introduces a variety of management issues facing the NPS and the nation as a whole. This part concludes with some thoughts about how readers and visitors can help protect the parks by becoming friends and stewards of the national parks.

References

Catlin, G. (1876) *Illustrations of the Manners, Customs, and Conditions of the North American Indians. With letters and notes, written during eight years of travel and adventure among the wildest and most remarkable tribes now existing.* Volume I. Chatto & Windus, London. Available at: https://www.gutenberg.org/cache/epub/68768/pg68768-images.html (accessed July 18 2024).

Howe, J. (2006) The rise of crowdsourcing. *Wired*, June 1. Available at: https://www.wired.com/2006/06/crowds/ (accessed July 18 2024).

Muir, J. (1912) *The Yosemite*. The Century Company: New York. Available at: https://vault.sierraclub.org/john_muir_exhibit/writings/the_yosemite/ (accessed July 16 2024).

National Park Service (2024) *America's National Park System: the Critical Documents*. Available at: https://www.nps.gov/parkhistory/online_books/anps/anps_1a.htm (accessed July 17 2024).

Olmstead, F.L. (1865) The Yosemite Valley and the Mariposa Big Tree Grove: Olmstead report on management of Yosemite. As reprinted in *Landscape Architecture* 43, 1952, 12–25. Available at: https://www.nps.gov/parkhistory/online_books/anps/anps_1b.htm (accessed July 16 2024).

Stegner, W. (1999) The best idea we ever had. In: *Marking the Sparrow's Fall: the Making of the American West*. Henry Holt and Company, New York, p. 137.

Thoreau, H.D. (1862) Walking. *The Atlantic*, June 1862. Available at: https://www.theatlantic.com/magazine/archive/1862/06/walking/304674/ (accessed July 17 2024).

Tilden, F. (2008) *Interpreting our Heritage*, 4th edn. University of North Carolina Press, Chapel Hill, North Carolina.

United States Government (2019) *National Park Service Organic Act*. An Act to establish a National Park Service, and for other purposes. Public Law (United States) 64–235, H.R. 15522, 39 Statute 535, enacted August 25, 1916. Available at: https://www.govinfo.gov/content/pkg/COMPS-1725/pdf/COMPS-1725.pdf (accessed July 18 2024).

Part 1: The National Parks

Introduction

1 Names and Titles of the National Parks

Post

Loui responded to an article about National Park Service (NPS) terminology on the *National Parks Traveler* website, noting the confusion in naming. Particularly, *Loui*'s post referenced the Baltimore-Washington Parkway, a 29-mile national park and highway connecting the capital area.

> *I'm just an average, literate American. This is a perfect example of ... inward focused bureaucracy ... I'm sure the BW Pkwy is probably administered by some overarching official unit, but that's government speak. I'm just reading the words on the page. And our government should speak to We the People in plain language. I am only making this observation to highlight how worthless these designations really are.*

Response

"What's in a name?" Shakespeare famously asked this enduring question in his iconic play, *Romeo and Juliet* (Shakespeare, 1974). Juliet spoke this line, complaining that she was not allowed to associate with Romeo because his family name was Montague (and hers was not). She continues, "That which we call a rose by any other name would smell just as sweet", suggesting that names can be meaningless (and, paradoxically, also meaningful).

Loui taps into that same vein of contemplation in his/her post, considering the myriad titles of national parks. The names and titles of national parks is a complex topic that can cause confusion—even heartburn—among members of the public (and even among the professionals who study and manage these places). But there can be no argument (well, not much) that there are currently more than 400 "units" of the National Park System, distinct geographic areas that federal law has proclaimed to be important manifestations of the nation's natural and cultural history and that are managed by the NPS. But be aware that this number continues to inch upward as our collective conscience adopts more expansive notions of what constitutes this common heritage (see Conversation 23). (There have even been places that have been deleted from the National Park System, but this is rare.) Together, these places comprise more than 85 million acres and are scattered across all 50 states and four US territories (Puerto Rico, US Virgin Islands, American Samoa, and Guam).

In the process, these places have been given a great variety of titles: national parks, national monuments, national preserves, national historic sites, national recreation areas, and, yes, national parkways too, etc. Only Congress can establish "national parks" (though, like all federal legislation, the president must sign these acts of Congress), but the president can establish "national monuments" under the provisions of the 1906 Antiquities Act (see Conversation 5). The following titles are the most common, and the number of parks included in each title is shown in parentheses.

- *National parks* (63) tend to be large, mostly natural places having a wide range of attributes (e.g. mountains, rivers, deserts, wildlife), generally remaining in their natural condition, and where consumptive activities such as timbering and mining are generally prohibited. A few national parks were established primarily for their cultural resources; examples include Mesa Verde National Park, Gateway Arch National Park, and Hot Springs National Park, and these tend to be smaller than most national parks. The names of many of the national parks are familiar to most people and include Yellowstone National Park, Yosemite National Park, Grand Canyon

© Robert Manning and Elizabeth Perry 2024. *Conversations About Visiting and Managing the National Parks* (R.E. Manning and E.E Perry)
DOI: 10.1079/9781800626768.0001

National Park, and Great Smoky Mountains National Park.

- *National monuments* (85) also tend to be large areas of natural, historic, and scientific interest (though often smaller than national parks and sometimes featuring less diversity). As noted above, many have been established by the president under the 1906 Antiquities Act; this allows for speedy designation (compared to what can be a lengthy Congressional legislative process to establish a national park) when such areas are threatened. In many cases, national monuments have been established and then ultimately designated as national parks by Congress; Grand Canyon National Park is an early example.

- *National historic sites* (75) are usually relatively small sites that have important historical and cultural meaning. Many were established by the Secretary of the Interior under the provisions of the Historic Sites Act of 1935, but most have been authorized by Congress. (There is one international historic site: Saint Croix Island International Historic Site located in the US and Canada.)

- *National historical parks* (63) are typically larger than national historic sites and include more than one property or building and may include some surrounding open space.

- *National memorials* (31) commemorate a historic person or episode and are generally small.

- *National battlefields* (11) preserve important battlefield and military sites; other associated titles include national battlefield parks (4), national military parks (9), and national battlefield sites (1).

- *National recreation areas* (18) have been established as important opportunities for outdoor recreation; some are in association with large reservoirs around the nation and others are in or proximate to large urban areas.

- *National seashores* (10) are located on the Atlantic, Pacific, and Gulf coasts and are designed to protect these fragile environments and offer recreation opportunities.

- *National lakeshores* (4) are similar to national seashores and are located on the Great Lakes.

- *National parkways* (4) are scenic roadways and surrounding park lands, as *Loui* shares as a naming example.

- *National scenic trails* (11) and National Historic Trails are trails that have been authorized under the provisions of the National Trails System Act of 1968.

- *National rivers* (4) and *national wild and scenic rivers* (10) preserve free-flowing streams that have been designated by Congress under the provisions of the Wild and Scenic Rivers Act of 1968.

- *National preserves* (19) are similar to national parks but have been permitted by Congress to offer public hunting, trapping, and oil/gas exploration and extraction.

- *Other designations* (11) carry site-specific names/titles and are located in the Washington, DC, region. Examples include The White House and President's Park, National Mall and Memorial Parks, Prince William Forest Park, and Wolf Trap National Park for the Performing Arts.

There are many other "related areas" that have a strong connection to the National Park System and that are managed in whole or in part by the NPS, or for which the NPS provides technical or financial assistance. These include affiliated areas (27) authorized areas (7), co-managed areas (1), commemorative sites (3), national heritage areas (62) (see Conversation 30 for more about these areas), units of the National Trails System (32), and units of the National Wild and Scenic Rivers System (50).

These designations offer a general sense of the types of resources and attractions that visitors can expect to find in each national park, as well as the management policies that are likely to apply. However, there are many inconsistencies and vagaries in this "system". For example, Dinosaur National Monument is big (210,000 acres) and diverse, including its world-famous fossil quarry, the confluence of the Green and Yampa Rivers, and more than 1000 species of plants and wildlife, while Gateway Arch National Park is small (90 acres) and features the Gateway Arch constructed in the 1960s to celebrate the history of the westward march of the American frontier. To add to this confusion, some types of parks are also managed by other federal agencies; for example, many national monuments are managed by the US Forest Service and the Bureau of Land Management.

However, these distinctions are not absolute and many units include more than one type of resource and attractions. In fact, it may be more accurate to recognize that many—perhaps most—units of the National Park System include both natural and cultural resources and may be most accurately recognized as "cultural landscapes" that protect the integrity of much of the nation's natural and cultural heritage and offer visitors rewarding opportunities to learn about and enjoy these places (see Conversations 10, 11, and 30).

Other complications about the names of national parks include the fact that some units have been retitled over the years (e.g. changed from national monuments to national parks), and some units are comprised of multiple locations (e.g. Klondike Gold Rush National Historical Park is comprised of two units, one in Alaska and one in the state of Washington).

The complex and sometimes inconsistent titling of units of the National Park System has caused some confusion among the public and scorn among national park professionals. *Loui's* response highlights this frustration with government structure not always matching public use. To some, the status of "national park" designation bestowed upon just some (currently 63) units has resulted in elevating them over the rest of the deserving units of the National Park System. One observer caustically suggests that we have created a national park "caste system" rather than a National Park System, that these many titles are "distinctions without difference", that this confusing jargon amounts to "a towering tower of bureaucratic babble", and that this terminology is "oversubtle and underinformative" (Harmon, 2012). Of

course, this is made even more complicated by: (i) the other types of public lands in the US (see Conversation 4 for more about this); and (ii) other often overlapping categories of parks and protected areas such as national heritage areas and World Heritage Sites. (See Conversations 30 and 31, respectively, for more about these two types of areas.) There may be some potentially harmful management implications of all this as well, as the bulk of park funding, personnel, and public attention are traditionally allocated to the 63 "national parks" that are often referred to as the "crown jewels" of the National Park System and are found mostly in the West.

An answer to this problem may be to rename all units of the National Park System "national parks". The National Parks Second Century Commission, formed to help celebrate the centennial of the NPS in 2016 and chart a course for the future, generally agreed with this sentiment, concluding that the titling of units of the National Park System should be greatly simplified (the commission recommended five basic categories). A more uniform system of titles would lessen the potential problem of a perceived hierarchy of park units and, therefore, might more effectively use the national park "brand" to more evenly distribute visitation throughout the National Park System.

Despite these problems with nomenclature, we can celebrate the grand diversity of the National Park System. All of the more than 400 units of the National Park System are important to the nation's natural and cultural history and are rewarding places to visit, enjoy, and appreciate. Understanding the basics of the naming system will allow you to recognize these places by their titles and craft a plan to visit those of greatest interest to you. For the sake of simplicity, we call all units of the National Park System "national parks" in this book (Latson, 2022; Shakespeare, 1974).

References

Congressional Research Service (2013) *National Park System: What Do the Different Park Titles Signify?* Available at: http://npshistory.com/publications/r41816.pdf (accessed 28 June 2024).

Harmon, D. (2012) Beyond the 59th park: Reforming the nomenclature of the US National park system. *The George Wright Forum* 29(2), 188–196.

Latson, R. (2022) What's with all these different park units, anyway? *National Parks Traveler,* August 4. Available at: https://www.nationalparkstraveler.org/2022/08/whats-all-these-different-park-units-an yway (accessed 28 June 2024).

Lower, R. and Watson, R. (2023) How Many National Parks are There? National Park Foundation. Available at: https://www.nationalparks.org/connect/blog/how-many-national-parks-are-there (accessed 28 June 2024).

National Park Service (2015) Designations of National Park System Units. Available at: https://www.nps. gov/goga/planyourvisit/designations.htm (accessed 28 June 2024).

National Park Service (2016) The National Parks: Index 2012-2016. National Park Service, Washington, DC. Available at: https://www.nps.gov/aboutus/upload/npindex2012-2016.pdf (accessed 18 July 2024).

National Park Service (2017) What's In a Name? Discover National Park System Designations. Available at: https://www.nps.gov/articles/nps-designations.htm (accessed 28 June 2024).

Shakespeare, W. (1974) *Romeo and Juliet.* In: Blakemore Evans, G. (ed.) *The Riverside Shakespeare*, Vol. 2. Houghton Mifflin, Boston, Massachusetts, pp. 1307–1342.

2 Geographic Diversity of the National Parks

Post

On the popular Reddit thread r/nationalparks, *SmokedMango*—an Australian planning a trip to the US—inquired about what a "top five" list of US national parks might entail. Many chimed in with favorites, but user *rsnorunt* centered discussion on the landscape diversity throughout the US National Park System to better hone a vacation selection:

> *We've got a huge number of amazing and diverse parks over here, and almost any of them will be worth the trip. The main thing to ask yourself is what sorts of scenery you want to see, and what sorts of activities you want to do. You're coming from Australia, so would you be wanting things that are very different from home? Or are you interested in comparing and contrasting e.g. American deserts to Australian ones? ... International tourists usually flock to the more famous parks: Yellowstone, Grand Teton, Yosemite, Zion, Arches, Grand Canyon, Death Valley. Those are all famous for a reason, but there are lots of others too.*

Response

The National Park System is big and diverse (and certainly "amazing" too, *rsnorunt*!); it includes more than 400 national parks that represent much of the natural and cultural history of the nation. Also, by definition, it's widely dispersed across the American landscape. There's at least one national park in every state, Washington, DC, and four US territories (American Samoa, Guam, Puerto Rico, and US Virgin Islands). California has the most national parks (28), but three states have more than 20 (Alaska, Arizona, and New York) and most states have more than one. This can certainly make the decision about which national parks to visit difficult, as *SmokedMango* is aware, and the need to consider the geographic breadth imperative.

The size of the national parks varies just as widely. The National Park System totals just over 85 million acres, or an area a little smaller than the State of Montana. Although this is a big area, it accounts for only about 3.6% of the US. The largest national park is Wrangell-St. Elias National Park and Preserve in Alaska; it's 13.2 million acres (about the combined size of the states of Vermont, New Hampshire, and Rhode Island). The smallest national park, Thaddeus Kosciuszko National Memorial (celebrating the life of this international champion of human rights), is only 0.02 acres.

The number of recreation visits to the national parks also varies dramatically. The most visited park is Blue Ridge Parkway at 16.8 million visits in 2023. The only other national parks to accommodate more than ten million annual visits are Golden Gate National Recreation Area (15 million) and Great Smoky Mountains National Park (13.3 million). It's no coincidence that all three are found near large urban areas. The least visited national park is Aniakchak National Monument and Preserve in Alaska, with only 199 visits in 2023, and this is strongly related to its location far from population centers.

The National Park System includes the highest point in the US (20,350 ft Denali, located in Denali National Park and Preserve) and the lowest point in the US (Badwater Basin in Death Valley National Park is 282 ft below sea level). Crater Lake in Crater Lake National Park is the deepest lake in the US at 1949 ft, Great Sand Dunes National Park includes the highest sand dunes in the US, and Mammoth Cave in its namesake national park is the largest cave in the world. The National Park System is highly diverse, indeed, and is a land of superlatives. It lends itself nicely to a great game of geographic trivia, though it complicates trip planning!

© Robert Manning and Elizabeth Perry 2024. *Conversations About Visiting and Managing the National Parks* (R.E. Manning and E.E Perry)
DOI: 10.1079/9781800626768.0002

References

National Park Service (2024) About Us: National Park System. Available at: https://www.nps.gov/aboutu s/national-park-system.htm (accessed 1 July 2024).

Wikipedia (2024) List of the United States National Park System official units. Available at: https://en.w ikipedia.org/wiki/List_of_the_United_States_National_Park_System_official_units (accessed 1 July 2024).

3 Visits to the National Parks

Post

The NPS estimated the number of visits to Gateway Arch National Park (which has no entrance gates) based on the number of visitors that entered the park's visitor center. But it recently updated this method to include cell-phone location data of visitors in the park. Based on this new approach, it was found that visitation to the park was chronically underestimated. *The Gateway Arch Park Foundation* (the non-profit "friends group" of the park; see Conversation 97) shared this posting on LinkedIn:

> *A new visitor counting methodology from the NPS points to much higher visitation at Gateway Arch National Park! Using location-based mobile device data to track visitors' movement throughout the park, it's estimated that for every person who enters the Gateway Arch Visitor Center, there are an additional 1.1 visitors in the park that did not enter the visitor center.*

This led to enthusiastic responses about the higher numbers, such as *Ruth* responding with hashtags of #StLouisRising, #touristinmyownhometown, and #explorestlouis.

Response

How many annual visits are there to the national parks? That's a familiar question, but the answer is a little more complicated than it might seem. First, what is a "visit"? According to the NPS, a visit is defined as "the entry of any person ... onto to lands or waters administered by the NPS". But not all people entering the park are there for recreation: some are NPS employees, some deliver supplies like food and fuel, some are scientists conducting research, some are students on field trips, some work for the private businesses that run the commercial facilities and services in the parks (e.g. hotels,

restaurants, gift shops), some people commute through parks (Blue Ridge Parkway is an example), and so forth. These ancillary entries are classified as "non-recreation visits" or "non-reportable visits" and are typically excluded from data on "visits". When the NPS reports visitor use statistics, it almost always refers to *recreation* visits: the entry of a person into a park for recreation (or more specifically, for purposes for which the park has been established; in a paradoxical sense, people attending a funeral at Andersonville National Cemetery—a unit of the National Park System—are included in the count of recreation visits). If a person enters a park, leaves it, and re-enters the same day, only one visit is counted, but if a person enters a park, leaves it, and enters another park that same day, that's counted as two recreation visits.

But how does the NPS count these visits (really estimates)? It would be pretty simple if there were only one or maybe even just a few entrances to each park and if these entrances were always staffed. But neither of these "if statements" is true. In fact, the National Park System is exceptionally more diverse than this. Many national parks have what the NPS calls "porous" borders: (i) roads wander in and out of the park; (ii) many parks include vast areas of backcountry/wilderness where visitors can walk in; (iii) parks might border large bodies of water where visitors arrive by boat; and (iv) parks in urban areas are generally accessible to pedestrians, etc. The postings about Gateway Arch National Park at the beginning of this conversation certainly exemplify these porous entry points and how updated counting technologies might be more sensitive to counting such visitation. Moreover, the NPS doesn't have the personnel to staff entrance stations all the time. In these instances (and most parks fall into this category), the NPS uses "proxy" counts or what is sometimes called "double sampling". This approach is to conduct detailed counts of visits (sometimes including a

© Robert Manning and Elizabeth Perry 2024. *Conversations About Visiting and Managing the National Parks* (R.E. Manning and E.E Perry)
DOI: 10.1079/9781800626768.0003

visitor survey) for a short period of time while at the same time counting something that's more easily measured and that's correlated with visits. An example of the latter is the number of motor vehicles entering a park as recorded by automated traffic counters like the ones used in transportation management. (The NPS uses inductive-loop traffic detectors, magnetometer-style traffic counters, and pneumatic-tube traffic counters on roads, and infrared-beam counters on trails; the agency uses nearly 1000 traffic counters.) If there's a strong statistical relationship between the two measures (the actual counts of visits and the proxy), then visits can be estimated from the proxy. If visitor counts are extended to key sites in the park (in addition to the entrance station), then the number of visits to these sites can be estimated too.

Infrared trail counters are used in backcountry contexts. However, these counters aren't foolproof, especially given the unusual conditions encountered in many parks. For example, it can be challenging to power and maintain counters in remote locations; visitors sometimes spot, tinker with, and even take counters; and bears and other wildlife—and even falling leaves—can sometimes "trip" counters. Location data from cellphones (ever give permission for a weather app to know your location?) and vehicle GPS (Global Positioning System) trackers are now routinely purchased and examined as part of the "visitation" question, though of course these measures don't catch everyone either. Other eccentricities of estimating the number of visits include the need for "multipliers" for the number of people entering in cars and other vehicles (buses, boats, airplanes, motorcycles, snowmobiles, cruise ships, etc.) and changes in visitation patterns by season.

The NPS makes a valiant attempt to measure visitor use but notes that "estimating visitor use is a complex and difficult task", that resulting data are "coarse", and that "everything we do is an estimate" (NPS Stats, 2024). As the Gateway Arch example in this post demonstrates, location data are part of the conversation because they can capture "visits" beyond those that are actively seen by park staff or registered at particular park locations via vehicle and trail counters. But, it is not entirely accepted yet as a routine means to gather visitation data, as such

a "big brother" approach to counts across parks, and in wilderness management in particular, raises challenging issues of privacy.

Now to some of the data … (Note: we use data from calendar year 2022, the most recent complete year for which data were available when preparing this book.) First, let's consider the number of (recreation) visits to the National Park System over the years. The first year that data were collected was 1904, and there were a total of 120,690 visits to the National Park System. By 2022, that number had grown to an impressive 311,985,998 (keep in mind, however, that there are many more national parks now than in 1904). (A footnote: if you add the number of visits for each year from 1904 to 2022, it totals a staggering 15,703,311,966!)

Now let's begin to dig into these data by national park. Three parks recorded the number of visits in the eight digits: (i) Blue Ridge Parkway (15,711,004); (ii) Golden Gate National Recreation Area (15,638,911); and (iii) Great Smoky Mountain National Park (12,937,633). The important characteristic that's shared by these parks is their accessibility to population centers. But 75 parks estimate their number of annual visits in the millions. The least-visited national park is Aniakchak National Monument and Preserve, with a few hundred per year.

Another potentially useful way to look at these data is to add in the size of the parks, because this varies dramatically. Wrangell-St. Elias National Park and Preserve is the largest at 13.2 million acres, while Thaddeus Kosciuszko National Memorial is 0.02 acres. Dividing the number of visits by the size of the park provides a rough (very rough) sense of how "densely" they are visited and how crowded they might be. Not surprisingly, most of the parks with the lowest visitor densities are in Alaska; Gates of the Arctic National Park and Preserve hardly registers with a density coefficient of 0.001; that is, there are only 0.001 visitors/acre over the course of a year. (This may be because not only are there no roads *in* the park, there are no roads *to* the park!) But there are other national parks in the "lower 48" with density coefficients of less than 1: prominent examples include Isle Royale, North Cascades, Death Valley, Big Bend, and Everglades. If you're looking for some solitude, these parks might be good choices. Some of the better known parks such as Bryce Canyon, Acadia, Zion, Great Smoky Mountains, Arches, and Rocky Mountain have double-digit densities and you'll have to work harder to find some moments of solitude. However, if you are local to a national park like *Ruth* is, perhaps larger numbers are exciting signals of more people caring for a place you care about too!

The density-of-use statistic is useful for comparing visits across parks, but it must be interpreted properly; it is based on annual visits and doesn't represent a daily use level. In other words, a visitor would encounter only a small proportion of annual use in any single day. Moreover, it inherently spreads visits over a whole park when the reality is that visits are typically concentrated in a relatively small portion of a park. This is a very important point as national parks are typically managed in a way that concentrates visits on roads and developed facilities and services, leaving the vast majority of the parks for lighter, dispersed use. It also doesn't factor in seasonality: although nearly all national parks are open year-round, most accommodate the majority of their use during selected seasons of the year. See Conversation 55 on how to avoid the crowds when visiting a national park.

References

National Park Service (2024) About Us: Visitation Numbers. Available at: https://www.nps.gov/aboutus/visitation-numbers.htm (accessed 1 July 2024).

NPS Stats (2024) Visitor Use Statistics. National Park Service. Available at: https://irma.nps.gov/Stats/ (accessed 1 July 2024).

4 National Parks and Other Public Lands

Post

Sharing a post on LinkedIn about land designations, *Susan* noted the diversity of US public lands and activities allowed on each:

> *Public lands are not all the same … Understanding the mission and intention of the entity gives a great head start on navigating the differences for public access. Game lands or wildlife management areas are a quick example – wildlife-associated activities, including hunting, are very likely to have priority. In a national park hunting is rarely an option and other uses have priority … At the end of the day, there's a public land to suit everyone! Go find yours! #publiclands #recreation #recreateresponsibly #parks #forests.*

Response

The national parks are often referred to as "America's crown jewels", and with parks like Yellowstone, Yosemite, and Grand Canyon, along with historical sites such as Statue of Liberty, Independence Hall, and Gettysburg, it is hard to argue this point. But as described in Conversation 2, the National Park System is large and diverse and all of the more than 400 national parks are important manifestations of American history and natural history, are worthy of protection, and make fine places to visit. The National Park System totals more than 85 million acres, but this is only a fraction of all public land in the US—lands owned and managed by federal, state, and local governments—most of which are available for public recreation. *Susan* is spot-on, though, that the types of public recreation allowed will vary across public land management agencies. Given the popularity of the national parks, along with the remarkable character and outstanding recreation opportunities of many

other public lands, it's wise to understand and appreciate the full spectrum of these opportunities.

Before briefly outlining the major types of US public lands, it may be surprising to learn that such a large percentage of the country—about 35%—is owned and managed by federal, state, and local governments. Early immigrants were attracted to America because of the opportunities for religious and economic freedom, and private land ownership was a pillar of the latter. But the desire to preserve elements of American history and its iconic landscapes, and to offer the finest outdoor recreation opportunities to its citizens, stimulated governments at all levels to reserve many areas of public land for parks and related purposes, and some private lands were purchased for these uses as well.

Another important dimension of US public lands is their longstanding relationships with Indigenous peoples and claims of ownership by other sovereign nations, including the UK, Spain, Mexico, Russia, and France. Most of today's public lands were taken from Indigenous people who had lived there since time immemorial, and many of these people were relegated to distant reservations. Recent recognition of this injustice has led to inclusion of local tribal nations in management of these areas. Indian reservations in the US total approximately 56 million acres, but they are generally not considered public land and may not be accessible to the general public. As noted above, much of the land in the US was once claimed by other countries, and this land was either purchased by the US or ceded to it as a result of military action.

Because there are a number of federal land management agencies, as well as 50 states, several territories, and a multitude of local governments, it can be challenging to gather current and authoritative data on public land ownership. As *Susan* astutely notes, understanding the mission and intention of these agencies is a good first step in understanding their recreation character and access. Most of the public land estate is managed by the four largest federal agencies: (i) the NPS; (ii) the US Fish and Wildlife Service; (iii) the Bureau of Land Management; and (iv) the US Forest Service. The first three of these agencies are part of the US Department of the Interior. The NPS manages lands that make up the National Park System, and these lands total more than 85 million acres, or about 3.6% of the US. As described in Conversation 1, units of the National Park System have many titles, but this book refers to all of them as "national parks". National parks are managed to keep them unimpaired for future generations and to provide recreation opportunities. The US Fish and Wildlife Service manages an extensive system of national wildlife refuges across the country that total 89 million acres, or about 3.7% of the US. Wildlife refuges protect a great variety of wildlife populations and their habitats and most are available for public recreation. The Bureau of Land Management manages public lands that were not claimed or purchased by private citizens through the Homestead Act or other programs. This is a vast collection of areas in the western US that total 245 million acres, or about 10% of the US. This land is managed for multiple uses (e.g. forestry, mining, grazing, water, and recreation) and offers many dramatic landscapes and outdoor recreation opportunities.

The fourth large federal land management agency is the US Forest Service and is part of the US Department of Agriculture. The agency manages an extensive system of national forests throughout the US; these national forests total 193 million acres, or about 8.5% of the country. National forests are managed for multiple uses that include forestry, mining, water, grazing, fish and wildlife, and recreation. Many national forests are heavily used for outdoor recreation.

There are several other federal agencies that manage public lands, but these tend to involve other, more specialized uses, are smaller than those noted above, and may not be generally available for outdoor recreation. Examples include the Department of Defense, the Army Corps of Engineers, the Bureau of Reclamation, and Tennessee Valley Authority.

As noted above, state and local governments also own and manage land for outdoor recreation. Although most of these areas are small compared to the federal land management agencies, they are large in aggregate—estimated to total nearly 200 million acres, or 8.7% of the US—and the location of most of them in close proximity to population centers makes them especially attractive options for outdoor recreation.

Given the surprising amount of land in public ownership, there is a wealth of opportunities for outdoor recreation throughout the US, and we agree with *Susan*—public lands provide something for everyone! Many of these lands are of exceptional beauty, are ecologically and historically important, and offer outstanding recreation. While many people consider the national parks to be the very finest of these places, consider visiting other areas as well and you will be richly rewarded.

References

Callaghan, A. (2024) What are Public Lands in the U.S.? Available at: https://www.publiclands.com/blog/a/public-lands-in-the-united-states (accessed 18 July 2024).

US Department of the Interior (2023) America's Public Lands Explained. Available at: https://www.doi.gov/blog/americas-public-lands-explained (accessed 1 July 2024).

5 Antiquities Act

Post

Soft_Cranberry6313 posed a very common question on Reddit:

> *Can someone tell me what's the difference between a national park and a national monument? Are national monuments smaller areas?*

And others chimed in with responses, including *leehawkins*:

> *In a word, politics. National Monuments are designated via executive order by the President under the Antiquities Act, and National Parks are established by acts of Congress.*

Response

Ah, *Soft_Cranberry6313*, this is indeed a bit of a puzzling question—and a ubiquitous one—for those curious about the National Park System. In the Introduction to this book, we note that many national parks are officially called "national monuments"; examples include Devils Tower National Monument, Muir Woods National Monument, and Natural Bridges National Monument. We also note that many other national parks were originally established as national monuments before eventually being re-established by Congress as "national parks". (Only Congress can establish national parks, as *leehawkins* notes.) For example, Grand Canyon National Park was originally established as Grand Canyon National Monument in 1908 by President Theodore Roosevelt, and then "elevated" to Grand Canyon National Park by Congress in 1919. Establishment of national monuments has been (and still is) integral to the protection of federal lands, and this has been facilitated by Congressional legislation titled "An Act for the Preservation of American Antiquities", more widely known as "The Antiquities Act".

During the last few decades of the 19th century, westward expansion and development revealed many antiquities (e.g. dwellings, ceremonial sites, historic and prehistoric artifacts) associated primarily with the long presence of Indigenous peoples. Unfortunately, these antiquities were being improperly and insensitively gathered and removed, and often looted for private gain. Scientists, government officials, and private citizens encouraged Congress to enact legislation to protect such antiquities on federal lands, and the Antiquities Act was passed in 1906, signed by President Theodore Roosevelt, and became law.

The act requires that permission must be granted by federal land managers to conduct archeological investigations and to remove related objects from federal land. The act further allowed presidents to establish "national monuments" on federal lands to protect the prehistoric/historic, scientific, commemorative, and cultural values of these locations. This provision allows timely protection of such sites without having to wait for the sometimes lengthy Congressional legislative process of establishing a "national park". As noted above, Congress has sometimes chosen to re-establish national monuments as national parks.

Since its passage in 1906, the Antiquities Act has been used by most presidents to establish many national monuments. In fact, the Antiquities Act has been used many times to help protect the nation's historical and cultural resources. Moreover, most of these sites have been incorporated into the National Park System and are managed by the NPS. Prominent examples include Mesa Verde National Park, Chaco Culture National Historical Park, Casa Grande National Monument, and Hopewell Culture National Historical Park. Thus, the Antiquities Act is instrumental in protecting public lands; for example, 28 of the current 63 national parks include lands originally protected by the act.

© Robert Manning and Elizabeth Perry 2024. *Conversations About Visiting and Managing the National Parks* (R.E. Manning and E.E Perry)
DOI: 10.1079/9781800626768.0005

References

Congressional Research Service (2022) *National Monuments and the Antiquities Act*. Library of Congress, Washington, DC.

Harmon, D., McManamon, F. and Pitcaithley, D. (2006) *The Antiquities Act: a Century of American Archaeology, Historic Preservation, and Nature Conservation*. University of Arizona Press, Tucson, Arizona.

Lee, R.F. (1970) The American Antiquities Act of 1906. National Park Service, Washington, DC. Available at: https://irma.nps.gov/DataStore/DownloadFile/675601 (accessed 18 July 2024).

6 Organic Act

Post

Every August 25th, social media and blogs erupt with birthday wishes for the NPS and fond memories of favorite national park experiences. For example, *alexahope* shared such a wish on Instagram:

> *On August 25, 1916, President Woodrow Wilson signed the National Park Service Organic Act into law, establishing the National Park Service ... Happy birthday @nationalparkservice #findyourpark.*

Response

Passage of the Organic Act is indeed the NPS's "birthday" and honored annually as such, as noted by *alexahope*. But, this origin story is a bit complicated. As mentioned in the Introduction to this book, Yellowstone was the first national park in the US, established by Congress in 1872. This is also widely recognized as the first national park in the world. A suite of other US national parks soon followed, including Sequoia (1890), Yosemite (1890), Mount Rainier (1899), Crater Lake (1902), and Wind Cave (1903). However, no new federal agency had been established to manage and care for these and other national parks. Consequently, the US Army was called upon to manage the parks, and their principal duty was to help ensure that the parks were not subject to illegal timber harvesting, mining, grazing, and other prohibited activities. The Army's Buffalo Soldiers, an African American cavalry unit of the Army, famously helped with this assignment. Evidence of the Army's presence in the early years of the national parks is plainly seen today in the remaining buildings of Fort Yellowstone in its namesake park; in fact, one of these buildings houses the park's visitor center at Mammoth Hot Springs.

But as the number of national parks increased, along with their popularity, it became increasingly evident that a new federal agency was needed to manage the nascent National Park System. The first decades of the 20th century saw a professional and citizens' movement to encourage Congress to establish a management agency in the US Department of Interior. Noted organizations and individuals were active in this movement, including the American Civic Association, the General Federation of Women's Clubs, the Sierra Club, and landscape architect Frederick Law Olmstead, Jr. In 1915, influential industrialist and national park advocate Steven Mather was hired by the Secretary of Interior to help lobby Congress for establishment of the NPS, and Congress did so the following year. The act was titled the "National Park Service Organic Act", but it is popularly called the "Organic Act". The legislation was sponsored by Representative William Kent of California and Senator Reed Smoot of Utah. Mather was appointed the first director of the agency and paid an honorary salary of $1/year.

The most important clause in the act is the statement of the fundamental purpose of the agency, which is "to conserve the scenery and the natural and historic objects and the wildlife therein and to provide for the enjoyment of the same in such manner and by such means as will leave them unimpaired for the enjoyment of future generations" (United States Government, 2019, p. 1). The objective of maintaining the parks in an "unimpaired" condition remains a foundational goal of national park management and the guiding principle on which all management decisions are made. A number of management policies, director's orders, handbooks, and reference manuals have been developed to help guide this decision making.

As the number of visits to the national parks has risen, the "dual mandate" of the

DOI: 10.1079/9781800626768.0006

NPS implicit in the above clause—specifying that national parks are to be protected in an unimpaired condition but are to be enjoyed by the public as well—has become increasingly problematic. Hundreds of millions of annual visits to the national parks can cause substantial impacts to park resources and the quality of the visitor experience. Thus, balancing park use and preservation has become increasingly urgent and challenging. This issue is addressed in Part 3: Managing the National Parks of this book in Conversations 73, 74, 85, 86, and 89.

References

Manning, R. (2007) *Parks and Carrying Capacity: Commons Without Tragedy*. Island Press, Washington, DC.

United States Government (2019) National park service organic act. An act to establish a National Park Service, and for other purposes. Public Law (United States) 64-235, H.R. 15522, 39 Statute 535, enacted August 25, 1916. Available at: https://www.govinfo.gov/content/pkg/COMPS-1725/pdf/CO MPS-1725.pdf (accessed 18 July 2024).

US Department of the Interior (2005) NPS Organic Act. Available at: https://www.doi.gov/ocl/nps-organi c-act (accessed 1 July 2024).

7 NPS Arrowhead

Post

Missvain posted this photo of the entrance sign to Great Smoky Mountains National Park on Wikimedia Commons:

Great Smoky Mountains National Park, Wikimedia Commons/*Missvain*.

Response

Many visitors to the national parks like to stop and take a photo of the entrance sign as a reminder of their visit, and *Missvain* has taken an especially nice one at Great Smoky Mountains National Park. If you look closely, you'll notice the NPS "arrowhead" on the sign, the official emblem of the agency that's on most NPS signs, brochures, etc. This design was authorized as the agency's official emblem by the Secretary of the Interior in 1951. The elements of the emblem reference the major components of the National Park System: (i) the sequoia tree and bison represent the diverse plants and animals featured in the parks; (ii) the mountains and water represent the scenic and recreational values of the parks; and (iii) the arrowhead itself represents the historical and cultural themes of the parks.

To prevent inappropriate use of the arrowhead design, a notice was published in the Federal Register in 1962 designating it as the official symbol of the NPS and regulating commercial use. The arrowhead emblem is allowed to be used in a limited number of situations, and only when it contributes to the work of the NPS. The websites below have more information about use of the arrowhead and how to request permission to use it. Otherwise, enjoy the symbolism the emblem represents and its comforting familiarity as you visit the national parks.

References

National Park Service (2022a) Arrowhead Artwork. Available at: https://www.nps.gov/subjects/hfc/arrowhead-artwork.htm (accessed 1 July 2024).
National Park Service (2022b) Requesting permission to use the NPS arrowhead. Available at: www.nps.gov/subjects/partnerships/arrowhead-requests.htm (accessed 1 July 2024).

© Robert Manning and Elizabeth Perry 2024. *Conversations About Visiting and Managing the National Parks* (R.E. Manning and E.E Perry)
DOI: 10.1079/9781800626768.0007

8 NPS Uniforms

Post

David R. uploaded this image to Wikimedia Commons of an NPS ranger at Glacier National Park, talking with visitors at a scenic location. The ranger is in field uniform, with the classic campaign hat ("flat hat") and "gray and green" outfit.

Park Ranger at St. Mary Falls, Wikimedia Commons/GlacierNPS.

Response

When you close your eyes and imagine a park ranger, what distinguishes them? The NPS ranger uniform is an iconic image. The image above shows a ranger "in action", talking with visitors at a waterfall in Glacier National Park. Such an image has long-captured what we envision as a NPS employee: gray shirt with the NPS "arrowhead" (see Conversation 7) and a badge, green pants, hiking boots, and, of course, the flat-brimmed campaign hat with brown NPS buckled band ("flat hat" in popular terms).

However, not all NPS employees wear the "gray and green" or the flat hat of the agency. Only staff who come into regular public contact are required to wear the uniform. These typically include: (i) park managers; (ii) law enforcement rangers and US Park Police officers; and (iii) those who are often in the field and/or with the public such as those working in maintenance, interpretation, natural resources, and cultural resources. Staff required to wear a uniform are provided with an annual allowance for it (about $400/year for updated outfits), layers such as NPS jackets or cold weather hats, and shoes.

There are three classes of uniform that visitors might see park staff wearing:

- service uniform—standard uniform with formal dress details for public contact;
- field uniform—a more practical uniform for public contact in difficult environmental conditions (as seen above); and
- work uniform—a uniform for backcountry use and work projects, perhaps with less public contact.

The design of the uniform is standardized in some aspects but will vary across job duties for safety and function. For example, maintenance staff have gray shirts made of more breathable fabric for comfort and without the epaulets that may cause safety hazards around machinery.

Because the national parks pre-dated the NPS (see Introduction and Conversations 5 and 6), the US Cavalry was tasked with park protection in 1886. Therefore, the first uniformed rangers in the parks wore military dress, which distinguished them from park visitors and game poachers. As a "national park ranger" identity began to coalesce from these early park-protection personnel and the NPS became the managing agency with the Organic Act of 1916, the uniform was inspired and adapted from this military style with an outdoorsy twist. The gray-and-green color scheme has been present in the NPS since 1920—over 100 years!

As with any uniform, there have been changes over time to reflect our ideas of fashion and function, but the basics of the NPS "look"

© Robert Manning and Elizabeth Perry 2024. *Conversations About Visiting and Managing the National Parks* (R.E. Manning and E.E Perry)
DOI: 10.1079/9781800626768.0008

have remained remarkably constant. For example, the iconic straw or felt campaign hat has remained relatively unchanged from the early days of the NPS. An enduring rumor is that go-go boots were part of the women's dress uniform in the 1960s and 1970s, in part due to images of models in the "fashionable" updates to the uniforms for women. In truth, types of shoes during this time were suggested and not mandated, as long as they met certain criteria. Shoes in the go-go boot style and of the appropriate colors/materials did meet these criteria, so it is likely that some women chose to wear them out of popularity, not regulation. While they may have presented a sharp image, they lacked practicality for fieldwork!

Chances are, the NPS staff you encounter in a park will be identifiable through a uniform—and that's a good thing! The NPS encourages public contact and easy recognition via a uniform, and this is a good way for the public to seek out those who might provide answers or assistance. However, research suggests that not all park visitors have a positive reaction to the uniform and may avoid rangers when in national parks because of it. As noted above, the uniform shares similarities to law enforcement uniforms and can be imposing. For people who have had, or who fear, negative interactions with law enforcement, the uniform may dissuade them from approaching such staff, either because of the symbolism or the perception of real danger in an interaction. This has been disproportionately pronounced by visitors of color in the parks listing it as an "uncomfortable" aspect of park experiences; and people of color outside the national parks who cite it among their reasons for not visiting these areas. In parks along the country's southern border, this is compounded with the similarities to border patrol and immigration uniforms. The NPS has recognized this potential barrier to welcoming all to the national parks and is working toward lessening these associations through outreach in communities as well as parks.

References

National Park Service (2024) NPS Uniform Collection FAQs. Available at: https://www.nps.gov/subjects/hfc/nps-uniform-collection-faqs.htm (accessed 1 July 2024).
Workman, R.B. (2024) National Park Service Uniforms. Available at: http://npshistory.com/publications/nps-uniforms/index.htm (accessed 1 July 2024).

Themes of the National Parks

9 Natural History

Post

PointiestHat posted the following question on Reddit:

> What national park is best for seeing unique wild animals?

This post received a lot of helpful replies. Yellowstone National Park was the most frequent suggestion, but other less well-known parks were good suggestions as well. For example, *houinator* suggested:

> If it's unique species you are looking for, Haleakalā National Park in Hawaii is probably your bet. Most endangered species of any US national park.

Response

As the number and diversity of the replies to *PointiestHat*'s question suggest, the National Park System includes representative examples of much of the natural diversity of the US. In a way, that's surprising because protecting natural diversity wasn't a high priority during the formative decades of the national parks in the late 19th and early 20th centuries. At that time, the science of ecology was relatively unknown and concepts such as ecosystems and biodiversity were yet to be developed. In fact, top predators such as wolves, mountain lions, and grizzly bears were still being killed, even in the national parks, because they endangered cattle, killed game animals such as deer and elk, and were the subjects of unfortunate mythologies.

Nevertheless, the more than 400 national parks that make up the National Park System help preserve much of the wide-ranging natural diversity of the US (including the top predators noted above). But, given contemporary advances in natural history and ecology, how well do the national parks represent the natural diversity of the nation? That's a challenging question because there are so many ways to measure natural diversity. But two foundational and wide-ranging measures are landforms and biodiversity. Let's start with landforms.

Landforms

Landforms are one way to think about the natural diversity of a large region such as the US. Geologists and geographers often classify and describe natural diversity based on how the land is shaped and sculpted into a wide diversity of landscapes called landforms. Landforms are influenced by underlying bedrock and geological processes over long periods of time such as the forces of water, wind, ice, and gravity, as well as tectonic and volcanic activity. The National Park Service (NPS) divides the landforms of the US into eight categories, and it's fortunate that all of them are pretty well represented in the National Park System.

For example, one of the eight types of landforms is *tectonics and mountain building*, which refers to landforms that have been shaped by the movement of tectonic plates and resulted in the uplift of most of the country's major mountain ranges such as the Appalachians, Rockies, and Sierras. These mountains are well represented in the national parks, with primary examples of Great Smoky Mountains National Park, Rocky Mountain National Park, and Yosemite National Park. *Glacial landforms* are a second category; these are lands that have been shaped by the advance and retreat of glaciers over very long time periods and that result in characteristic features such as the presence of contemporary glaciers themselves, moraines, U-shaped valleys, cirques, fjords, and kettle ponds. Many national parks are representative, including Glacier National Park and Kenai Fjords National Park.

© Robert Manning and Elizabeth Perry 2024. *Conversations About Visiting and Managing the National Parks* (R.E. Manning and E.E Perry)
DOI: 10.1079/9781800626768.0009

Arid and semi-arid landforms are marked by their relatively little precipitation, the types of vegetation that have adapted to this, and erosion that results in characteristic features such as mesas and buttes, canyons, and "badlands". Badlands National Park and Death Valley National Park are good examples. *Beaches and coasts* are the distinctive landforms at the margins of the land and the sea and other large bodies of water; common features include rocky shorelines, sand beaches, estuaries, and deltas. All of the more-than-a-dozen national seashores and lakeshores are good examples.

Dunes (technically aeolian areas) are a fifth type of landform. These are areas that are shaped largely by the wind, and sand dunes are the primary example. There are many examples in the national parks, including namesake Great Sand Dunes National Park and Preserve. *Rivers* (technically fluvial areas) are a sixth type of landform, shaped by the flow and deposition of streams. Perhaps the world's greatest example is Grand Canyon National Park, eroded by the Colorado River and other geological forces.

Volcanic landforms are shaped by volcanic action such as eruptions and lava flows; common features include volcanic mountains, craters, lava tubes, and a variety of thermal features. Hawaii Volcanoes National Park exemplifies this. *Karst landforms* are the result of dissolving bedrock; their characteristic feature is caves and associated speleothems such as stalactites and stalagmites. Mammoth Cave National Park is a quintessential example.

Biodiversity

A second important way to think about the natural diversity of the national parks is the concept of biodiversity, generally defined as the variety of living things and their interactions. Applying this concept to the National Park System, it quickly becomes apparent that the more than 400 national parks represent a great deal of the biodiversity of the nation and much of North America. Perhaps this is best illustrated by using a few examples. It was noted in the brief history of the national parks presented in this book's Introduction that Everglades National Park was the first national park to be established (in 1947) primarily for its biodiversity (rather than its strictly scenic value). This vast shallow river (punctuated with tree islands, pine uplands, and coastal mangrove forests) is often called "the river of grass" and supports enormous biodiversity. For example, the park includes more than 350 species of birds, along with the American alligator, American crocodile, West Indian manatee, Florida panther, and four species of endangered sea turtles. Great Smoky Mountains National Park features the largest intact eastern deciduous hardwood forest in what may be the nation's most biodiverse national park. Its wide range of elevations and plentiful precipitation support more than 1500 species of flowering plants and more than 100 species of trees. Resident animals include white-tailed deer, black bears, coyotes, turkeys, raccoons, woodchucks, and elk.

Desert plants and animals are found in abundance at a number of national parks, and Joshua Tree National Park is a good example. The park features many plants that have adapted to the harsh conditions of little precipitation and high temperatures, such as its namesake the Joshua tree (a tree-like yucca). Channel Islands National Park, sometimes called "the Galapagos of North America", lies off the coast of Southern California and supports as many as 40,000 marine mammals, including dolphins, seals, sea lions, sea otters, porpoises and several species of whales, along with vast "forests" of kelp. Foxes were stranded on the islands by rising sea levels and have adapted to their limited habitat by evolving into the present-day diminutive cat-size foxes. The park is also a nesting and feeding site for many seabirds. Six-million-acre Denali National Park and Preserve in Alaska supports populations of large mammals and predators, including grizzly bears, Dall sheep, moose, caribou, and wolves, all of which roam the park as in historic and prehistoric times. Washington's Olympic National Park includes a wide range of habitats from tall mountains and glaciers to miles of wild ocean beaches and ancient rainforests. Consequently, the park's biodiversity is especially high.

Certainly, the biodiversity of the nation isn't yet fully represented in the National Park System, but a great deal is. This is likely to continue to expand as new parks are added to the system.

References

Graber, D. (2016) Conserving biodiversity. In: Manning, R., Diamant, R., Mitchell, N. and Harmon, D. (eds) *A Thinking Person's Guide to America's National Parks*. Braziller Publishers, New York, pp. 69–81.
National Park Service (2019) Park Landforms. Available at: https://www.nps.gov/subjects/geology/landforms.htm (accessed 2 July 2024).

10 Cultural History

Post

Reviewing the Pueblo Alto Trail at Chaco Culture National Historical Park on AllTrails, *Gretchen* noted that this is an excursion steeped in cultural history:

> *What a unique, interactive experience! I don't think I've ever done a trail that is basically a walking museum. I would recommend getting a pamphlet/ little book, so that you can stop at the sights and really feel/understand the significance of an amazing history of over 300 years starting in 800. We had a fun scramble up after visiting the great houses on the valley floor. Then, we meandered on this amazing loop linking historic sites and just beautiful vistas! The overlook down onto the great houses was a real plus as well. It took longer than expected because of the investigation on these historic remains.*

Response

What a wonderful excursion, *Gretchen*, and we similarly delight in finding unexpected nuggets of history and culture at Chaco Culture National Historical Park and the many other historical and cultural national parks. The NPS protects the breadth of the American story (or more accurately, stories) of both nature *and* culture. Although the original parks were considered solely for their natural beauty, cultural sites were quickly added with passage of the Antiquities Act in 1906 (see Conversation 5)—including Chaco in 1907. This was a highly empowering act of Congress that advanced cultural preservation and allowed active protection of cultural history on federal lands. Now, it's increasingly acknowledged that all national parks include strong components of culture and human history, either in terms of the resources protected or the ways in which they are interpreted (see Conversation 52 about "interpretation" in the national parks). In fact, we embrace history and culture as primary narratives in two-thirds of our more than 400 national parks, and an additive narrative in the remainder. Despite this, national parks are still considered by many visitors as primarily majestic flora, fauna, and natural scenery.

The breadth of culture stewarded by the NPS and included in the National Park System is impressive and represents stories from Indigenous peoples' histories since time immemorial, to our birth and growth as a nation, to contemporary challenges and celebrations, to our ideals for future Americans. Here are a few broad categories of cultural history represented in this stewardship, with a selection of illustrative examples.

Stories of conflict and distress

National park visitors may consider many cultural parks as focusing primarily on the context and events of American conflicts and their aftermath. Examples include conflict-related parks such as the American Revolution at Boston National Historical Park, the War of 1812 at River Raisin National Battlefield Park, the Civil War at Fort Sumter and Fort Moultrie National Historical Park, World War II at Pearl Harbor National Memorial, and 9/11 at the Flight 93 National Memorial. Other cultural national parks extend to stories related to conflicts, such as: (i) many of the war memorials across Washington, DC, and the state-side war effort in Rosie the Riveter/World War II Home Front National Historical Park; (ii) recognition of our shameful history of internment camps at Manzanar National Historic Site, Tule Lake National Monument, and Minidoka National Historic Site; and (iii) a growing presence of narratives throughout many parks of atrocities

© Robert Manning and Elizabeth Perry 2024. *Conversations About Visiting and Managing the National Parks* (R.E. Manning and E.E Perry) DOI: 10.1079/9781800626768.0010

committed against Indigenous peoples and marginalized groups. Some national parks recognize other tragedies, such as at the Johnstown Flood National Memorial.

Stories of ideals and progress

Other culturally related national parks focus on stories of progress, advancement, and overcoming challenges. Examples include the struggle for racial equity and justice in school integration at Brown v. Board of Education National Historical Park and Little Rock Central High School National Historic Site. More broadly, the National Park System has a number of parks related to the Civil Rights Movement such as the recently established Emmett Till and Mamie Till-Mobley National Monument (three sites in Illinois and Mississippi) and the Birmingham Civil Rights District (12 sites significant to the 1963 Birmingham Campaign). Other social/cultural movements represented in the National Park System include suffrage (Women's Rights National Historical Park), workers' rights (César E. Chávez National Monument and Pullman National Historical Park), and lesbian, gay, bisexual, transgender, intersex, queer/questioning, asexual (LGBTIQA+) rights (Stonewall National Monument), among others. Other historical/cultural parks include progress toward industrial development (e.g. Lowell National Historical Park, Saugus Iron Works National Historic Site, Hopewell Furnace National Historic Site), technological progress (e.g. Thomas Edison National Historical Park, Minuteman Missile National Historic Site, and Manhattan Project National Historical Park), and advances in transportation (e.g. Wright Brothers National Memorial, Dayton Aviation Heritage National Historical Park, and Golden Spike National Historical Park).

Stories of extraordinary individuals

Some iconic Americans are recognized in the national parks for their remarkable accomplishments. For example, many parks have presidential affiliations, such as Ulysses S. Grant National Historic Site, Abraham Lincoln Birthplace National Historical Park, Franklin Delano Roosevelt Memorial, Lyndon B. Johnson National Historical Park, President William Jefferson Clinton Birthplace Home National Historic Site, and of course Mount Rushmore National Memorial (depicting Presidents Washington, Jefferson, Lincoln, and Theodore Roosevelt). Other important Americans celebrated in the national parks are recognized in the names of these parks, including Martin Luther King, Jr. National Historical Park, Lewis and Clark National Historical Park, George Washington Carver National Monument, Carl Sandburg Home National Historic Site, and Saint-Gaudens National Historical Park. Other cultural national parks may not feature the names of famous Americans, but these national figures are celebrated in the stories these parks tell, such as John Brown's Raid against slavery at Harpers Ferry National Historical Park.

Stories of daily living

Many cultural national parks capture the American experience throughout the centuries and provide a glimpse of what life was like for those before us. These include places for which we have limited written history available but do have artifacts, structures, landscape modifications, and oral traditions, such as Chaco Culture National Historical Park, Mesa Verde National Park, Hopewell Culture National Historical Park, Pu'uhonua o Hōnaunau National Historical Park, and Effigy Mounds National Monument. Historic forts are also good examples, parks such as Fort Union Trading Post and Fort Vancouver National Historic Sites. Of course, stories of American history and culture are also found in the many historic structures found across the National Park System: (i) historic homes; (ii) cultural landscapes; and (iii) urban landmarks. Here, the NPS's robust ability to care for and interpret artifacts, collections, documents, and archives plays a vital role in telling the many varied stories of American history and culture. For example, Homestead National Historical Park describes and illustrates the lives of those who used the Homestead Act of 1862 to "settle" the American West and "improve" the lands of those who were displaced from their traditional homelands. Pullman National Historical Park describes the lives of the Pullman Porters, the establishment of a Black middle class, the constraints of life in a company town, and the push for workers' rights. Increasingly, national parks address contemporary events and lives as ways to safeguard the connections between past and present and experiences of those today. These could be considered the cultural history of "living traditions" and are presented through interpretive materials and programming on Indigenous and cultural practices, traditional farming practices, and craftsmanship. (See Conversation 30 on how national heritage areas preserve and promote stories of daily living within whole regions.)

All of these parks speak to progress in expanding our understanding and protection of cultural history. Early on, national parks' cultural resources were viewed as secondary and confined only to those that were "ancient" subjects of archeology and prehistory (e.g. the artifacts in Chaco Canyon of peoples 1500 years ago). Over the 1900's, though, the NPS's consideration of cultural history continued to evolve. For example, the Historic Sites Act (1935), about 20 years after the NPS's founding, broadened the agency's mandate to include parks significant to the telling of American history. This opened the possibility for many of the types of national parks outlined above.

In the ensuing decades, our understanding of archeology became more sophisticated and our inclusion of diverse Indigenous and marginalized peoples' histories became more

sensitive, further emphasizing the cultural history alive in every national park. Although the telling of such stories is taking a while to catch up with the traditional emphasis on natural history, the broadening of cultural history to extend beyond the usual narrow and sometimes biased stories of colonialism continues to progress in the NPS. For example, at Arlington House, The Robert E. Lee Memorial, the NPS is engaging with the descendent groups of the formerly enslaved peoples at the plantation (and with the Custis and Lee families who owned the property) about how to interpret not just the Lee legacy, but those of all the peoples who played such important roles at the site and the artifacts and written and oral histories they have left. Chaco Culture National Historical Park is another example of telling rich stories of people and place, weaving both together through the visitor experience as *Gretchen* describes at the beginning of this conversation on the park's trails.

An organizational culture shift within the agency has advanced over time to help expand the acceptance and relevance of cultural history as a valued part of the National Park System and the NPS as well. The movement has evolved from interpreting "relics" as solely of the past to recognizing their vibrant connections to today's stories and peoples, and this has helped solidify historical and cultural resources as integral components of the National Park System. The emphasis on the diversity of parks within the National Park System, such as urban parks (see Conversation 19) and national heritage areas (see Conversation 30) continues to normalize cultural history as part of the NPS mandate.

11   Cultural Landscapes

Post

Christine recently visited Pecos National Historical Park, New Mexico, and posted the following comment on Tripadvisor:

> *There is a lovely walk among the ruins of the Pueblo and the church and you can see how the history of this area changed from the 1st people to the Spanish, then the frontiersmen and even the Civil War.*

Response

Pecos National Historical Park is a lovely area that shows off much of the region's impressive geology and native plants and animals. But it also tells the important stories of the human history of this area, and that is what has caught the attention of *Christine* in her post. Much of the National Park System consists of large natural areas such as Yellowstone National Park, Yosemite National Park, Grand Canyon National Park, and Great Smoky Mountains National Park. Many other national parks are typically smaller historical and cultural sites such as Statue of Liberty National Monument and Independence National Historical Park. However, another emerging and important type of national park is "cultural landscapes", a blend of natural and cultural lands that feature the often long-term relationships between people and place. In fact, from this perspective, most national parks are really cultural landscapes.

Geographers generally recognize three types of cultural landscapes: (i) landscapes that have been designed for their aesthetic qualities ("designed landscapes"); (ii) those that have been shaped by people working the land ("working landscapes"); and (iii) those that are associated with culture, traditions, and beliefs ("associative landscapes"). All three types are increasingly found in the National Park System.

An example of a designed cultural landscapes is the historic and beautiful 469-mile Blue Ridge Parkway that was designed and constructed between 1935 and 1987, and is often called "America's favorite drive" and "a museum of the managed American countryside". It's also the most heavily visited national park. The parkway is designed for a slow-paced and relaxing drive through the beautiful Appalachian highlands, strategically connecting Shenandoah National Park in the north with Great Smoky Mountains National Park to the south. Acadia National Park's carriage roads are another example of an important designed cultural landscape. This 45-mile network of carriage roads—designed primarily for horse-drawn carriages, but now used mostly by walkers and bikers (cyclists)—was constructed at the direction of John D. Rockefeller. Designed by landscape architects, the non-motorized roads wind through the beautiful natural landscapes of what is now Acadia, and include 17 artful bridges constructed of native granite. Frederick Law Olmsted National Historic Site celebrates this famous American landscape architect who designed so many of the nation's celebrated cultural landscapes such as New York's Central Park, and this is a great place to learn about designed cultural landscapes.

Examples of working cultural landscapes include the ancient Indigenous places that feature the homesites and surrounding agricultural and hunting grounds of these tribes and peoples. Well-known examples include Mesa Verde National Park, Chaco Culture National Historical Park, and Canyon de Chelly National Monument. Cuyahoga Valley National Park near Cleveland

© Robert Manning and Elizabeth Perry 2024. *Conversations About Visiting and Managing the National Parks* (R.E. Manning and E.E Perry)
DOI: 10.1079/9781800626768.0011

and Akron, Ohio, is a more contemporary site. This innovative national park protects a large historic valley that includes a pleasing mix of small towns and farms. Park management works with the local non-profit group, Countryside Conservancy, to revitalize the area's small-scale working farms to recreate this historic working landscape. Grant-Kohrs Ranch National Historic Site is another working landscape that celebrates America's legacy of cattle ranching and the role this played in American history.

Examples of associative cultural landscapes include sites that reference a great variety of historical and cultural places and issues. Minute Man National Historical Park and its iconic North Bridge commemorate the very beginnings of the American Revolution, and some of the lands in and adjacent to Glacier National Park are the homelands and sacred spaces of the Blackfeet Indians.

America's growing system of national heritage areas (NHAs) are also good examples of cultural landscapes. Although NHAs aren't part of the National Park System, they receive financial and technical assistance from the NPS (see Conversation 30). NHAs are often very large areas composed mostly of private lands and reflect the sense of place of these distinctive regions, including their natural and cultural history, educational offerings, and outstanding collections of visitor attractions and recreation opportunities. NHAs and other cultural landscapes are much like the national parks found in many other countries, particularly in Europe, where the population density is high compared to the US and where it's especially challenging to find large areas of public lands.

In fact, nearly all of the national parks are increasingly being recognized as cultural landscapes, places that reflect the interrelationships between nature and culture. See more about this in Conversation 82.

Reference

Mitchell, N. (2016) Storied landscapes. In: Manning, R., Diamant, R., Mitchell, N. and Harmon, D. (eds) *A Thinking Person's Guide to America's National Parks*. Braziller Publishers, New York, pp. 163–174.

12 America's Playground

Post

Michael, who's earned the status of "local guide" on Google Reviews, effused about all the ways to play at Boston Harbor Islands National Recreation Area:

> *A bunch of rare gems that few venture out to see. Well worth taking a day to explore an island or two. (Or even go camping!) Shuttles are inexpensive but keep an eye on times so you're not stranded and make sure the shuttle goes back to your original starting point. Seals can be spotted in the summer lounging on the rocks on some of the islands! It's a Beachcombers paradise since very few people go to some of the islands that do not have public shuttles. Take a kayak or small boat to explore!*

Response

Wow—*Michael* has really earned his status as "local guide" by noting the variety of recreation activities at this national park. Now multiply that by the more than 400 national parks and you get a sense of why the national parks are sometimes called "America's Playground". In fact, national parks and outdoor recreation have been close companions from the beginning. Congress granted Yosemite Valley and the nearby Mariposa Grove of giant sequoias to the state of California in 1864, explicitly reserving these areas for "public use, resort, and recreation" (Senate Bill 203, 13 Statute 325, June 30, 1864, cited in National Park Service, 2024). (These sites ultimately became part of Yosemite National Park in 1890.) Yellowstone National Park was established in 1872—widely recognized as America's (and the world's) first national park—to serve as a "pleasuring ground", again emphasizing the importance of recreation (National Archives, no date). The very word "park" suggests recreation's centrality, and whole categories of national parks reference recreation even more explicitly: "national recreation areas" (e.g. Lake Mead National Recreation Area), "national parkways" (e.g. Blue Ridge Parkway), and "national trails" (e.g. Appalachian National Scenic Trail).

National parks emerged as a response to the Romantic Movement that swept much of the Western world in the 18th and 19th centuries. This was a growing sentiment that civilization, in the form of big cities with increasing social and environmental problems, along with the environmental and social abuses of the Industrial Revolution, needed parks, wilderness, and outdoor recreation as an antidote. Recreation is, after all, "re-creation", recovery from the stress of the work-a-day world. John Muir, one of the founders of the American national park movement, was among the most influential prophets of these ideas, famously writing that "Everybody needs beauty as well as bread, places to play in and pray in" (Muir, 1912).

Attention to recreation—and its close cousin, tourism—dominated national park management for most of the early decades. Legendary first director of the National Park Service, Steven Mather, was a wealthy businessman and skilled marketer who believed that for the fledgling National Park System to prosper, parks needed to be more accessible; Americans must see, enjoy, and appreciate the national parks for themselves to rally around them with their support. Mather found an eager ally in the railroads, which saw the burgeoning eastern cities as a reservoir of potential park visitors (and, of course, railroad customers!). The Northern Pacific Railway provided service to Yellowstone National Park, the Southern Pacific to Yosemite National Park, the Great Northern Railway to Glacier National Park, and the Santa Fe Pacific Railway to Grand Canyon National Park. To welcome and accommodate these mostly well-to-do visitors, the railroads financed

© Robert Manning and Elizabeth Perry 2024. *Conversations About Visiting and Managing the National Parks* (R.E. Manning and E.E Perry)
DOI: 10.1079/9781800626768.0012

construction of grand lodges in the national parks, many of which remain important visitor attractions today (see Conversation 68).

Soon, mass production of automobiles and, ultimately, development of the interstate highway system, popularized and democratized recreation in the national parks. The NPS responded to this increased demand with construction of dramatic, scenic roads through the parks, campgrounds, visitor centers, and extensive networks of trails.

Recreation infrastructure in the national parks received a substantial boost from the Civilian Conservation Corps during the Great Depression, a nationwide public works project that included many national parks, and the NPS's Mission 66 initiative, a 10-year program of planning and construction designed to meet growing post-World War II recreation demand and to celebrate the agency's 50-year anniversary in 1966. Many of the national parks' roads, buildings, trails, and campsites date from these periods and still serve the needs of the nation today. The annual number of visits to the national parks rose sharply during the post-war years, climbing to well over 100 million by 1966.

Today, the National Park System might well be considered "America's Playground". Most of the more than 400 national parks offer outstanding opportunities for recreation, and the parks accommodate more than 300 million visits/year (see Conversation 3 about the number and pattern of recreation visits to the national parks). With so many good choices of activities and parks, it is challenging to describe the number and range of recreation opportunities in the national parks, but here are some representative examples.

Let's start with scenic drives, traditionally one of America's favorite recreation activities. Many of the roads in the national parks were designed by landscape architects who planned them to lie gracefully on the land and offer the very best views. Driving these roads (or better yet, taking public transit where available; see Conversations 62 and 92) remains a vital part of the national park experience. Prominent examples include the Going-to-the-Sun Road in Glacier National Park, Grand Loop Road in Yellowstone National Park, Tioga Road in Yosemite National Park, West Rim Drive in Grand Canyon National Park, Trail Ridge Road

in Rocky Mountain National Park, and the Park Loop Road in Acadia National Park. In fact, there are four national parks titled "National Parkways" that were established explicitly for scenic driving.

Now it's time to park the car (or get off the shuttle bus!) and set out on foot. With an estimated 21,000 + miles of trails in the national parks, there are lifetimes of hiking to be done. The Anhinga Trail at Everglades National Park winds just under a mile through a sawgrass marsh, where you're likely to see alligators, turtles, herons, egrets, and the namesake anhingas. The trail to Delicate Arch in Arches National Park is another relatively short but iconic walk that winds over expanses of slickrock and leads to the magical Delicate Arch, a massive, improbable sandstone formation sitting on the edge of a huge slickrock bowl with the snow-capped La Sal Mountains in the background. Walk a portion of the lovely and historic 185 mile C&O Canal in Chesapeake and Ohio Canal National Historical Park in Maryland and Washington, DC. Feeling more ambitious? Hike across the Grand Canyon on the historic North and South Kaibab Trails or the 210 mile John Muir Trail through Yosemite, Sequoia, and Kings Canyon National Parks; these are world-class adventures, but you must prepare carefully for them (see Conversation 33 on planning a visit). The NPS also administers the National Trails System, a network of trails that crisscross the nation; the national scenic trails alone (e.g. Appalachian National Scenic Trail) total nearly 18,000 miles. Other types of national parks that feature outstanding opportunities for recreation include the 85 national monuments, 18 national recreation areas, and the 14 national seashores and national lakeshores. Even most of the national historical parks are large enough to include trails and other recreation-related facilities.

All that recreation can tire you out, so consider spending the night in one of the grand lodges of the national parks noted earlier (see Conversation 68); these lovely and historic hotels date from the early period of the national parks. Or maybe better still, pitch a tent in one of the many campgrounds scattered through most of the larger national parks. For example, Acadia National Park includes two large drive-up campgrounds, Blackwoods and Seawall; Yellowstone has 12. Utah's Capitol Reef

National Park has one of the sweetest camp-grounds (Fruita) in the National Park System, with pick-your-own fruit orchards nearby. There are even camping opportunities in some of the urban national parks; for example, Boston Harbor Islands National Recreation Area allows camping on four of the islands where you can take in some great sunrises and sunsets as well as stunning views of the Boston skyline. Most of the larger national parks allow more primitive backcountry or wilderness camping (though a permit is usually required).

This is a small but suggestive sampling of the recreation opportunities in the national parks, and *Michael*'s posting at the beginning of this conversation does a good job of illustrating this. See Conversations 38–49 for more information about a host of recreation activities—hiking, camping, biking, snowmobiling, river rafting, mountain climbing, hunting, fishing, and more.

References

Muir, J. (1912) The Yosemite. The Century Company: New York. Available at: https://vault.sierraclub.org/john_muir_exhibit/writings/the_yosemite/ (accessed 16 July 2024).

National Archives (n.d.) Act Establishing Yellowstone National Park (1872). Enrolled Acts and Resolutions of Congress, 1789-1996; General Records of the United States Government; Record Group 11. Available at: https://www.archives.gov/milestone-documents/act-establishing-yellowstone-national-park (accessed 18 July 2024).

National Park Service (2024) *America's National Park System: The Critical Documents*. Available at: https://www.nps.gov/parkhistory/online_books/anps/anps_1a.htm (accessed 17 July 2024).

13 America's Classroom

Post

The recent coronavirus (COVID-19) pandemic caused many colleges and universities to switch to remote learning formats. *Nathaniel* reacted creatively by making the national parks a vital part of his graduate education program, as he describes in this Facebook posting:

> *When it was announced that my graduate program would be online, I decided to use the opportunity to travel and study from various national parks. I converted my car into a camper and took to the road in September ... This semester has been incredible and the beauty that I've witnessed has provided a lot of outlets for me to apply what I'm learning in school.*

Response

Congratulations, *Nathaniel*—what a clever way to capitalize on the educational value of the national parks and the freedom of remote learning! It shouldn't be surprising that the national parks are great places to learn about our nation's natural and cultural history. As discussed in Conversations 9 and 10, the National Park System features a great diversity of the country's natural landscapes and cultural history. Conversation 52 outlines the NPS program of "interpreting" these places to visitors. As a visitor to the national parks, it's easy and engaging to learn about these places and the ways they contribute to understanding and appreciating our common heritage. NPS interpreters present entertaining programs about the parks, and park visitor centers and museums are designed and managed to offer informative educational materials and displays (see Conversations 50 and 51). As *Nathaniel* mentions, these parks are also places to see and apply educational concepts in action!

The NPS has invested heavily in maximizing the educational value of the national parks to visitors—and to those who may not be able to visit as well—and this includes a great variety of materials that can be used by teachers at all levels of learning. While *Nathaniel* was able to enhance his learning by visiting the national parks directly, the national parks can help advance learning through virtual visits too. You can begin to appreciate the national parks as an educational resource by exploring the NPS website for teachers (see National Park Service (2024) listed in the References at the end of this conversation). Here, you'll find a wealth of materials that can be used in a variety of teaching and learning contexts. In addition, explore the "For Teachers", "Nature and Science", "History and Culture", and "For Kids" options on the official website of most of the national parks.

For example, educational materials have been developed on how to use the rich collection of historic sites in the National Park System to teach American history. This "Teaching and Learning with Historic Places (TwHP)" program, and associated suite of materials, includes teaching tools and lesson plans to help teachers address American history. Parallel science-based programs and materials are available for national parks that feature the natural environment.

The NPS program, "A Park for Every Classroom", focuses on using parks as extensions of the classroom. In conjunction with park staff, teachers develop service-learning projects that engage students in real-world issues. For example, students in the Salem, Massachusetts, area use Salem Maritime National Historic Site to explore the connections between the Latino families in the community and the American maritime history in the Caribbean region.

Also the NPS helps arrange virtual visits to many national parks through a variety of distance-learning opportunities. For example,

© Robert Manning and Elizabeth Perry 2024. *Conversations About Visiting and Managing the National Parks* (R.E. Manning and E.E Perry)
DOI: 10.1079/9781800626768.0013

students can "visit" a kelp forest at Channel Islands National Park in real time with an NPS ranger/diver, helping to monitor ecological conditions, learning about marine protected areas, and discussing the impacts that humans have on these fragile ecosystems. Students can even ask the ranger questions.

The NPS Teacher-Ranger-Teacher (TRT) program is an option for professional development of teachers. This program links national parks and teachers from Title one school districts (those that have a high percentage of lower-income families). Teachers complete a three-credit college course on experiential education and also learn about national parks by shadowing NPS staff. Teachers who successfully complete both the online graduate course and the NPS program requirements receive a stipend that can help cover living expenses and local travel costs to participate in the program. Teachers are expected to engage their students in park-based experiential learning, including an on-site visit to a national park.

Contemporary research in education documents the values of what is being called "place-based education" and "experiential learning", learning that's connected to real places. These are often called "high-impact" educational experiences. The national parks offer great opportunities for this kind of learning, and the more than 400 national parks located throughout the nation, many of them in urban or urban proximate areas, magnify their educational potential. That's why national parks are increasingly called "America's Classroom"!

References

Hudspeth, T., Camp, M. and Cirillo, J. (2016) Lifelong learning. In: Manning, R., Diamant, R., Mitchell, N. and Harmon, D. (eds) *A Thinking Person's Guide to America's National Parks*. Braziller Publishers, New York, pp. 57–68.

Manning, R. (2016) How America's best idea can be colleges' best opportunity. *The Chronicle of Higher Education*, April 13. Available at: https://www.chronicle.com/article/how-americas-best-idea-can-be-colleges-best-opportunity/ (accessed 2 July 2024).

National Park Service (2024) Educators: National Parks are America's Largest Classrooms. Find lesson plans about these great places. Available at: www.nps.gov/teachers/index.htm (accessed 2 July 2024).

Thompson, J. and Houseal, A. (2020) *America's Largest Classroom: What We Learn from Our National Parks*. University of California Press, Berkeley, California.

14 Civil Rights

Post

After her visit to Women's Rights National Historical Park, *Eugenia* posted this Google Review:

This was really interesting, and they did a good job of explaining why the women's rights movement began and how it had ties to Native American culture and Abolition of Slavery. There were lots of images to see and artifacts. It was also very smart how they used traditionally women's crafts like quilting and fashion in their exhibits.

Response

The issue of civil rights is a vital part of American history, and this is powerfully represented in the National Park System. The NPS counts nearly a quarter of the more than 400 national parks as making substantive contributions to civil rights themes (still more such sites are found within the NPS-managed National Historic Landmarks program—see Conversations 1, 24, and 84). As *Eugenia* notes, interconnections among civil rights causes are often found within these parks. These sites and the powerful network of associated NPS websites effectively tell and document this story.

A logical time and place to begin to explore this issue is the Declaration of Independence, which famously states that "all men are created equal" and that they are endowed with "unalienable Rights that among these are Life, Liberty, and the pursuit of Happiness" (National Archives, no date). It has taken all of our history to advance this objective, and this struggle is far from complete (National Archives, n.d).

But the story begins even earlier with the mistreatment of Indigenous peoples. The very act of taking possession and occupying the lands originally inhabited by Indigenous peoples denied them rights that were originally theirs, marking the beginning of a long and continuing period of their disenfranchisement. This policy of discrimination was made more formal when Congress passed the Naturalization Act in 1790, specifying that a citizen must be "a free white person, of good character" (DocsTeach, no date). Moreover, while women could become citizens, they were not allowed to vote in most states and had limited property rights, particularly if married.

Despite ratification in 1791 of the original ten amendments to the US Constitution, popularly known as the Bill of Rights, many groups of people have been denied the full benefits of equal rights. Of course, African Americans were enslaved in the Southern States until after the Civil War and have continued to be subjected to various forms of discrimination including the Dred Scott Decision of the US Supreme Court in 1857, post-Civil War Jim Crow laws, poll taxes, immigration quotas, segregated schools, and widespread social ostracization. The Treaty of Guadalupe Hidalgo in 1848 ending the Mexican American War promised Mexican-Americans the rights of US citizenship, but these rights were not immediately and fully forthcoming. The Chinese Exclusion Act of 1882 denied citizenship rights to Chinese Americans. The 19th Amendment to the US Constitution in 1920 gave women the right to vote, but many forms of discrimination persisted. The long and continuing struggle for the rights of full citizenship continues today, and is now being extended to include LGBTIQA+, neurodiverse, and disabled people.

The following national parks illustrate the power and diversity of ways in which the issue of civil rights is addressed, but these sites are only suggestive of the ways in which the issue of civil rights is included and treated in the National Park System. The website National Park Service (2024) noted at the end of this conversation

© Robert Manning and Elizabeth Perry 2024. *Conversations About Visiting and Managing the National Parks* (R.E. Manning and E.E Perry)
DOI: 10.1079/9781800626768.0014

includes a more complete listing of civil rights-related national parks.

- *Martin Luther King, Jr. National Historical Park*—Located in Atlanta, Georgia, this national park includes several sites that help tell the story of this iconic civil rights leader. Visit his birth home and historic Ebenezer Baptist Church where he was baptized and served as co-pastor with his father. The park also includes a visitor center and the Martin Luther King, Jr. Center for Nonviolent Social Change, and offers ranger-led tours.
- *Women's Rights National Historical Park*—This national park tells the story of the nation's first Women's Rights Convention in 1848 held in Seneca Falls, New York (where the park is located). The convention is generally considered the beginning of the US Women's Rights Movement. The park includes the Wesleyan Chapel where the convention was held, several historic homes associated with the convention, a visitor center, and ranger programs. As *Eugenia* mentions in her post, the depth and creativity of displays are powerful educational tools.
- *César E. Chávez National Monument*—César Chávez led California farmworkers in the establishment of the nation's first permanent agricultural union, and is widely recognized as the most important Latino leader in 20th-century America. The park is located in Keene, California, and is part of *Nuestra Señora Reina de la Paz*, the home and workplace of the Chávez family and farmworker-movement organizations. Visitors are welcome at the park's visitor center, memorial garden, and desert garden.
- *Manzanar National Historic Site*—At the beginning of World War II, the US government incarcerated more than 110,000 men, women, and children of Japanese descent in ten remote military-style camps.

Manzanar, located in eastern California, was one of these camps. The park's visitor center tells this story and visitors can also learn about daily life in the camp by touring the replica buildings and exhibits of Block 14, driving or biking the park's self-guided auto tour road, and taking a guided tour.

- *Little Bighorn Battlefield National Monument*—Located in south-central Montana, this national park memorializes the 1876 Battle of Little Bighorn in which Lt. Col. George Custer and his troops of the US Army's 7th Cavalry were defeated by Lakota, Cheyenne, and Arapaho warriors. Originally called Custer Battlefield National Monument, the name of the park was changed in 1991, and the site's history and story were broadened to include a more balanced view of the conflict between westward expansion of the nation and the traditional presence of Indigenous peoples (see Conversation 15).
- *Stonewall National Monument*—In the 1960s, homosexual activities were illegal in New York City and much of the rest of the US. A police raid at the city's Stonewall Inn precipitated a riotous protest that spilled into nearby Christopher Park, and this marked the beginnings of the LGBTIQA+ Movement. This park is located in Christopher Park in historic Greenwich Village, but is relatively new (established in 2016) and has few visitor facilities and services at this time.

In addition to the many national parks that address civil rights, the NPS has developed a large and sophisticated network of websites that address this issue. Examples include a "We Shall Overcome Travel Itinerary", a list of all national parks that address civil rights, a history of the Civil Rights Movement, and materials designed for public education, including lesson plans, classroom materials, field experiences, and distance-learning opportunities.

References

DocsTeach (n.d.) Naturalization Act of 1790. Available at: https://www.docsteach.org/documents/docum ent/naturalization-act-of-1790 (accessed 18 July 2024).

National Archives (n.d) The Declaration of Independence (U.S. 1776). Available at: https://www.archives. gov/founding-docs/declaration-transcript (accessed 18 July 2024).

National Park Service (2024) Civil Rights in America. Available at: https://www.nps.gov/subjects/civilright s/index.htm (accessed 2 July 2024).

15 Contested Landscapes

Post

Cindy and *Carl* both visited Little Bighorn Battlefield National Monument. But their postings on Google Reviews about this park were quite different as a function of their backgrounds and personal situations. *Cindy* posted the following:

> The Visitor Center has done an amazing job of telling the story with respect to both sides which is important. It's a time in history that may not be looked upon favorably but they have done an amazing job with facts about that time and the events that occurred.

But *Carl* had a different take based on the feelings this park evoked:

> Great place with proud native American history. This is where Custer was killed for trying to attack local natives. Was disappointed to see that it's used as a cemetery by relatives of the soldiers that were killed during the battle. As a native I found this spot very inspiring as a location where natives stood their ground and fought back against the murderous U.S. soldiers.

Response

Most Americans take pride in celebrating our national parks, iconic places such as Yellowstone National Park and Statue of Liberty National Monument. But sometimes things are more complicated than they might seem. For example, Yellowstone was once an important hunting ground for Indigenous people, but these people were forcibly displaced. Although "Lady Liberty" carries the Declaration of Independence in her left hand, this powerful document's foundational statement that "all men are created equal" hasn't been fully realized by all segments of American society.

In this way, many national parks might be considered "contested landscapes", places where people might legitimately disagree about the history and meaning of such sites. In other words, there may be different stories about these places, told by different voices. What do we do about this? While this can be troubling, it's also an opportunity to adopt what some scholars and park managers call "civic engagement", a concept that was advanced in a landmark report by a group of historians working in concert with the NPS. Titled "Imperiled promise: the state of history in the National Park Service" (Whisnant et al., 2012), the report celebrates the opportunity to involve the public in such discussions, to take advantage of this opportunity for critical thinking and civic engagement, and to perfect the interpretive and management programs of so many national parks. In the process, this can only help us be more informed citizens and enrich the national parks at the same time. Some national parks where people frequently express the "contested" part of such landscapes will have areas specifically designated for First Amendment activities—free speech, assembly, protest, etc.—to help balance their right to free expression with others' right to a peaceful visit.

Many national parks are especially well suited to public engagement approaches. As noted above, most national parks were once occupied by Indigenous people. While some of these parks were established to honor this heritage, contemporary Indigenous people and tribes may rightfully feel a measure of resentment. A process of civic engagement, public dialogue, and appropriate follow up can be helpful in these cases. For example, tribal nations are increasingly consulted in park management, even taking on the role of co-managers, and interpretive programs are often expanded and enhanced to tell the stories of these parks from Indigenous points of view, enriching the parks and the educational programs they offer. For

© Robert Manning and Elizabeth Perry 2024. *Conversations About Visiting and Managing the National Parks* (R.E. Manning and E.E Perry)
DOI: 10.1079/9781800626768.0015

instance, the national park associated with what many Americans learned in their school history classes as "Custer's Last Stand" was originally called Custer Battlefield National Monument. However, after public discourse and consideration, the park has been appropriately renamed the more objective and inclusive Little Bighorn Battlefield National Monument. In addition, a memorial was established to honor the Indigenous warriors who died there (complementing the existing monument to the Army soldiers who perished), the park's interpretation of the site has been substantially broadened, and the park actively seeks Indigenous staff. The postings by *Cindy* and *Carl* beginning this conversation exemplify the contested landscapes that national parks like Little Bighorn Battlefield National Monument represent. Similar approaches to park management and interpretation have been taken at Sand Creek Massacre National Historic Site and Washita Battlefield National Historic Site, both places where many Indigenous people died—many of whom were women and children—at the hands of the US Cavalry. San Antonio Missions National Historical Park offers a different kind of learning opportunity, a place where Indigenous people were encouraged to adopt

the Christian religion by Spanish military and religious figures (Linenthal, 2016).

Other types of national parks that are benefiting from civic engagement include those that address the extension of human rights such as Eleanor Roosevelt National Historic Site, Women's Rights National Historical Park, and the Ellis Island portion of Statue of Liberty National Monument. But perhaps the best example is the extensive network of national parks addressing the Civil War (and Reconstruction and Jim Crow periods) and American Civil Rights Movement, more than 100 of them. A few examples include Fort Sumter National Monument, Shiloh National Military Park, Harpers Ferry National Historical Park, Selma to Montgomery National Historic Trail, Little Rock Central High School National Historic Site, Brown v. Board of Education National Historic Site, and Martin Luther King, Jr. National Historic Site. The causes and consequences of the Civil War are still debated in American society, and the Civil Rights Movement has a long history of struggle and contentiousness. But the national parks that are the direct manifestations of this history can play a vital and productive role in stimulating the thinking, debate, and action of visitors, students, and the general population.

References

Linenthal, E. (2016) Civic engagement. In: Manning, R., Diamant, R., Mitchell, N. and Harmon, D. (eds) *A Thinking Person's Guide to America's National Parks*. Braziller Publishers, New York, pp. 127–136.
Whisnant, A., Miller, M., Nash, G. and Thelen, D. (2012) Imperiled promise: the state of history in the National Park Service – Opening the discussion. *The George Wright Forum* 29(2), 246–263.

16 Mechanization, Industry, and Technology

Post

National parks can bring seemingly distant histories of technological change back to life. Reacting to a Facebook post about the world record for laying railroad track (10 miles in a single day!) in 1869 by Irish and Chinese laborers working for the Central Pacific Railroad—an event commemorated at Golden Spike National Historical Park—*Jan* noted:

I think it's harder for us to imagine the achievement and the change to our nation after the transcontinental railroad was complete.

Response

The national parks are traditionally associated with natural areas such as Yosemite National Park and Yellowstone National Park, but they also include a strong historical theme, as represented by parks such as Gettysburg National Historical Park and Independence National Historical Park (see Conversations 9 and 10 for more about natural areas and historical areas, respectively). But other important components of the history of the nation represented in the National Park System include development of the nation's industrial heritage, including mechanization, industry, technology, and other sectors of economic and military development, and *Jan*'s posting to start this conversation is representative.

Lowell National Historical Park is a good example. Here, 30 miles north-west of Boston, entrepreneurs dammed the Merrimack River to power a textile mill in 1823, marking the beginning of the American Industrial Revolution. The location, renamed Lowell after one of the investors, became the largest producer of cotton

fabric in the world, enriching its owners. But the thousands of "mill girls" recruited from surrounding farms and towns to work in the mills were subjected to the shameless rigors of 14-hour work shifts and unhealthy living and working conditions.

Mining and metallurgy is another important topic addressed in several national parks. For example, Saugus Iron Works National Historic Site near Boston commemorates the very early process (in the mid-1600s) of smelting local iron ore and fashioning nails, hinges, axes, horseshoes, and other necessities. A waterwheel was adapted to power a forge to melt the iron ore, and the resulting raw material was fashioned by heat and hammer into implements. Even earlier, Indigenous people mined copper at what is now Keweenaw National Historical Park in Michigan, fashioning the malleable material into useful implements and decorative objects. Later, European immigrants continued this practice, but at a larger scale. Still later, the Kennecott Copper Company developed an industrial-scale copper mine in Alaska that's preserved and interpreted as part of Wrangell-St. Elias National Park and Preserve (the country's largest national park).

Multiple components of the transportation industry are celebrated in several national parks. For example, Golden Spike National Historical Park (as noted by *Jan* above) commemorates completion of the nation's first transcontinental railroad in 1869, and Steamtown National Historic Site is located in a former roundhouse and railroad yard in Pennsylvania and features a large collection of historic locomotives, freight cars, and passenger cars, many still in operating condition. San Francisco Maritime National Historical Park and Salem Maritime National Historic Site commemorate the nation's maritime heritage. The former documents the

DOI: 10.1079/9781800626768.0016

region's maritime history starting with the arrival of the first ship in San Francisco Bay (the Spanish sailing vessel, *San Carlos*) and continuing to the present-day container ships that dominate commercial shipping. The latter tells the story of American privateering during the American Revolution (local seaman confronting some 600 British ships) and later development of trade with China and other Asian ports.

Of course, another vital form of transportation is air travel, and this is celebrated at two important sites. Wright Brothers National Memorial at Kitty Hawk, North Carolina, is where it all began, and the site commemorates and interprets that famous first flight by brothers Wilber and Orville. Floyd Bennett Field was New York City's first municipal airport and the site of many historic flights, such as Howard Hughes' 1938 flight around the world. The airfield is now part of Gateway National Recreation Area.

American military technology is another theme that's well represented in the National Park System. For example, Springfield Armory National Historic Site in Massachusetts tells important parts of this story beginning in 1777 when the US made ammunition, stored weapons, and maintained artillery during the American Revolution and ending with the production of rifles used in World Wars I and II. Minuteman Missile National Historic Site in South Dakota is an example of the large network of missile silos constructed during the cold war throughout much of the country as a national defense strategy; the site includes silo D-09 and an underground control center. A recent addition to this category of military parks is Manhattan Project National Historical Park, telling the chilling story of development of the first atomic bombs during World War II. This is a serial national park that includes sites in: (i) Los Alamos, New Mexico; (ii) Oakridge, Tennessee; and (iii) Hanford, Washington (Corn, 2016).

Of course, the story of American technological advancement wouldn't be complete without reference to Thomas Edison, and Thomas Edison National Historical Park named in his honor. He and his colleagues working in their laboratories (Edison called them "an invention factory"; Bellis, 2023) in West Orange, New Jersey, are best known for the invention of electric lighting, but their innovations included a range of other technological advancements such as the phonograph. Perhaps future national parks will commemorate the development of computers, the Internet, and social media!

References

Bellis, M. (2023) What was Menlo Park? Thomas Edison's Invention Factory. Thought.Co. Available at: https://www.thoughtco.com/what-was-menlo-park-1992136 (accessed 17 July 2024).

Corn, J. (2016) Machines and ingenuity. In: Manning, R., Diamant, R., Mitchell, N. and Harmon, D. (eds) *A Thinking Person's Guide to America's National Parks*. Braziller Publishers, New York, pp. 149–162.

17 Indigenous Peoples

Post

electric dresses recently posted the following question on Reddit:

> How did Native American tribes indigenous to Yellowstone National Park (e.g., Shoshone, Blackfeet, Crow, etc.) perceive the land (e.g., thoughts on geothermal activity) and what was their relationship like with white/European trappers and explorers entering the region in the early 1800s?

This posting generated a number of helpful and thoughtful responses, including citations for a number of authoritative sources. Indigenous peoples have strong connections to many national parks and raise important issues of civil rights. Moreover, the relationships between Indigenous peoples and the natural environment have increasingly vital application to contemporary environmental issues.

Response

There is a long and sometimes sorry history that links the national parks and Indigenous peoples (including Alaska Natives and Native Hawaiians). Of course, much of the North American continent was home to many tribes of Indigenous peoples long before—perhaps as many as 15,000 years, or "time immemorial" as spoken by Indigenous peoples—the land that is now the US was "discovered" and occupied by European settlers and their descendants. Indigenous peoples were generally treated with disdain (or often worse) as the nation was "settled" from east to west. In many cases, Indigenous peoples were simply pushed aside, coerced into signing treaties that were ultimately broken by the US government, forced to relocate to reservations that were sometimes far from their homelands, and too often killed.

Yosemite National Park in California's Sierra Nevada mountains is a representative example. In 1851, the Mariposa Battalion of the US Army was sent to Yosemite Valley, now the heart of the park, to drive out the Miwok Indians who had occupied the area for generations. This military action was taken to protect American settlers who were looking for gold. The Army troops forced the Indigenous peoples out of the valley, calling them "barbarians", killing some in the process, and burning their homes and food supplies. The valley and the surrounding 750,000 acres of land were ultimately established by Congress as Yosemite National Park in 1890. Similar stories played out across the American landscape and the formative years of American history (National Park Service, 2021).

This is a difficult chapter in the story of America, and the national parks in particular, but these stories are now being told with remarkable and refreshing candor by the NPS and by contemporary Indigenous peoples themselves. This current period of American history is playing out in at least two ways. First, many national parks have been established to honor the historic and prehistoric presence of Indigenous peoples, and tell their stories in the process. For example, Mesa Verde National Park was established in 1906 to protect the remarkable cliff dwellings of the Indigenous peoples—now known as Ancestral Pueblo people—who lived in the region for 700 years. The NPS lists over 100 national parks that celebrate the heritage of Indigenous peoples (see links/resources in the References at the end of this conversation).

Secondly, Indigenous peoples themselves are telling these stories in an increasing number of national parks and are active participants in park management. For example, Grand Canyon National Park was established in 1919 to protect this remarkable natural feature that has now been honored as a World Heritage

© Robert Manning and Elizabeth Perry 2024. *Conversations About Visiting and Managing the National Parks* (R.E. Manning and E.E Perry)
DOI: 10.1079/9781800626768.0017

Site (see Conversation 31 on World Heritage Sites). But lands included in this park have been considered a sacred site for thousands of years by 11 federally recognized tribes of Indigenous peoples, including the contemporary reservations of three tribes that directly border the park. Park staff have been working directly with these tribes for more than 40 years, developing many innovative and collaborative tribal partnerships. For example, the park is now establishing the Desert View Inter-Tribal Cultural Heritage Site, where Indigenous peoples will tell their own stories of this land, including its natural and cultural history. The NPS superintendent of the park notes that "this project was conceived of by our tribal partners who continue to collaborate with us to expand first-voice tribal interpretation" (Grand Canyon Conservancy, 2024).

Other diverse examples include the Huna Tlingit Tribal House that was recently constructed in Glacier Bay National Park and Preserve. This facility honors the Indigenous peoples who occupied park lands for thousands of years and serves as a gathering place where tribal members can reconnect with their homeland and park visitors can learn about Huna Tlingit history, culture, and traditions. Congress established the Trail of Tears National Historic Trail in 1987 commemorating the forced removal of the Cherokee Tribe and other Indigenous peoples from the American Southeast to reservations in Oklahoma. The trail passes through eight states. Congress also established what was then called Custer Battlefield National Monument in 1879 to commemorate the famous battle between the US Army and tribes of Indigenous peoples that was fought there 3 years earlier. But more recently, the name of the site was changed to the more inclusive Little Bighorn Battlefield National Monument and the park now honors both Lt. Col. George Armstrong Custer and his troops as well as the Lakota, Sioux, and Cheyenne warriors who fought there. Responding to more recent history of Indigenous peoples, management of Alcatraz Island, part of Golden Gate National Recreation Area in the San Francisco Bay area, has been expanded to the tell the story of occupation of the island by Indigenous peoples for 19 months from 1969 to 1971 as part of the contemporary American Indian Movement and the larger American Civil Rights Movement. These are just a few ways in which the National Park System is changing in response to a greater national sensitivity to the plight of Indigenous peoples and their contributions to American history and society.

There are other examples as well. A new park brochure for Haleakala National Park was prepared in the Native Hawaiian language (with English translation) by local Native Hawaiians. Alaska Natives are granted "subsistence rights" in many Alaskan national parks, allowing them to hunt and gather as they once did. The Indigenous community of American Samoa led the successful movement to establish the National Park of American Samoa, part of the US National Park System. Grand Portage National Monument, commemorating the historic North American fur trade, is now working with the Grand Portage Band of Ojibwa to expand the park's interpretation, and Kaibab Paiute are leading the effort to protect the quality of night sky viewing at Grand Canyon—Parashant National Monument and Pipe Spring National Monument. Washita Battlefield National Historic Site and Sand Creek Massacre National Historic Site candidly tell the story of the injustices perpetrated on Indigenous peoples by the US Army.

Perhaps most powerfully, some contemporary observers have noted that as environmental problems in the US have become more apparent and urgent, American society has begun to adopt attitudes that are more in keeping with the worldviews of Indigenous peoples, attitudes that express greater concern for the natural environment and a healthier respect of it. These ideas are being presented in an increasing number of national parks, increasingly often by Indigenous peoples themselves, and we should be grateful for this gift.

References

Grand Canyon Conservancy (2024) Desert View Inter-tribal Cultural Heritage Site. Available at: https://www.grandcanyon.org/protect-grand-canyon/projects/desert-view-inter-tribal-cultural-heritage-site (accessed 17 July 2024).

Lane-Kamahele, M. (2016) Indigenous voices. In: Manning, R., Diamant, R., Mitchell, N. and Harmon, D. (eds) *A Thinking Person's Guide to America's National Parks*. Braziller Publishers, New York, pp. 117–126.

National Park Service (2021) American Indian Heritage. Available at: www.nps.gov/subjects/americanind ians/index.htm (accessed 2 July 2024).

Spence, M.D. (1999) *Dispossessing the Wilderness*. Oxford University Press, Oxford, UK.

Treuer, D. (2021) Return the national parks to the tribes. *The Atlantic,* May.

18 Models of Sustainability

Post

Many news stories have been shared on Facebook about the "Decarbonize the Parks Project", a collaboration between the National Parks of Lake Superior Foundation and the five national parks on Lake Superior. This is part of the NPS's *Green Parks Plan* for net-zero energy goals across the National Park System. *Phillip* responded to one of these, noting that the national parks around Lake Superior are putting words into action to decrease the NPS's carbon footprint:

> *As national parks around the country try to raise awareness about climate change, those around Lake Superior are taking steps to cut their emissions ... The country's national parks emit 179,000 tons of carbon dioxide annually ... equal to about 40,000 gasoline-powered cars driven over a year.*

Response

Although Congress may not have known much about it at the time, they started a social and environmental movement that's become widely known as sustainability when they voted in 1872 to establish Yellowstone National Park. By setting aside 2.2 million acres of public domain lands to be conserved, they saved this place from being exploited for timber, mining, market hunting, and other forms of environmental exploitation. This marked the beginning of a nascent concern over sustainability. More recently, sustainability has been widely recognized throughout society as an increasing priority. The 1987 report, *Our Common Future*, published by the United Nations' World Commission on Environment and Development, famously defined sustainability as "meeting the needs of the present without compromising the ability of future generations to meet their own needs" (Brundtland, 1987, p. 16). Today,

sustainability is one of the world's most important priorities, and the National Park System has continued its leadership role (National Park Service, 2020).

Many of the national parks have become models of sustainability, and the NPS *Green Parks Plan* (National Park Service, 2023c) is their textbook. Released on Earth Day, 2012, the plan is now in its third edition (published in 2023) and crafts a blueprint for conserving energy, fuel, and water, and addressing the increasingly urgent challenges of global climate change. The plan sets forth five strategic goals: (i) to be climate friendly and climate ready; (ii) to be energy smart and water wise; (iii) to buy green and reduce, reuse, and recycle; (iv) to green our rides; and (v) to foster a sustainability ethic. These goals are monitored and progress is evaluated (National Park Service, 2023a).

As you explore many of the more than 400 national parks, be sure to notice the many ways in which sustainability has been integrated into their design and management (National Park Service, 2023a). For example, visitor centers are being retrofitted and new visitor centers are being designed in keeping with newly emerging environmental principles and priorities. The New River Gorge National Park and Preserve's Sandstone Visitor Center is a case in point. The building is located on the site of a former quarry and school, leaving undeveloped park lands undisturbed. The south-facing building allows maximum natural daylight and heating, and the light-colored roof minimizes the need for cooling. A geothermal system circulates water underground to reach the Earth's constant temperature, then returns water to the visitor center to heat or cool the building. All of this minimizes electrical and fossil fuel consumption. Environmentally certified wood, which comes from trees harvested in a manner that doesn't damage the integrity of the forest, has been used throughout the

© Robert Manning and Elizabeth Perry 2024. *Conversations About Visiting and Managing the National Parks* (R.E. Manning and E.E Perry) DOI: 10.1079/9781800626768.0018

visitor center. Native plants are used for landscaping, requiring less water, fertilizer, and pesticides than non-natives, and plants are watered with roof and stormwater runoff. These and other sustainability principles and practices are being used in visitor centers and other buildings throughout the National Park System (National Park Service, 2024).

An increasingly vital sustainability issue is global climate change, and the NPS's Climate Friendly Parks Program is an initiative designed to help address this. The program provides parks with tools and resources to help address the cascading effects of climate change across the National Park System. Components of the program include: (i) measuring park-based greenhouse gas emissions; (ii) educating park staff, partners, stakeholders, and the public about climate change; and (iii) assisting parks in addressing their climate change impacts (National Park Service, 2023b).

One of the most obvious effects of climate change is sea level rise, combined with more severe storms and associated storm surges (see more on climate change in Conversation 76). About a quarter of all national parks are found on or near the coastline, and a variety of actions are being taken to protect these places from sea level rise, now and in the future. For example, important historic and prehistoric shell mounds, some of them among the largest, most intact, and most significant in North America, are found at Canaveral National Seashore, Florida, and these are threatened by rising sea levels. The NPS is mapping and documenting these cultural resources to gather vital archeological, environmental, and paleontological data before these mounds are damaged or lost. At the same time, these sites are being stabilized through soft armoring and living-shoreline techniques. More aggressive action was needed at Cape Hatteras National Seashore where sea level rise was threatening the structural integrity of the site's historic lighthouse. After ultimately futile attempts to thwart shoreline erosion, the lighthouse was moved inland more than half a mile, a drastic and costly action, but the only way to save this structure that's so important to the park and history of the region.

The national parks have been especially active in implementing alternative transportation systems—modes of transportation other than private motor vehicles—that reduce energy consumption and emission of greenhouse gasses (see Conversation 92). For example, park visitors no longer drive into Zion Canyon, the principal visitor attraction at Zion National Park, instead riding a system of propane-powered shuttle buses. These quiet, clean-burning vehicles are a convenient and more energy-efficient means of accessing the park. Moreover, this public transit system helps relieve traffic congestion and the stress associated with finding a parking spot, and helps protect the natural quiet of Zion Canyon (see Conversations 79 and 86). The transit system at Zion and an increasing number of other national parks provide direct connections to surrounding gateway towns. Nearly 100 national parks have adopted alternative transportation systems—shuttle buses, ferries, bike paths—that contribute to their environmental and experiential sustainability.

There are many facets of sustainability that are being addressed throughout the National Park System, enhancing climate resilience and lowering greenhouse gas emissions. Examples include alternative fuels to oil, gas, and other petroleum products, local foods, organic agriculture, electric vehicles, energy efficiency, recycling and reuse, green buildings, water conservation, adaptive use of historic buildings, public transit, and more. But one of the most ironic examples of potential threats to the sustainability of the national parks is the high and growing number of visitors. As described in Conversations 73 and 74, 85 and 86, and 89, this issue is often called "carrying capacity": how much and what kinds of recreational uses can the national parks accommodate before the impacts of use—trampling vegetation, disturbing wildlife, water and air pollution, traffic congestion, crowding—begin to degrade park resources and the quality of the visitor experience to an unacceptable degree. Given the foundational democratic character of the parks and the desire to accommodate as many visitors as possible, this is a challenging issue and another application of the concept of sustainability.

In addition to managing these kinds of issues in the national parks, the NPS is integrating information about them into its educational programming (see Conversation 52), and using the work it's doing to address sustainability as models for the public to take back into their communities when they return home. Look for this type of programming in the visitor centers of many parks and enjoy interpretive programs—guided walks, campfire talks, educational displays and exhibits throughout the parks—that address these topics for visitors of all ages.

References

Brundtland, G. (1987) *Our Common Future*. Report of the World Commission on Environment and Development. United Nations General Assembly document A/42/427. United Nations, New York.

National Park Service (2020) Alternative Transportation Program. Available at: https://www.nps.gov/orgs/1548/multimodal-transportation.htm (accessed 15 October 2024).

National Park Service (2023a) Sustainability in the National Park Service. Available at: www.nps.gov/sustainability/index.htm (accessed 2 July 2024).

National Park Service (2023c) *Green Parks Plan: Advancing the National Park Service Mission Through Sustainable Operations*, 3rd edn. National Park Service, US Department of the Interior, Washington, DC.

National Park Service (2024) Climate Friendly Parks Program. Available at: https://www.nps.gov/subjects/climatechange/cfpprogram.htm (accessed 2 July 2024).

National Park Service (2023b) Green Parks. Available at: www.nps.gov/subjects/sustainability/green-parks.htm (accessed 2 July 2024).

Reynolds, J. and Diamant, R. (2016) Practicing sustainability. In: Manning, R., Diamant, R., Mitchell, N. and Harmon, D. (eds) *A Thinking Person's Guide to America's National Parks*. Braziller Publishers, New York, pp. 241–250.

19 Urban National Parks

Post

Uptownflunk (many of the usernames on social media are very entertaining) posted this image of Pullman National Historical Park in Chicago on Reddit:

From Reddit.

Tree1Dva responded:

I've been to Pullan three times over the last decade and every time I learn about some other crazy important historical/social/technological thing with roots there. Per square mile, one of the most significant sections of America.

Response

For many, the classic image of a national park is a rural, remote location with iconic scenery. Yes, those parks are flagship examples of the National Park System, but our spectrum of national parks extends far beyond wild spaces and rural areas. Some of these other national parks have been long standing, such as the national memorials and monuments in Washington, DC, that collectively constitute the National Mall and Memorial Parks. Others are more recent. For example, President Lyndon B. Johnson's War on Poverty included a push for more urban national parks designed to elevate the well-being of all Americans. From this effort and others in the 1960s and 1970s, an impressive number of urban national parks were established—recreation areas, historical parks, monuments, etc. Pullman National Historical Park in Chicago (the subject of this post) is one of our newer national parks in an urban area, established in 2016. This push for new national parks in, or proximate to, urban areas continues today, and these parks now constitute about a third of the National Park System (National Park Service, 2019).

As *Tree1Dva*'s post suggests, these parks are important for visitors from far-flung areas and can be a wonderful and enriching experience to add into a city trip. They may be even more important for locals. Urban national parks embody the foundational democratic notion of "parks for the people", offering nearby recreation opportunities for the more than 80% of Americans who live in urban areas. In this way, they offer an important component of social equity. These nationally recognized sites and stories are more accessible to urban residents than conventional rural national parks, allowing places for recreation, rejuvenation, and reflection without long-distance travel. They also help build community and pride in place, supporting a sense of community and the knowledge that these places are as much of the fabric of America as the grand landscapes of America's hinterlands. Many of the national parks in urban areas are predominantly historic, cultural, and/or heritage spaces and the narratives they tell are welcome additions (see Conversation 10). Moreover, most of these parks have natural features (some even have large swaths of natural landscaping, such as Crissy Field in Golden Gate National Recreation Area

© Robert Manning and Elizabeth Perry 2024. *Conversations About Visiting and Managing the National Parks* (R.E. Manning and E.E Perry)
DOI: 10.1079/9781800626768.0019

in the San Francisco Bay area and Cuyahoga Valley National Park just outside of Cleveland and Akron, Ohio), and these parks provide crucial ecosystem services such as shading and cooling urban heat islands, stormwater capture and filtration, and microhabitats for wildlife.

Reference

National Park Service (2019) The Urban Agenda. Available at: https://www.nps.gov/subjects/urban/index .htm (accessed 15 October 2024).

20 Marine Parks

Post

Alyssa posted a glowing Google Review about her fall experience at Apostle Island National Lakeshore:

> *Gorgeous scenery. A variety of ways to see it, kayak, boat tour, hiking the shoreline ... but gorgeous any way you choose. Especially beautiful in October. Was like a slice of Heaven*❤

Response

Ah yes, Apostle Islands! *Alyssa*, you are absolutely right. The NPS's collection of marine parks—those lining the country's seashores, in the open ocean, and along the Great Lakes like the one *Alyssa* visited—are truly wonderful. Although national parks were originally envisioned as land-based/terrestrial resources, the National Park System now encompasses 88 marine-related parks. Early efforts at national marine conservation included Pelican Island National Wildlife Refuge in Florida (1903) and Channel Islands National Monument (now National Park) in California (1938). Both of these were designated as wildlife sanctuaries, recognizing the unique vulnerabilities of animals relying on coastal and ocean conditions. As our understanding grew about vulnerabilities beyond single species to whole ecosystems (see Conversations 26 and 75), Congress and the NPS responded with the National Seashore Act (1961) and National Coastal Zone Management Act (1972). Coastal shores and waters we now enjoy as national parks such as Cape Hatteras National Seashore (North Carolina), and Cape Cod National Seashore (Massachusetts) were created in this period, with Great Lakes-based national lakeshores soon thereafter—Apostle Islands (Wisconsin), Pictured Rocks (Michigan),

Sleeping Bear Dunes (Michigan), and Indiana Dunes (Indiana; now a national park). Marine protected areas, a designation for offshore resources, were established beginning in the 2000s, an example of how we've continued to advance our ideas about, research on, and protections of marine life and related ecological systems.

For example, the NPS now works with other conservation partners like the National Oceanic and Atmospheric Administration, the California Water Resources Control Board, and The Nature Conservancy to manage more than just the originally preserved Channel Islands National Park (see Conversations 83 and 95 for more on "parknerships"). Together, they rely on integrated sciences—natural, social, and economic—to guide decisions about marine park policies and engagement. Through a series of expansions, the limited area protected in the 1930s now encompasses an international biosphere reserve and a national marine sanctuary, as well as more lands and waters within the national park itself. It also complements the system of state-administered marine reserves and conservation areas established in the early 2000s. Each of these areas that comprise the conserved lands and waters in and around Channel Islands National Park was sparked by a different focus—preservation, conservation, and/or protection (see Conversation 73). Yet so far, the results center on a key idea of "connectivity" between conserved spaces with restrictions on use, and areas between them with fewer or no restrictions on use or with different management aims (National Park Service, 2022).

We're encouraged that *Alyssa*'s post (and many others) highlight the "gorgeous scenery" of Apostle Islands and the many activities you can do there. Our coastal parks have a diversity of ways you can enjoy them from land and water. Whether taking in the sights by land or exploring via kayak or tour boat, these places

© Robert Manning and Elizabeth Perry 2024. *Conversations About Visiting and Managing the National Parks* (R.E. Manning and E.E Perry)
DOI: 10.1079/9781800626768.0020

offer a variety of recreation. Narrated boat tours provide opportunities for learning and seeing sights such as lighthouses and ice caves that might be too far apart for someone to travel by boat or kayak on their own. Also, they can provide an idea of the "lay of the land" for further exploration later. These all represent ways in which the NPS tries to facilitate connections between people and our marine resources. Heavenly indeed, as *Alyssa* notes.

Although we are not an aquatic species, more than half of the world's population lives within 100 miles of the ocean. This indicates the opportunity these places have for connection and learning, as well as their continued fragility. Issues like climate change, ocean acidification, unnatural lake level fluctuations, overfishing, and increased commerce continue to present challenges requiring good science and engaged people in these areas.

Reference

National Park Service (2022) National Parks Protect our Ocean and Coasts. Available at: https://www.nps.gov/subjects/oceans/index.htm (accessed 15 October 2024).

21 Wilderness

Post

Nook recently used Google Reviews to post the following comments about a visit to Grand Teton National Park:

Grand Teton National Park is a gem of the American wilderness, offering a perfect blend of natural beauty, adventure, and tranquility. Whether you're seeking adrenaline-pumping activities or peaceful moments of reflection, this park has something for everyone, making it a must-visit destination for nature enthusiasts of all ages.

Response

The Environmental Movement of the 1960s and 1970s led to passage of a suite of important Congressional legislation to protect the environmental quality of the nation. Examples include the National Environmental Policy Act, the Clean Water Act, the Clean Air Act, and the Endangered Species Act. The Wilderness Act of 1964 is an early example of this sweeping program of environmental legislation that has increasingly important implications. The act defines wilderness as "an area where the earth and its community of life are untrammeled by man, where man himself is a visitor who does not remain" (Wilderness Connect, no date). Congress directed the four largest federal land management agencies—NPS, US Forest Service, US Fish and Wildlife Service, and the Bureau of Land Management (see Conversation 4 for more about these and other types of public lands)—to recommend to Congress which areas of public land should be designated as wilderness and become part of the National Wilderness Preservation System (NWPS).

As *Nook* suggests, much of the National Park System is often referred to as "wilderness", referencing its wild character. But the word "wilderness" also has a specialized meaning in the context of national parks (and other federal lands, such as national forests). Sometimes this is suggested by capitalizing the word. We're sorry to be so technical about this, but designation of an area by Congress as "wilderness" makes a big difference about how these areas are managed and what visitors are likely to find there. We explain a little more about this issue as follows (National Park Service, 2023b).

The Wilderness Act specifies that areas proposed for wilderness designation should "generally appear to have been affected primarily by the forces of nature, with the imprint of man's work substantially unnoticeable" (Wilderness Connect, no date). Moreover, the following uses are not allowed on lands designated as wilderness: (i) commercial enterprises; (ii) construction of temporary or permanent roads and aircraft-landing facilities; (iii) use of motorized equipment, motor vehicles, motorboats, or other forms of mechanical transport; (iv) timber harvesting; and (v) construction of structures or other installations. Non-motorized recreation is generally allowed, though it is regulated to help protect the environmental integrity of the area. The NWPS has grown substantially and now totals nearly 112 million acres, an area slightly larger than the state of California.

Much of the National Park System—more than 44 million acres or about half the system—is included in the NWPS. This land is found in about 50 national parks (this number continues to rise), and these parks are found throughout the nation, ranging from Fire Island National Seashore (that ironically offers outstanding views of the New York City skyline) to Gates of the Arctic National Park and Preserve (that features more than seven million acres of wilderness). Some national parks are almost entirely wilderness; for example, 90% of Yosemite National Park is wilderness, 93% of Glacier National Park, and 99% of Isle Royale National

DOI: 10.1079/9781800626768.0021

Park. The website National Park Service (2024) in the References at the end of this conversation lists national parks that include wilderness. However, much of the remaining land in the National Park System is eligible for wilderness designation and is therefore managed to protect the wilderness character of these lands. Consequently, more than 80% of the National Park System is managed for its wilderness values.

Some people might wonder why the national parks should be protected through wilderness designation, because the national parks were already established to preserve these places. But portions of most national parks have been developed to allow visitor use; examples include roads, visitor centers, campgrounds, hotels, and other visitor facilities and services. Areas of the national parks that are designated as wilderness (or are eligible for this designation) must remain undeveloped, with the primary exception of trails and campsites. So wilderness designation adds another layer of protection to national parks.

Recreational use of wilderness areas (e.g. hiking, camping, fishing) is generally encouraged by the NPS, though use levels are generally kept substantially lower than in the developed portions of the parks. In fact, the Wilderness Act specifies that wilderness areas are to be managed "to provide opportunities for solitude" (Wilderness Connect, no date). Wilderness recreation is generally managed to emphasize the naturalness of these areas, provide recreation opportunities that offer quality time together for family and friends, inspire reflection and inspiration, and provide a sense of discovery and adventure. The NPS's (2023a) America's Wilderness Webisode Series (listed here in the References) features short videos that highlight the special connections that are often shared between visitors and NPS wilderness areas.

The concept of wilderness can be as complex as it is compelling. While the focus is obviously on the naturalness of the environment, it is hard to ignore the fact that the world is increasingly affected by climate change (see Conversation 76), expanding urbanization, extinction of species, and widespread air and water pollution. Together, these and related issues suggest that we have entered the "Anthropocene", the "age of humans", and that little or no true wilderness is left on the planet (see Conversation 82 for more about the management implications of all this). Moreover, some observers argue that we do a disservice by relegating humans as somehow "unnatural", especially considering that our evolutionary ancestors lived on Earth for several million years. Further, defining wilderness as a place "where man himself is a visitor who does not remain" (Wilderness Connect, no date) ignores the Indigenous presence of many centuries (see Conversation 17).

Wilderness management can also be controversial. For example, mountain bikes are not allowed in wilderness areas because they are mechanical conveyances that are specifically prohibited in wilderness areas (see Conversation 41 about biking). Mountain climbing is also controversial because it sometimes employs power drills to set anchors (installations that are also sometimes left on the landscape), and some people feel this violates the provisions (and the spirit) of the Wilderness Act. Wildfire policy can also be controversial as management agencies may be more inclined to allow natural fires to burn in wilderness areas (see Conversation 77).

References

Aldo Leopold Wilderness Research Institute (2024). Available at: https://leopold.wilderness.net/ (accessed 3 July 2024).

Arthur Carhart National Wilderness Training Center (2024). Available at: https://carhart.wilderness.net/ (accessed 3 July 2024).

Minteer, B. and Manning, R. (2016) Wilderness preserves. In: Manning, R., Diamant, R., Mitchell, N. and Harmon, D. (eds) *A Thinking Person's Guide to America's National Parks*. Braziller Publishers, New York, pp. 105–116.

National Park Service (2023a) America's Wilderness Webisode Series. Available at: https://www.nps.gov/subjects/wilderness/multimedia.htm (accessed 3 July 2024).

National Park Service (2023b) Wilderness is for All. Available at: https://www.nps.gov/subjects/wilderness/index.htm (accessed 3 July 2024).

National Park Service (2024) National Parks with Wilderness. Available at: https://www.nps.gov/subjects/wilderness/wilderness-parks.htm (accessed 3 July 2024).

The Wilderness Society (2024) The Wilderness Act. Available at: https://www.wilderness.org/articles/article/wilderness-act (accessed 3 July 2024).

Wilderness Connect (n.d) The Wilderness Act. An Act to establish a National Wilderness Preservation System for the permanent good of the whole people, and for other purposes. Public Law 88-577 (16 U.S.C. 1131-1136). 88th Congress, Second Session, September 3, 1964. Available at: https://wilderness.net/learn-about-wilderness/key-laws/wilderness-act (accessed 16 July 2024).

22 Spirituality in the National Parks

Post

OldF4therTime posted on Reddit about the spiritual meaning of national parks:

> *I'm really sad about my asthma. I'll never hike to the top of Old Rag* [in Shenandoah National Park] *or up Guadalupe peak* [in Guadalupe Mountains National Park] *and that makes me very sad. But the parks have enough amazing beautiful things that I can do that are still out of this world that keep my love of the outdoors alive. I'm very religious and I believe that these parks and nature in general are some of God's greatest artistic expressions. It's a spiritual experience.*

Response

We're sorry about your asthma, too, *OldF4therTime*, but it sounds like you're making the best of it, visiting and hiking in the national parks as much as you can; and your observations about the spiritual values of the national parks are shared by many other national park visitors. Although the separation of religion and state is a foundational principle of American government, expressly stated in the First Amendment to the Constitution, there's no denying that many people find spiritual meaning in the national parks.

The earliest expression of this spirituality in nature is found in Indigenous mythology. Many groups of Indigenous people consider their homelands and other sites to be sacred based on a variety of origin stories and the practice of giving thanks for the multiple blessings bestowed upon them by a variety of creators. This sacredness of many national parks based on these ideas is now an important part of the ways these parks are interpreted to the public by the NPS (see Conversation 52 for more on interpretation).

Nineteenth-century European Americans also found great spiritual values in nature and this began to be part of the rallying cry for protecting the first national parks such as Yellowstone, Yosemite, and Grand Canyon (see the Introduction to this book for a short history of the national parks). This was part of the Romantic Movement of the 19th century that focused on the values of nature as an antidote to the growing ills of the Industrial Revolution and concentration of people and associated problems in large urban areas. The spiritual teachings of transcendentalism, embraced by conservationists such as Ralph Waldo Emerson, Henry David Thoreau, and John Muir, posited that nature was God's most pure creation, and that getting close to nature was the best way to find spiritual truths. Arguing for the preservation of Yosemite, Muir famously wrote that "Everybody needs beauty as well as bread, places to play in and pray in, where nature may heal and cheer and give strength to body and soul alike" (Muir, 1912). Many national park visitors continue to write about the "sublime" character of powerful national park landscapes.

The National Park System includes a number of parks that celebrate religious traditions more directly. For example, San Antonio Missions National Historical Park in Texas preserves a string of four Spanish missions that advanced the Catholic religion. The NPS ensures the protection of these historic and sacred sites, while the San Antonio archdiocese oversees contemporary church services at these missions, including Sunday mass and weddings. Tumacacori National Historical Park includes the ruins of a 1691 Jesuit mission founded near present-day Tucson. Also the National Register of Historic Places, managed by the NPS (see Conversation 24 on the variety of conservation-related programs administered by the NPS) includes more than 400 Catholic churches, including the California missions established

DOI: 10.1079/9781800626768.0022

by Spanish Franciscan missionary St. Junipero Serra.

Some writers suggest that the US has adopted a "civic religion" that has strong connections to the National Park System. This is partly a reflection of the early American concept of Manifest Destiny and its strongly religious connections, the notion that the nation was given to us by the Divine. Moreover, the great nation that we've created reflects the ascendance of our ideals of freedom and democracy, and these accomplishments are celebrated in so many of the national parks, such as Independence National Historical Park, Statue of Liberty National Monument, Mount Rushmore National Memorial, and the many Revolutionary War battlefield parks.

Given the spirituality of the national parks to many visitors, it may be appropriate to think that at least some of the hundreds of millions of annual visits to the national parks are as much pilgrimages as recreation.

References

Bremer, T.S. (2021) The Religious and Spiritual Appeal of National Parks. *Sacred Wonderland,* August 29. Available at: https://www.sacredwonderland.us/religious-and-spiritual-appeal-of-national-parks/ (accessed 3 July 2024).

Bremer, T.S. (2023) In America, national parks are more than scenic – they're sacred. But they were created at a cost to Native Americans. *The Conversation,* November 20. Available at: https://theconversation.com/in-america-national-parks-are-more-than-scenic-theyre-sacred-but-they-were-created-at-a-cost-to-native-americans-215344 (accessed 3 July 2024).

Dallas, K. (2021) The religious significance of America's national parks. *Deseret News,* September 21. Available at: https://www.deseret.com/faith/2021/9/21/22683320/state-faith-newsletter-us-national-parks-religious-significance-arches-bryce-canyon-rocky-mountain/ (accessed 3 July 2024).

Muir, J. (1912) The Yosemite. The Century Company: New York. Available at: https://vault.sierraclub.org/john_muir_exhibit/writings/the_yosemite/ (accessed 16 July 2024).

Weichec, N. and Muth, C. (2016) National parks: places of wonder, history, spiritual refuge. *National Catholic Reporter,* October 29. Available at: https://www.ncronline.org/blogs/eco-catholic/national-parks-places-wonder-history-culture-spiritual-refuge (accessed 3 July 2024).

Other Dimensions of the National Parks

23 The Next National Parks

Post

Stonewall Inn (Greenwich Village, New York City), a catalyst location for the contemporary struggle for lesbian, gay, bisexual, transgender, intersex, queer/questioning, asexual (LGBTIQA+) rights, was declared a national monument in 2016 (Stonewall National Monument), only weeks after the Pulse Nightclub shooting in Orlando, Florida. This designation highlights the NPS's commitment to expanding themes of the American story represented in our national parks. This image by *Rhododendrites* posted on Wikimedia Commons sadly shows how civil rights for the LGBTIQA+ community are still not secure.

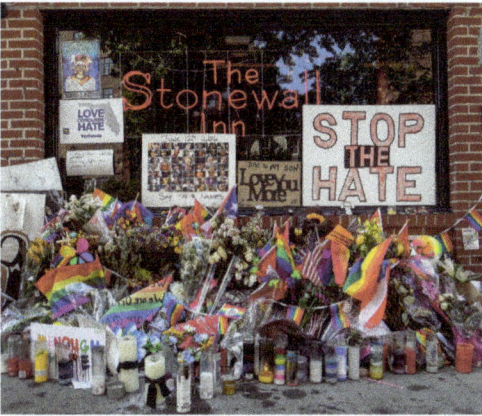

Stonewall Inn with Orlando nightclub shooting memorial during Pride 2016, Wikimedia Commons/*Rhododendrites*.

Response

How are decisions made about establishing new national parks? There are some stories of the American experience, such as the contemporary struggle for civil rights for LGBTIQA+ communities, that are underrepresented or absent in the National Park System and are therefore examined for potential establishment of new national parks. Similar consideration is periodically given to adding new types of natural areas that are unrepresented in the National Park System. Establishment of potential national parks normally precedes the needed Congressional action (in the case of national parks) or presidential action (in the case of national monuments) (see Conversation 5). Stonewall National Monument was added to the National Park System in 2016 to commemorate the mistreatment of LGBTIQA+ people following a brutal police crackdown there; this national park serves as a major catalyst in the Gay Rights Movement (now more inclusively referred to as LGBTIQA+ or Queer Rights). Let's briefly explore some of the major steps involved in establishing a new national park or monument.

The NPS process for evaluating additions to the National Park System is well structured. Many petitions come into the NPS from communities of place and communities of identity to consider a particular site as a new national park. To thoughtfully consider these, as well as apply their own filters and considerations of needs, the NPS considers three main criteria as a first pass. First, does the site contain nationally significant resources? These could be natural, cultural, and/or recreational resources (see Conversations 9 and 10) that hold "exceptional value" for the country. Second, can the site be effectively managed and protected within the National Park System? This is a consideration of suitability and feasibility (e.g. location, size, challenges). Third, is the NPS the best management agency for this site? This is an assessment of the need for federal management or if other agencies or entities can adequately protect the site and its resources (National Park Service, 2022a).

© Robert Manning and Elizabeth Perry 2024. *Conversations About Visiting and Managing the National Parks* (R.E. Manning and E.E Perry)
DOI: 10.1079/9781800626768.0023

These questions are addressed over a study process that can often be lengthy and that also consists of three steps. First, nominations for new national parks come through in the Proposal Initiation. These nominations may be from communities, members of Congress, local officials, tribal nations, or even from within the NPS itself. Second, if a site looks promising, a Reconnaissance Survey is undertaken. In this, the NPS conducts a preliminary assessment about the resources and potential challenges. Finally, if this basic information also looks promising, a Detailed Study is undertaken. In this, Congress may authorize an in-depth study about how well the site fares against the criteria and questions noted above. If all of these steps indicate that national park designation and management is appropriate, then the site may be put forward as a new national park or monument, either through congressional approval or presidential executive action (National Park Service, 2022b).

As the subject of the post precipitating this conversation indicates, there are parts of the American story that warrant further attention within the NPS and may lead to establishment of a new national park or monument. This process is called a "theme study" and pertains to ideas, identities, events, and places that have potential to be included as a National Historic Landmark, or perhaps a national park. Theme studies examine the specific historical context of a theme or a time period, such as LGBTIQA+, civil rights, women's rights, aviation, geology, the Underground Railroad, labor, or Asian American Pacific Islanders' histories. (The diversity of such theme studies is listed in the NPS links in the References at the end of this conversation.) Theme studies may be requested by Congress or within the NPS itself and often include collaboration with various interested communities and/or professional groups.

The processes outlined above normally govern how new national parks and monuments are established. But the reality is that Congress can establish new national parks with a majority vote and presidential signature, and the president can establish national monuments with a simple Executive Order (National Park Service, 2024).

What do you feel is an underrepresented theme in the National Park System, or a place worthy of NPS designation? If you feel passionately about such a theme or place, reach out to others and you may gather momentum toward the next national park.

References

National Park Service (2022a) Telliing all Americans' Stories: Introduction. Available at: https://www.nps .gov/subjects/tellingallamericansstories/index.htm (accessed 15 October 2024).

National Park Service (2022b) National Historic Landmarks: Theme Studies. Available at: https://www.nps .gov/subjects/nationalhistoriclandmarks/theme-studies.htm (accessed 15 October 2024).

National Park Service (2024) National Historic Landmarks: Full List of Theme Studies. Available at: https://www.nps.gov/subjects/nationalhistoriclandmarks/full-list-of-theme-studies.htm   (accessed 15 October 2024).

24 Beyond the National Parks

Post

This historic photo of New York City's iconic Penn Station was posted on Wikimedia Commons by the New York Public Library's Miriam and Ira D. Wallach Division of Art, Prints, and Photographs. This grand, Beaux-Arts style building was a city landmark for decades. However, the building was demolished in the 1960s as a part of "urban renewal", and this galvanized a social movement to preserve the nation's historic architecture. The NPS administers the resulting National Historic Preservation Act of 1966 which has helped save many of the nation's historic buildings from the wrecking ball.

Penn Station, East Facade, New York City, Wikimedia Commons/Detroit Publishing Company.

Response

Of course, the NPS is widely known for its management of the extensive US National Park System, a collection of more than 400 national parks that total more than 85 million acres and that extend to all 50 states and several US territories (see Conversation 2). But, as if that weren't enough, the agency's responsibilities and work extend to a number of related activities that are important in protecting the nation's natural and cultural resources and providing outdoor recreation opportunities, many of them at the state and local levels. Most of these programs have their genesis in important Congressional legislation that assigns NPS the responsibilities needed to carry out these national mandates. Many apply to the federal government, but also extend to—in fact, are directed at—state and local governments, and frequently include a suite of non-profit citizen groups as well.

One of the most prominent programs is NPS administration of the US Land and Water Conservation Fund (LWCF). Derived from royalties paid to the federal government for offshore oil leases, up to $900 million is invested annually in acquiring park and outdoor recreation lands at all levels of government and development/redevelopment of outdoor recreation facilities. Since its inception in 1965, the LWCF has funded billions of dollars through tens of thousands of grants to federal agencies, states, tribal nations, local governments, and cities. More recently, the 2020 Great American Outdoors Act committed to permanently and fully funding the LWCF. Examples of projects funded by the LWCF include the Allagash Wilderness Waterway (Maine), Liberty State Park (New Jersey), Willamette River Greenway (Oregon), Platte River Park (Denver), Herman Brown Park (Houston), and Illinois Beach State Park (Chicago).

In an analogous way, the National Historic Preservation Act of 1966 is directed at saving many of our nation's cultural resources. The act was precipitated by the demolition of New York's Penn Station in 1962, a large, iconic Beaux-Arts style building that was a city landmark. Loss of this building and many others around the country was devastating much of the country's cultural history. The National Historic Preservation Act is instrumental in helping save and reuse/repurpose many historic

© Robert Manning and Elizabeth Perry 2024. *Conversations About Visiting and Managing the National Parks* (R.E. Manning and E.E Perry)
DOI: 10.1079/9781800626768.0024

buildings and neighborhoods, and the NPS plays an important role in administering this program. In particular, the NPS administers the National Register of Historic Places, the official list of nearly 100,000 of the nation's historic places that have been judged the most worthy of preservation. Related programs include the National Historic Landmarks Program, the Historic Preservation Tax Incentives, the Historic American Building Survey, the Historic American Engineering Record, the NPS Heritage Documentation Program, and the Historic American Landscapes Survey. The NPS plays an important role in administering these programs, and this work is a natural extension of the many historic sites that are included in the National Park System.

The NPS also helps administer two other important national conservation programs: (i) the National Trails System; and (ii) the National Wild and Scenic Rivers System. The National Trails System was established by Congress in 1968 and includes national scenic trails (iconic long-distance trails such as the 2200-mile Appalachian National Scenic Trail), long-distance national historic trails (such as the 1,200-mile Juan Bautista de Anza National Historic Trail), and a large number of national recreation trails that have been designated in many states and local communities. The National Wild and Scenic Rivers System was also established by Congress in 1968 and includes exceptional rivers around the country that have been designated to protect their free-flowing condition, water quality, and outstanding natural, cultural, and recreational values. The NPS manages wild and scenic rivers that flow through national parks and offers technical assistance to states and local communities regarding river management issues.

The NPS created and administers the Rivers, Trails, and Conservation Assistance Program (RTCA) to provide conservation and recreation technical support to communities across the nation. While the NPS doesn't provide funding for these projects, it does provide professional services to help communities achieve their conservation and outdoor recreation objectives.

25 Economics of National Parks

Post

Responding to a report shared on Facebook by Carlsbad Caverns National Park staff that visitors to the park spent $25.1 million in communities near the park, supporting 312 local jobs and creating a cumulative benefit of $27.4 million to the local economy, *Ann Marie* responded:

> *Trying to do our part*❣

Response

Many of us enjoy visiting national parks, but we probably don't often think about the economic implications of this. But, in fact, the national parks generate quite a large economic impact that's enjoyed by those who live near the parks and the larger US economy as well. The NPS conducts periodic studies in which park visitors report the amount of money they spend on their trips to the national parks, and the results are impressive. For example, study findings for 2022 estimate the 312 million visits to the national parks generated $23.9 billion of spending in the communities within 60 miles of a national park (National Park Service, 2023). Moreover, these expenditures supported 378,400 jobs in park gateway communities. In the post above, Carlsbad Caverns details numbers from one such study and *Ann Marie* kindly lends moral support beyond the statistics. All this is part of the new science of "parkonomics".

It's interesting to compare this economic impact with the expenditures from the federal government to manage and maintain the national parks. The 2022 budget for the NPS was $3.3 billion, "effectively turning a $1 investment in national parks into a more than $10 boost to the nation's economy" according to the National Park Service (2023). That sounds like a pretty good investment.

But it's even better than that—much better. As discussed in Conversation 26, the national parks also: (i) protect air and water quality; (ii) help reduce the impacts of climate change by sequestering carbon in trees and other plants; (iii) help to regulate flooding, stabilizing soils; (iv) help to pollinate agricultural crops; and (v) contribute to human health and well-being. These kinds of benefits from parks and other protected areas are often called "ecosystem services". Economists have begun to estimate the economic value of ecosystem services and the results are staggering. The value of the natural environment to the world's economy is estimated well into the trillions of dollars, and this suggests that the contemporary decline of environmental quality is undercutting the robustness of the economy. This, in turn, suggests the substantial and increasing value of national parks and related areas. A study more specific to the US national parks estimates the economic value of the ecosystem services derived from the National Park System to be $98 billion annually (Flyr and Koontz, 2023).

So while we appreciate the national parks for all the enjoyment they offer (as *Ann Marie* puts it in her post: ❣), we should also appreciate them for the multiple ways they contribute to local, national, and global economies.

DOI: 10.1079/9781800626768.0025

References

Flyr, M. and Koontz, L. (2023) National Park Visitor Spending Effects: Economic Contributions to Local Communities, States, and the Nation. Natural Resource Report NPS/NRSS/EQD/NRR—2023/2551. Fort Collins, Colorado. Available at: https://www.nps.gov/nature/customcf/NPS_Data_Visualization/docs/NPS_2022_Visitor_Spending_Effects.pdf (accessed 3 July 2024).

National Park Service (2023) National Park Visitation Sets New Record as Economic Engines. Available at: https://www.nps.gov/orgs/1207/national-park-visitation-sets-new-record-as-economic-engines.htm (accessed 3 July 2024).

26 Ecosystem Services

Post

On X, *PEERorg* shared a quote from a staffer, *Hudson*, about the value of the ecosystem of the Mississippi National River and Recreation Area in St. Paul, Minnesota:

> *These spaces allow you to access wild areas that rejuvenate you and remind you how the land may have been before the urban areas built up around them … a real treasure.*

Response

Most people would probably agree that national parks are great places to visit because they offer beautiful scenery, teach us so much about our human history, and offer great opportunities for outdoor recreation. "A real treasure," as *Hudson* points out (and we agree). National parks do all these things and so much more. In fact, we've only recently become more conscious about the many ways the parks and related areas contribute to human well-being. These benefits of national parks are increasingly called "ecosystem services" and represent the multiple ways that protecting our natural and cultural environment contribute to human welfare and the quality of life (see Conversation 25 for more about the economic benefits of ecosystem services).

Ecosystem services are generally thought of in four categories. "Provisioning services" reflect the ability of humans to gather useful products from the natural environment; examples include food, water, wood, minerals, and medicines. "Regulating services" reference the benefits obtained from natural processes; examples include air and water purification, sequestration of carbon to help counterbalance the carbon emissions that contribute to climate change, flood regulation, soil stabilization, and pollination of agricultural crops. "Cultural services" include non-material benefits that flow from natural environments, including aesthetic appreciation, recreation, spiritual enrichment, and intellectual stimulation (see Conversations 78 and 79 that discuss the recent recognition of natural darkness and natural quiet as cultural ecosystem services). "Supporting services" are related to naturally functioning ecosystems that help support human life; examples include photosynthesis, water and nutrient cycles, soil creation, and maintenance of genetic diversity. *Hudson*'s words support the cultural benefits of the Mississippi National River and Recreation Area and also hint at the regulating and supporting services that this national park plays in an urban area and for the central US more broadly (Flyr and Koontz, 2023).

The concept of ecosystem services suggests that when we help preserve natural ecosystems we are also contributing to human welfare, including the economy. In fact, economists have begun to estimate the economic values of ecosystem services and the results are staggering. The value of the natural environment to the world's economy is estimated well into the trillions of dollars, and this suggests that the contemporary decline of environmental quality is undercutting the robustness of the economy. This, in turn, suggests the substantial and increasing value of national parks and related areas. A study more specific to the US national parks estimates the economic value of the ecosystem services derived from the National Park System to be $98 billion annually.

© Robert Manning and Elizabeth Perry 2024. *Conversations About Visiting and Managing the National Parks* (R.E. Manning and E.E Perry)
DOI: 10.1079/9781800626768.0026

References

Costanza, R., de Groot, R., Sutton, P., Ploeg, S., Anderson, S.J. *et al.* (2014) Changes in the global value of ecosystem services. *Global Environmental Change* 26, 152–158. Available at: https://doi.org/10.1016/j.gloenvcha.2014.04.002

Flyr, M. and Koontz, L. (2023) National Park Visitor Spending Effects: Economic Contributions to Local Communities, States, and the Nation. Natural Resource Report NPS/NRSS/EQD/NRR—2023/2551. Fort Collins, Colorado. Available at: https://www.nps.gov/nature/customcf/NPS_Data_Visualization/docs/NPS_2022_Visitor_Spending_Effects.pdf (accessed 3 July 2024).

Millennium Ecosystem Assessment (2005) Ecosystems and Human Well-being: Synthesis. Island Press, Washington, DC. Available at: https://www.millenniumassessment.org/documents/document.356.aspx.pdf (accessed 4 July 2024).

Sutton, P.C., Duncan, S.L. and Anderson, S.J. (2019) Valuing our national parks: an ecological economics perspective. *Land* 8, 54. Available at: https://doi.org/10.3390/land8040054

27 International Connections

Post

In leaving a Google Review on Chamizal National Memorial in El Paso, Texas, *Ping* noted the park's cross-border history. This shared history informed a sister park arrangement between the park and Parque Chamizal in Ciudad Juárez, Chihuahua, Mexico.

Learnt a lot about Chamizal, specifically the history of the harmonious settlement of a 100-year boundary dispute between the United States and Mexico. The gentleman ... was very helpful. He told me a few facts that I didn't see from the brochure. (Thank you!)

Response

It is widely recognized that Yellowstone National Park—established in 1872—was the world's first national park, the first time a nation set aside a large area of its land for the benefit of all its citizens (see the Introduction to this book for more about the history of the national parks). Since then, the National Park System has grown to more than 400 national parks and is admired throughout much of the world. But the NPS also has a strong international component. In 1916, when the NPS was established, the agency was directed by the Secretary of the Interior to maintain contacts with national park leaders in other nations for their mutual benefit. A century after the establishment of Yellowstone, the US proposed the World Heritage Convention, an international treaty under the auspices of the United Nations to extend the national park idea on a global basis. The NPS Office of International Affairs was established to facilitate cooperation between the NPS and related agencies around the world.

For example, the Office of International Affairs coordinates US participation in the United Nations World Heritage Program and the related World Heritage List. In fact, the US helped establish this program through ratification of the World Heritage Convention as noted above, a landmark program designed to advance the cause of conserving "the heritage of humanity", the world's most important examples of our global natural and cultural history. Moreover, the US includes 25 World Heritage Sites, most of them directly associated with the National Park System (see Conversation 31 on World Heritage Sites).

Recognizing that individual parks are rarely large enough to encompass the full extent of important natural and cultural resources, the NPS also participates in the Sister Parks Program. For example, two national parks—one in the US and the other in Mexico, recently formed a sister parks arrangement to celebrate the peaceful resolution of the historic international border dispute between these countries. *Ping*'s post notes this history that precipitated the arrangement. Parque Chamizal (in Mexico) and Chamizal National Memorial (a US national park) are now sister parks and recognize their shared history and present in this example of international cooperation. A related program of such international parks is Waterton-Glacier International Peace Park, established in 1932, in which the US and Canada cooperate in protecting this section of the Rocky Mountains.

For many years, the NPS has participated in a number of technical assistance programs around the world. These programs include visits to other countries by NPS staff, and reciprocal visits by park staff of other nations to meet with NPS officials at the agency's Washington, DC, headquarters or in the field at selected national parks. Countries that have recently participated in this program include Japan, Lebanon, Senegal, South Africa, Estonia, Latvia, Lithuania, Georgia, and Rwanda.

The NPS also administers an International Volunteers in the Parks Program, whereby

© Robert Manning and Elizabeth Perry 2024. *Conversations About Visiting and Managing the National Parks* (R.E. Manning and E.E Perry)
DOI: 10.1079/9781800626768.0027

more than 100 people each year from all over the world volunteer in US national parks. Volunteers receive training in park management and related topics, and NPS staff gain new perspectives on managing national parks. The program is directed primarily at college students who are studying park management and closely related fields.

Reference

National Park Service (2023) Office of International Affairs. Available at: https://www.nps.gov/orgs/1955/index.htm (accessed 4 July 2024).

28 National Park Books

Post

Like a lot of us, *jervacious* wanted some suggestions for a holiday gift, so she posted the following question on Reddit:

> *My Partner Wants a Book About the National Parks for the Holidays. Anyone Have Any Recommendations?*

There were lots of replies such as the following:

> *WillinPin3949:* Desert Solitaire *by Edward Abbey. It's about Arches National Park, fantastic read.*
>
> *SirDwightSchrute: I just finished* Leave Only Footprints *by Conor Knighton. Heartbroken guy visits every national park in the country. Thoroughly enjoyed it :)*

Response

Given the importance of the national parks, it shouldn't be surprising that there are lots of books about them. Consulting some of them will help prepare you for your national park visits and enhance your understanding and enjoyment of the parks. These books vary widely in their subject matter and approach, and include guidebooks (see Conversation 71), histories, photography, research, and management. (There are also national park cookbooks, coloring books, knitting books, children's books, journaling books, calendars, books of stickers, novels, and more, but these aren't included here.) Here are short descriptions of several books about the national parks that are highly recommended.

- *National Geographic Books*—There's been a long and productive association between the National Geographic Society and the national parks, and this is reflected in the small library of National Geographic Books about the parks. These are primarily guidebooks, and they're all authoritative, well researched and written, and usually well illustrated with the highest quality photos. Recommended titles include *Guide to the National Parks of the United States*, *Complete National Parks of the United States*, *Secrets of the National Parks*, and *Atlas of the National Parks*.

- *Treasured Lands: a Photographic Odyssey Through America's National Parks* (QT Luong, 2022, Terragalleria Press)—There are a number of very good books that feature photographs of the national parks, but this is the best. Luong is the only photographer to capture photos of all 63 of the units of the National Park System that are titled "national parks" with state-of-the-art large-format equipment. The book has won a dozen national and international awards.

- *Wilderness and the American Mind* (Roderick Nash, 2014, Yale University Press)—Now in its fifth edition, this is a classic study of the evolving attitudes of Americans about nature and wilderness, and includes a strong emphasis on the national parks. This is a scholarly book, but is highly readable.

- *National Parks: the American Experience* (Alfred Runte, 2010, Taylor Trade Publishing)—Now in its fourth edition, this is a classic history of the US national parks. It's well researched and presented, though it needs a little updating. This is a scholarly book, but is highly readable.

- *To Conserve Unimpaired: the Evolution of the National Park Idea* (Robert Keiter, 2013, Island Press)—This is another history of the US national parks that is well researched and presented. It's also a scholarly book that is very readable.

- *Preserving Nature in the National Parks* (Richard Sellars, 1997, Yale University Press)—This is another history of the US

© Robert Manning and Elizabeth Perry 2024. *Conversations About Visiting and Managing the National Parks* (R.E. Manning and E.E Perry)
DOI: 10.1079/9781800626768.0028

national parks with a special emphasis on the need for a stronger emphasis on environmental protection in the national parks and more emphasis on science-based management of the parks. Written by a senior NPS historian, this book is well researched and respected.

- *A Thinking Person's Guide to America's National Parks* (Robert Manning, Rolf Diamant, Nora Mitchell, and David Harmon, 2016, Braziller)—Prepared to help celebrate the centennial of the NPS, this is an edited volume that discusses the many dimensions of the national parks and the NPS, including history, recreation, education, conservation, science, Indigenous people, civil rights, urban national parks, international connections, and the future of the National Park System. The book is richly illustrated with engaging photos.

- *Yosemite: the Embattled Wilderness* (Alfred Runte, 1990, University of Nebraska Press)—This book addresses the history and management of the national parks by focusing on Yosemite National Park. This is a scholarly book and generally readable, but is getting a little dated.

- *Wildland Recreation: Ecology and Management* (William Hammitt, David Cole, and Christopher Monz, 2015, Wiley Blackwell) and *Studies in Outdoor Recreation: Search and Research for Satisfaction* (Robert Manning et al., 2022, Oregon State University Press)—These are scholarly books that review and synthesize the research on parks and outdoor recreation with a special emphasis on national parks and wilderness. The former addresses ecological issues and the latter social science issues. These books are primarily used in college courses and by park and wilderness managers.

- *Managing Outdoor Recreation: Case Studies in the National Parks* (Robert Manning, Laura Anderson, and Peter Pettengill, 2017, CABI)—This book describes alternative practices for managing outdoor recreation in national parks and related areas, and presents a series of 25 case studies in the US national parks. This book is used primarily in college courses and by park and wilderness managers.

- *Walks of a Lifetime in America's National Parks* (Robert Manning and Martha Manning, 2020, Falcon/Rowman and Littlefield)—Hiking is the most intimate and authentic way to enjoy and appreciate the national parks. This award-winning book briefly describes all units of the National Park System that are titled "national parks" and recommends the best half dozen or so hikes in each; all of these trails have been hiked by the authors and have been chosen to best represent each park. The book is richly illustrated with high-quality photos.

- *Our National Parks* (John Muir, 1901)—Muir is generally considered the father of the national parks for the power and eloquence of his writing about the parks and advocacy for them. Sample the joy of his writing in this book that was originally published in 1901.

- *America's National Heritage Areas: a Guide to the Nation's New Kind of National Park* (Robert Manning, 2022, Globe Pequot Press)—Conversation 30 addresses national heritage areas (NHAs) as a new model of national parks, and this is a guidebook to the 54 NHAs scattered across the country. The book is richly illustrated with color photos.

- *Guide to U.S. World Heritage Sites: the Heritage of Humanity* (Robert Manning, 2024, Globe Pequot Press)—Conversation 31 addresses World Heritage Sites as a new model of national parks, and this is a guidebook to the 25 World Heritage Sites scattered across the country. The book is richly illustrated with color photos.

- *Desert Solitaire: a Season in the Wilderness* (Edward Abbey, 1968, Touchstone)—Based on his 2 years working for the NPS in Arches National Park, this book is a spirited and often irreverent defense of parks and wilderness by a prominent environmental writer of the 1960s. It's fun and thought-provoking (and is highly recommended by *WillinPin3949*!).

- *Dispossessing the Wilderness* (Mark Spence, 2000, Oxford University Press)—While the national parks are widely revered in American society, they were established at great cost to the Indigenous people who inhabited and used them for thousands of years. This book explores this dark dimension of the national parks and associated Indian removal.

- *The National Parks: America's Best Idea* (Dayton Duncan and Ken Burns, Alfred A. Knopf, 2016)—This is the companion book to the celebrated film by Burns and Duncan commemorating the centennial of the NPS (see Conversation 29 about the film of the same title). The book is richly illustrated.
- *Prophets and Moguls, Rangers and Rogues, Bison and Bears* (Heather Hansen, 2015, Mountaineers Books)—This is an eclectic and interesting collection of stories about the history of the national parks, prepared to help celebrate the centennial of the NPS.
- *The Wonder of It All: 100 Stories from the National Park Service* (Yosemite Conservancy, 2016)—In celebration of the 2016 centennial of the NPS, this diverse and engaging book presents short stories about the national parks told by 100 employees of the agency.

29 National Park Films

Post

Documentary films are a good way to learn about the national parks, and there are a number of films to choose from. *Andrew* recently watched Ken Burn's classic on the parks and raved about it on Letterboxd:

> The National Parks: America's Best Idea *is fantastic. It is of such incredible depth in these six episodes covering details I had absolutely no knowledge of. I mean, I'm a history major, and I have been to a bunch of parks and monuments, and I have a keen interest in environmentalism and the creation of these magical places. But the depth of this series is unreal.*

Response

The remarkable visual character of so many national parks lends itself nicely to films and documentaries, and there are lots of them out there to whet our appetites for visiting the parks and remind us why they are such important elements of our national landscape and history. In the process, many of these films tell the story of the national park idea, and the people and places that have helped establish and shape America's National Park System. Here are some of the best national park films and documentaries.

- *The National Parks: America's Best Idea*— Let's start with *Andrew*'s recommendation. It's a platitude to call a film "epic", but this one is. Produced by America's great documentary film-maker, Ken Burns, and written by Dayton Duncan, this is a six-episode series that tells the story of how the National Park System began and how it has evolved and expanded. It's a grand mix of the people who helped save these places

and stunning photography of the places themselves.
- *National Parks Adventure*—This documentary was originally released for IMAX theaters in 2016 to help celebrate the centennial of the NPS. Directed by Greg MacGillivray and narrated by Robert Redford, the film traces the history of the national parks and why so many people from around the world want to see them. One reviewer described the film as "equal parts adrenaline-pumping odyssey and soulful reflection on what the wilderness means to us all" (National Parks Adventure, 2015).
- *The Great Yellowstone Thaw*—This three-part series follows the iconic animals of Yellowstone National Park—bison, wolves, grizzly bears, beavers, and great gray owls— as the seasons change from the extreme cold of winter, through spring thawing, and summer wildfires. The film was co-produced by PBS (Public Broadcasting Service) and the BBC (British Broadcasting Corporation).
- *Into the Canyon*—Produced by National Geographic, this film follows Peter McBride and Kevin Fedarko as they hike 750 miles through the Grand Canyon. This is a compelling adventure, but the film also highlights the environmental threats to this flagship national park.
- *Our Great National Parks*—This is a five-part series produced by Netflix and narrated by Barack Obama that features iconic national parks from around the world, including the US. The film is breathtakingly beautiful in places, celebrates the foresight of so many nations in establishing these parks, and is educational and enlightening throughout.
- *America's National Parks at 100*—Produced by National Geographic, this film celebrates the 2016 centennial of the NPS. The film follows the story of America's National Park System from the wonders of nature at

DOI: 10.1079/9781800626768.0029

Yellowstone National Park in 1872 to the more than 400 national parks that now comprise the National Park System.

- **Films about specific national parks—** There are several good films/documentaries that feature specific national parks. For example, *The Everglades: Where Politics, Money, Race, and the Environment Collide* was produced by WFOR-TV in Miami and reports on the litany of environmental and social challenges that face the park. *Yosemite: the Fate of Heaven* is narrated by Robert Redford and traces the history of this iconic national park, including the pressures it faces from millions of annual visits. *Rocky Mountain National Park: Wilderness, Wildlife, and Wonder* was produced to celebrate the park's centennial in 2015 and features interviews with park rangers and stunning cinematography.

- **Films about rock climbing in Yosemite—**Yosemite National Park is world famous for its rock climbing, especially on iconic El Capitan. *Valley Uprising* was released in 2014 and traces the history and evolution of rock climbing in the park. *The Dawn Wall* tells the story of the 19-day ascent of El Capitan by Tommy Caldwell and Kevin Jorgeson. *Free Solo* traces the free-climb of El Capitan by Alex Honnold and captured the attention of so many Americans.

Finally, don't forget that most national parks show at least one film at their visitor centers.

Reference

National Parks Adventure (2015) MacGillivray Freeman's National Park Adventure. Available at: https://nationalparksadventure.com/about/ (accessed 22 July 2024).

30 National Heritage Areas

Post

Alan H. posted this comment on Tripadvisor about Atchafalaya National Heritage Area:

> *Louisiana is home to few areas which the National Park Service manages, but this large area (14 parishes) is expansive and representative of much of Louisiana. Focus most of your visit on the Atchafalaya Swamp. There's great fishing and dining throughout the area.*

Response

We're glad you've discovered this large and lovely national heritage area (NHA) in your home state of Louisiana, *Alan H*. Although the NPS doesn't manage this area, it's much like a national park and benefits from funding and technical advice provided by the agency. NHAs are relatively new places that are not yet well known among much of the public. They're much like national parks, except they're different in several important ways. President Ronald Reagan presciently noted to those in attendance at the dedication of the first NHA in 1984 that they were helping to establish "a new kind of national park". Fast forward to today and there's now a system of 62 NHAs scattered around the nation. NHAs are typically large areas—sometimes even vast expanses—that reflect the sense of place of these distinctive regions, including their natural and cultural history, educational offerings, and outstanding collections of visitor attractions and recreation opportunities.

While NHAs are not really national parks, they are close cousins. Jon Jarvis, recent Director of the NPS, echoed this idea when he spoke of NHAs as "part of the family" (Jarvis, 2016). In official bureaucratic language, NHAs are "related areas" of the NPS which describes them as "linked in importance and purpose to places managed directly by the National Park Service by preserving important segments of the nation's natural and cultural heritage" (National Park Service, 2024). NHAs receive some (limited) funds from the NPS and, perhaps more importantly, technical assistance and related guidance. Both national parks and NHAs can only be established by Congress. Moreover, national parks and NHAs share a strong sense of purpose; their conservation, education, and recreation-related objectives echo one another.

However, the methods employed by NHAs to achieve these objectives are different—very different—from those used in conventional national parks. National parks are generally large areas of public land owned and managed by the NPS, a federal agency. NHAs take a more inclusive, partnership-based approach; they offer non-profit organizations, private enterprise, interested citizens, and all levels of government the opportunity to help define, celebrate, conserve, and share the natural, historic, cultural, scenic, and recreational resources that have been vital in shaping the identity and destiny of the regions within their borders. Perhaps NHAs might best be described as "parknerships". Moreover, NHAs are composed primarily of private lands; they're "living landscapes" where residents live, work, and play.

NHAs are much like the national parks found in many other countries, particularly in Europe where the population density is high compared to the US, and it's especially challenging to find large areas of public lands (see Conversation 83 on new models of national parks). Instead, these national parks include a mix of public and private lands, even including whole communities. Former Director of the NPS, Jon Jarvis, once said that "America invented the idea of national parks, the idea went around the

© Robert Manning and Elizabeth Perry 2024. *Conversations About Visiting and Managing the National Parks* (R.E. Manning and E.E Perry)
DOI: 10.1079/9781800626768.0030

world, and it came back different" (Manning, 2024, p. 2). The US can benefit from the experience of other countries in establishing these new kinds of national parks.

Before establishment, Congress must be convinced that NHAs are (or can become) cohesive, distinctive, and nationally important landscapes organized around history, environment, industry, geography, and/or other themes. In other words, NHAs must be recognizable "places". This assurance often requires a feasibility study that may lead to establishment of an NHA by Congress. Once established, NHAs must conserve the resources that are important to their identity while balancing community needs for sustainable economic development that commonly focuses on heritage-based education, recreation, and

tourism. This program of work must be guided by a management plan. NHAs are usually managed (actually, the word "coordinated" is often preferred) by a local partner organization—often a local non-profit group—that is entrusted with planning and management responsibility. Many NHAs include units of the National Park System. For example, Great Basin National Park in Nevada is the core area of nearly 80,000 acres owned and closely managed by the NPS, and this is complemented by the vast—more than ten million acres— Great Basin National Heritage Area that links the park to surrounding national forests, tribal lands, and numerous small communities in the states of Nevada and Utah. Private land is generally not acquired by the federal government for the purposes of NHAs.

References

Jarvis, J. (2016) *My narrative: The administrative history of the National Heritage Areas Coordinating Office*. National Park Service Oral History Collection (HFCA 1817). Harpers Ferry, WestVirginia. Available at: https://www.nps.gov/npgallery/GetAsset/AA79D0BE-ECAC-45FD-9073-2B370F61BD FF (accessed 22 July 2024).

Manning, R. (2022) *America's National Heritage Areas: a Guide to the Nation's New Kind of National Park*. Globe Pequot Press, Guilford, Connecticut.

Manning, R. (2024) *A Guide to U.S. World Heritage Sites: the Heritage of Humanity*. Globe Pequot Press, Guilford, Connecticut.

National Park Service (2024) About Us: National Park System. Available at: https://www.nps.gov/aboutu s/national-park-system.htm (accessed 15 October 2024).

31 World Heritage Sites

Post

Packbj posted this image of Cliff Palace at Mesa Verde National Park on Wikimedia Commons:

Mesa Verde National Park, Wikimedia Commons/*Packbj*.

sheamus was also taken with her visit to this national park, writing on Google Reviews:

> *Mesa Verde National Park is a historical treasure trove, offering a captivating glimpse into the lives of the Ancestral Puebloan people. The awe-inspiring cliff dwellings and archaeological sites are a testament to the ingenuity and cultural richness of this ancient civilization. Walking through these well-preserved dwellings not only provides a sense of wonder but also a profound appreciation for the craftsmanship and resourcefulness of those who inhabited this land centuries ago. Mesa Verde National Park is an invaluable gem, a must-visit for history enthusiasts, nature lovers, and anyone seeking to explore the intriguing past of the Southwest.*

Response

Nice photo, *Packbj*, and well stated, *sheamus*. The world officially agrees with both of you,

inscribing this national park as a World Heritage Site in 1978. World Heritage Sites are the most iconic and well-known international conservation areas around the globe, and the US boasts 25 of them, most of them national parks. The international network of World Heritage Sites is the signature component of the World Heritage Convention, an outgrowth of global interest in conservation of the world's most significant natural and cultural places. While initial interest in the concept of the World Heritage Convention can be traced to the post-World War I period, it didn't begin its journey into reality until establishment of the United Nations in 1945. Later that year, the United Nations created a specialized agency, the United Nations Educational, Scientific and Cultural Organization, widely known as UNESCO. The objective of the agency is to promote world peace and security through international cooperation in education, arts, sciences, and culture. An early UNESCO initiative was the International Campaign to Save the Monuments of Nubia, begun in 1960 in response to the plan to construct the Aswan High Dam on the Nile River in Egypt. This planned project would have inundated many ancient treasures of Egyptian civilization. The 1960 campaign accelerated archeological research in the area that would be affected by the dam, and the vital Abu Simbel and Philae Temples were dismantled and reassembled on higher ground where they stand today.

Success with this and other initiatives eventually led to development by UNESCO of the Convention Concerning the Protection of the World Cultural and Natural Heritage (usually abbreviated as the "World Heritage Convention") in 1972, an international treaty. By 1975, the World Heritage Convention had been ratified by the required minimum number of nations belonging to the United Nations, and the convention went into effect. Some observers suggest that the World Heritage Convention may

© Robert Manning and Elizabeth Perry 2024. *Conversations About Visiting and Managing the National Parks* (R.E. Manning and E.E Perry)
DOI: 10.1079/9781800626768.0031

be one of the most important global conservation initiatives. Sites considered for inscription on the World Heritage List must be determined to have "outstanding universal value", a key term that is at the heart of the World Heritage Convention. This means that sites selected for inscription must meet the especially high bar of *global* importance, and not be of "just" national significance. Moreover, host nations must make an explicit commitment to uphold and protect the outstanding universal values of the sites they nominate. Once a site is inscribed on the list, periodic monitoring of the site must be conducted and reported.

Another key term in the World Heritage Convention is "heritage", and it's been taking on new and expanding meaning over the more than 50 years of the convention's existence. According to the *Oxford English Dictionary* (2024), "heritage" refers to "the full range of our inherited traditions, monuments, objects, and culture". Merrian-Webster (2024) builds on this by suggesting that heritage is "something transmitted by or acquired from a predecessor: legacy, inheritance". In the context of the World Heritage List, these are the vital places and ideas that helped shape the modern world, including its cultural and natural inheritance, and that civilization should pass along to future generations.

Equally important, heritage is increasingly recognized as having cultural and natural components, and this is evident in the wide-ranging list of historic and cultural monuments, as well as the diverse collection of distinctive landscapes and natural environments, that comprise the World Heritage List. The World Heritage Convention originally specified that two types of sites would be included on the World Heritage List, *cultural* and *natural*. However, more recently (and progressively), the meaning of heritage has begun to address the diverse and complex *inter-relationships* between culture and nature. Over the millennia of human history, culture has defined and expressed the many ways humans relate to nature, including the components of the natural environment that we value, and how we've shaped nature, often in distinctive, pleasing, and sustainable ways. Nature has helped mold culture as well as being manifested in the many expressions of the natural environment found in history, philosophy, art, literature, lifestyles, and the contemporary expression of environmental conservation.

Although history is clear that humans haven't always respected the lessons that have flowed out of healthy and productive relationships between nature and culture, the World Heritage List is a hopeful sign that this is changing. Given this evolution in the notion of heritage, the World Heritage List now includes a third category of sites that are called "mixed" or more eloquently "cultural landscapes" (see Conversation 11) in recognition that sites can (and often do) have both natural and cultural qualities that should be acknowledged, respected, and protected. The interaction between culture and nature, at least in some cases, might be just as important as either independently. For example, at Yellowstone National Park, one of the initial World Heritage Sites, the park's natural attractions—the world-famous thermal features, snow-capped mountains, wild rivers, rich meadows, iconic wildlife—justifiably overwhelm visitors. But the park has strong human and cultural connections as well—the presence of Indigenous people for 11,000 years, the historic European-American settlement of the area, and establishment of the world's first national park. Moreover, the interplay of the cultural and natural—the Indigenous worldview toward nature, the exploitation of nature by many European-American settlers, the commitment to preserving the area as a national park and now a World Heritage Site, and recognition of the ways in which nature can contribute to human well-being—are substantive and significant ideas that can and should enhance the power of this place to the world, and be celebrated as part of its outstanding universal values.

Other types of World Heritage Sites are "serial" and "transboundary". Serial sites are geographically discontinuous areas linked by their common natural and/or cultural values: the US World Heritage Site, "The 20th Century Architecture of Frank Lloyd Wright" is a good example. This site includes eight buildings across six states, each building designed and constructed by Wright, the American architect who had such a powerful influence on architecture across much of the world. The eight buildings illustrate the progression of Wright's distinctive architectural philosophy. Transboundary sites are located in more than one nation. For example, Kluane/Wrangell-St. Elias/Glacier Bay/Tatshenshini-Alsek World Heritage Site straddles the US/Canadian border and was the first transboundary World Heritage Site.

Americans can be proud of the leadership role the US has played in the establishment, administration, and participation in the World Heritage Convention. Some scholars trace at least part of the initiative for the convention to the concept of national parks that first emerged in the US with establishment of Yellowstone National Park in 1872, widely regarded as the world's first national park (see the Introduction and Conversations 1–6 for more on the history of the US National Park System). More recently, the US: (i) hosted the first World Parks Congress in 1962; (ii) initiated and conducted a long-running International Short Course on Administration of National Parks and Equivalent Reserves designed to share experience and expertise in park management with UNESCO member nations; (iii) carved out a special component of the nation's iconic Peace Corps program devoted to helping provide staff for parks in developing countries; (iv) was the first nation to ratify the World Heritage Convention; and (v) contributed the idea of combining natural and cultural heritage under a single international treaty (similar to the way that the US National Park System includes both natural and cultural heritage sites).

Ironically, the US has also had a checkered relationship with UNESCO, the United Nations entity responsible for administering the World Heritage Convention. The US has twice withdrawn from UNESCO, once for perceived mismanagement of the agency (though political considerations may have also been involved) and once as a protest against UNESCO's inclusion of Palestine as a UNESCO member. Despite these temporary withdrawals, the US has continued its active role in the World Heritage Convention during these periods. The US rejoined UNESCO in 2023.

There's a strong connection between World Heritage Sites and the US National Park System. More than half of the 25 US World Heritage Sites are national parks; examples include Yellowstone National Park, Mesa Verde National Park, and Statue of Liberty National Monument. Some are interesting combinations of sites that tell more comprehensive stories than individual national parks can. For example, Waterton-Glacier International Peace Park World Heritage Site includes the National Park System's Glacier National Park and Parks Canada's Waterton Lakes National Park. Together, these parks showcase and protect the core of the Northern Rocky Mountains and its substantive natural and cultural history. Other US World Heritage Sites are not part of the US National Park System; examples include the Monumental Earthworks of Poverty Point, Cahokia Mounds State Historic Site, and Taos Pueblo. US World Heritage Sites make great destinations for visitors interested in national parks and related attractions.

References

Manning, R. (2024) *A Guide to U.S. World Heritage Sites: the Heritage of Humanity*. Globe Pequot Press, Guilford, Connecticut.

Merrian-Webster (2024) Heritage (noun). *Merrian-Webster Dictionary*. Available at: https://www.oed.com/dictionary/heritage_n?tab=meaning_and_use#1764513 (accessed 23 July 2024).

Oxford English Dictionary (2024) Heritage (noun). *Oxford English Dictionary*. Available at: https://www.merriam-webster.com/dictionary/heritage (accessed 23 July 2024).

UNESCO World Heritage Convention (2024) World Heritage List. United Nations Educational, Scientific and Cultural Organization (UNESCO). Available at: https://whc.unesco.org/en/list/ (accessed 5 July 2024).

32 Biosphere Reserves

Post

Diane shared a posting on Facebook about her experience at Big Thicket Biosphere Reserve in Texas, which includes Big Thicket National Preserve:

> *Big Thicket Association hosted its 2nd Big Thicket Bus Tour today! We had so much fun sampling trails on the western side of the preserve plus a tour of the field research station where researchers lodge while conducting research in the Big Thicket National Preserve ...*

Response

That sounds like a delightful and informative day on the trails and in the field research station! It's nice to see the Big Thicket Biosphere Reserve celebrated, especially since it includes the national park of a similar name within its boundaries. Certainly the conceptual ties between the two areas are strong, but there might be some confusion between what differentiates Big Thicket *Biosphere Reserve* and Big Thicket *National Preserve*. (By the way, the name "Big Thicket" refers to the dense loblolly pine-hardwood forests included in both areas.)

Biosphere reserves are a newer model of protecting land and seascapes on the international level, administered by the United Nations Educational, Scientific, and Cultural Organization (UNESCO). These large landscape conservation initiatives encompass whole regions (similar to national heritage areas, see Conversation 30). They specifically focus on the coexistence of people and nature, balancing conservation and society. Because of this explicit and intentional focus on humans as part of nature, common themes of management and programming relate to: (i) sustainable human activities in the area; (ii) livable and thriving communities; (iii) local empowerment and economic well-being; and (iv) place-based attachments and stewardship. In this way, they're considered learning laboratories for sustainability (much like national parks—see Conversation 18), where we can try out and share different approaches about what may work best in one context, or across many contexts, in helping us learn to live with nature.

A biosphere reserve is typically divided into three zones. Within a designated reserve, there will be a core area or areas. These are the places with the tightest restrictions on human use. The focus here is on preserving natural habitats and intact ecosystems. If this sounds like the more nature-focused national parks to you, that's right. National parks often act as core areas within a biosphere reserve and therefore are at the heart of these conservation measures. Outside of the core area is a buffer zone. These areas allow for human activities that are compatible with the stated conservation goals of the reserve, such as traditional practices, research, and monitoring. These might be lands with fewer prohibitions that surround national parks, or conserved landscapes of other types (e.g. conservation easements). Finally, there are transition areas beyond the buffer zones. These bridges support sustainable human activities such as housing, recreation, and agriculture, with a focus on minimizing these activities' ecological impact.

There are hundreds of biosphere reserves internationally and 28 currently in the US. These 28 represent a variety of ecosystems—deserts, forests, grasslands, rivers, and coasts. Within the system of international biosphere reserves, the US Biosphere Network has opted for a new term in discussing these places. Instead of biosphere "reserve" in the US, you may find them called biosphere "regions". This is a move to emphasize the dual role of humans and nature in the making and maintenance of a place, opting for

© Robert Manning and Elizabeth Perry 2024. *Conversations About Visiting and Managing the National Parks* (R.E. Manning and E.E Perry)
DOI: 10.1079/9781800626768.0032

the geographic designation of "region" rather than one with connotations of limited human activities like "reserve".

Bringing it back to the Big Thicket Biosphere Reserve in Texas, some initiatives like the one referenced in *Diane*'s post focus on scientific research and education about the natural and cultural history of the Big Thicket region. Others focus on the seasonal replanting of longleaf pines and trash pickup (i.e. rubbish collection) along the trails and roads of the region. The national park is the heart of the biosphere reserve, encompassing over 100,000 acres representative of the region. It's complemented by other protected areas as buffer zones, such as the Angelina National Forest and McFaddin National Wildlife Refuge and state-level protected areas. There are many partners working together with the biosphere reserve, such as the NPS, Big Thicket Association, the National Parks Conservation Association, Big Thicket Natural Heritage Trust, and the Texas Conservation Alliance. These activities and partnerships, as well as science and societal considerations, are all aimed at sustaining human and non-human life in this "biological crossroads of North America", which is what people have called Big Thicket as it is one of the most biologically diverse assemblages of species in the world (National Park Service, 2024a).

References

Center for Large Landscape Conservation (2022) US Biosphere Regions. Available at: https://largelandsc apes.org/biosphere-regions/ (accessed 5 July 2024).

National Park Service (2024a) Big Thicket National Preserve. Available at: https://www.nps.gov/bith/learn /nature/index.htm (accessed 23 July 2024).

National Park Service (2024b) US Biosphere Network. Available at: https://www.nps.gov/subjects/conne ctedconservation/us-biosphere-network.htm (accessed 5 July 2024).

Part 2: Visiting the National Parks

Introduction

33 Plan Your Visit

Post

Some people create simple plans (if any at all) when they intend to visit national parks. Others, like *thefalcon3a* on Reddit, create detailed processes to plan the perfect trip:

> *I get my information from a variety of sources (NPS, AllTrails, Facebook groups, Instagram, etc.). When I'm in the research phase, I add pins to Google Maps of the places I want to hit. Once I've got a good amount built up, I use Google Docs to categorize and prioritize the top things I want to do ... Then I plan the route and accommodations, then fill in an itinerary. Once all of that is done, I use Google Calendar to lay it all out ... to make sure each day is realistic. In the Google Doc, I then go back to the original list and prioritize the things I wasn't able to fit in. That's helpful in the event that weather or something else unforeseen changes plans and we need to pivot.*

Response

Given the size and diversity of the National Park System, planning a visit to the parks can be a little complicated, even intimidating. But there are lots of tools that can help, as *thefalcon3a* lists in detail above. There are a number of good guidebooks to the parks (see Conversation 71), the National Park Service (NPS) has developed a helpful NPS App (see Conversation 36), the NPS "Find a Park" website is helpful in seeing all the national parks by state (see Conversation 35), and the large network of NPS websites—including a network of websites for each national park—provides a great deal of information for each of the more than 400 national parks (see Conversations 2 and 34). Also the NPS has even developed a "Trip Planning Guide" (see National Park Service (2023) listed in the References at the end of the conversation). Let's briefly walk through it.

The guide is organized into four sections: (i) know before you go; (ii) arrival at the park; (iii) during the trip; and (iv) after the trip. As described in Conversation 35, use the NPS website "Find a Park" to help you decide which parks to visit. Then use the Trip Planning Guide to help plan your visit. The first section of the guide, "Know Before You Go", includes nine basic steps. First, learn about the parks you're considering visiting by finding the park's official NPS website; a good way to find these websites is to enter "nps" followed by the name of the park. Make sure you're logging on to the official NPS website. Here you'll find a great deal of authoritative information about each park. Use the "Plan Your Visit" and "Learn about the Park" options. Then follow the other eight steps: (i) find out what activities you can do; (ii) know your limits; (iii) pick the right activity for you; (iv) look for regulations, permits, and reservations needed for your activity; (v) create a backup plan; (vi) pack the ten essentials; (vii) share your trip plan with a trusted contact; and (viii) create an emergency plan.

The second section of the Trip Planning Guide is "Arrival at the Park" and includes five steps: (i) check park conditions; (ii) check the ten essentials and your gear; (iii) ask yourself if you're ready for your planned activity; (iv) put a backup plan into action (if necessary); and (v) pick up any needed permits. The third section of the guide addresses "During the Trip"—the six steps include stick to your plan, stay within designated areas, stay together, stay aware of your surroundings, keep a safe distance from wildlife (see Conversation 45), and check in with yourself if you should continue your activity. The fourth section addresses "After the Trip"—the three steps include check in with your trusted contact, think about the lessons learned, and share your experience.

© Robert Manning and Elizabeth Perry 2024. *Conversations About Visiting and Managing the National Parks* (R.E. Manning and E.E Perry)
DOI: 10.1079/9781800626768.0033

The Trip Planning Guide even includes a sample trip plan and an Outdoor Emergency Plan. Also you can find some insider tips in the NPS article titled "Plan Your Vacation Like a Park Ranger" (see National Park Service (2024) in the References).

References

National Park Service (2023) Trip Planning Guide. Available at: https://www.nps.gov/subjects/healthands afety/trip-planning-guide.htm (accessed 5 July 2024).
National Park Service (2024) Plan Your Vacation Like a Park Ranger. Available at: https://www.nps.gov/a boutus/news/plan-like-a-park-ranger.htm (accessed 5 July 2024).

34 Digital NPS

Post

On Reddit, *hc2121* posted a wealth of resources about winter travel to Yosemite and how to know about park conditions using the nps.gov/yose web pages (accessed 5 July 2024). Many others chimed in about using this variety of web resources. When *STONEFREE_in_LA* asked about whether it was already winter conditions, *hc2121* was able to direct them to the park's webcam for current conditions:

> *Yes, it snowed a few feet last week. Take a look at the webcams linked above in daylight tomorrow.*

Response

The NPS has established an expansive, substantive, and user-friendly presence on the Internet and in the broader digital world. This includes websites, apps, social media, and more. As the agency was approaching its centennial in 2016, it redesigned and expanded its digital presence, starting with its flagship network of websites organized around its signature nps.gov address (accessed 5 July 2024). At this address, you'll find a vast amount of helpful, informative, and up-to-date information on all of the more than 400 national parks, the many programs offered by the NPS, helpful advice for visiting the parks, and much more.

Let's start with "mother site", the extensive network of websites organized around its signature address. This network of sites includes more than 100,000 web pages prepared by more than 1000 authors contributing authoritative content. Its value and popularity are reflected in its impressive annual use figures: more than 100 million annual visitors and more than 500 million page views. This is a clear signal of the popularity and power of this vast digital world

of the national parks. Begin your exploration on the nps.gov web page where you'll find options for "Plan Your Visit", "Learn & Explore", and "Get Involved" (see Conversation 33 for more about planning your visits to the national parks). You'll find all of these options interesting and useful, including the webcams streaming live feed from park locations.

In addition to the general nps.gov website, all of the national parks have their own network of websites to help you learn more specifically about them and plan your visits. Generally, the address of the official NPS website for each park is "www.nps.gov/____", the four letters at the end of the address are the official abbreviation of the park name. For example, the website address for Yosemite National Park is "www.nps.gov/YOSE". Since most people don't know these four-letter abbreviations, simply enter the name of the park in your browser. But be careful to *select the official NPS website* among the options that pop up; this site will feature the name "National Park Service" and the official NPS "arrowhead" emblem at the top (see Conversation 7 about the NPS arrowhead). Some of the other options will probably be commercial websites and none can be trusted to the degree that the official NPS website can.

Websites for most parks begin with any alerts (e.g. road closures) that might be in effect. These would be important for extreme conditions as well as seasonal travel, such as visiting Yosemite in the winter. Most then offer at least the three primary options noted above on the general NPS website (though these options offer much more specific information on the individual parks). The first is "Plan Your Visit" and has especially helpful logistical options such as "Basic Information", "Directions and Transportation", "Eating and Sleeping", "Places to Go", "Things to Do", "Calendar", "Safety", and "Accessibility". The "Learn About the Park" option will deepen your enjoyment and appreciation of the park,

© Robert Manning and Elizabeth Perry 2024. *Conversations About Visiting and Managing the National Parks* (R.E. Manning and E.E Perry)
DOI: 10.1079/9781800626768.0034

and includes options such as "History and Culture", "Nature", "Education", "Kids and Youth", and "Management". The third option is "Get Involved" and includes information on "Partner Organizations" (see Conversation 97 on this), "Volunteer" (opportunities to volunteer in the national parks; see Conversation 98 for more), and "Work With Us" (employment opportunities; see Conversation 99). Most park websites are rich in photos and some have additional "Photo Galleries" that can generate excitement about visiting.

While the network of NPS websites is the digital workhorse of the agency, the newer NPS App is a welcome and useful addition, especially for mobile devices that can be used while in the parks (see Conversation 36 about the app). The app was created by NPS staff, the people who know the parks the best, and provides up-to-date, authoritative, and helpful information in an easy-to-use format. Features include interactive maps, self-guided park tours, key park attractions, visitor facilities and services, accessibility resources (e.g. audio descriptions of popular park sites; see Conversation 54), creation and sharing of virtual postcards, and special alerts. This free app should be downloaded on your mobile device before you reach the park (especially for remote parks where cell service is spotty), is available for iOS and Android-powered devices, and is available from the APP Store and Google Play.

Like much of the world, the NPS is also active on social media. This presence is designed to reach new audiences, promote a wider and deeper understanding of the national parks, and expand the community of park advocates. Current media channels include Facebook, Instagram, Twitter, Flickr, LinkedIn, and YouTube. NPS on Instagram has become a big hit; check it out for both its information and entertainment value. All these platforms welcome discussion and debate, though postings must be respectful and family friendly. See the NPS social media website (National Park Service (2022) in the References at the end of this conversation) for more information and guidelines.

Other features of the NPS digital world include lots of photos and multimedia, a large collection of digital stories about the NPS and the national parks, and the NPS Data API (application programming interface) that allows NPS data and content to be used by internal and external developers of apps, maps, and websites. All of these links are listed in the References.

The digital world of the national parks is engaging and informative, and should be explored to help plan enjoyable and rewarding visits to the national parks. But be sure to leave time to actually visit these remarkable parks!

References

National Park Service (2019a) Digital Stories. Available at: https://www.nps.gov/subjects/digital/digital-st ories.htm (accessed 5 July 2024).

National Park Service (2019b) NPS Data API. Available at: www.nps.gov/subjects/digital/nps-data-api.ht m (accessed 5 July 2024).

National Park Service (2020) Transforming the NPS Digital Experience. Available at: https://www.nps.gov /subjects/digital/index.htm (accessed 5 July 2024).

National Park Service (2022) Social Media. Available at: https://www.nps.gov/subjects/digital/social-med ia.htm (accessed 5 July 2024).

National Park Service (n.d.) Multimedia Search. Available at: https://www.nps.gov/media/multimedia-sea rch.htm (accessed 5 July 2024).

35 Find a Park

Post

National parks can be found along many roads and routes through the US. On Tripadvisor, *itsanissue* titled a post "Amazing Impromptu Visit" about their surprise finding of the George Washington Carver National Monument in Missouri, after seeing the NPS signature "brown sign" along a highway:

> *We were on a road trip to Branson, MO ... Along I-44 there is a Brown Sign announcing the George Washington Carver National Monument (literally about 5 minutes before the exit). Since we were not in a hurry, we decided to go check it out ... We were pleasantly and overwhelmingly surprised! It is a fabulous tribute to a great scientist who changed farming for the nation! ... There is a phenomenal film that you can watch before walking through the "museum." It's not huge, but it is really powerful. DEFINITELY a must see ... We intended to just "stop by." Our stop was 2 hours!!!!*

Response

The NPS celebrated its centennial in 2016 with the slogan "Find Your Park". (See the Introduction to this book for a short history of the NPS.) The slogan was designed to illustrate the number and diversity of national parks and to encourage people to consider visiting the national parks. The more than 400 national parks feature many kinds of natural and cultural environments and attractions found across the nation. Moreover, it's likely that there are several national parks in or near where you live. As *itsanissue* found, there are also national parks to be discovered along routes to other destinations!

A good way to start your planning is to look at the map of all units of the National Park System on the NPS website (www.nps.gov

(accessed 5 July 2024)). Click on "Find a Park" and then search by state. Then enter the name of the national parks you might be interested in visiting followed by "NPS" to be sure you'll see the official NPS websites for these parks (other commercial websites that reference these parks are likely to pop up too). The official NPS website for each park offers a great deal of information, including a description of the park and its primary visitor attractions. Most websites are rich in photos (some even have "Photo Galleries"), so it's easy to get a good sense of each park.

You'll notice that some parks can easily be visited together, even some of the larger national parks. For example, there are several national parks (Zion, Capitol Reef, Bryce Canyon, Canyonlands, and Arches) across southern Utah that nicely complement one another. So do the three national parks in the State of Washington (Olympic, Mount Rainier, and North Cascades), the three in the northern Rocky Mountains (Grand Teton, Yellowstone, and Glacier), three in the Dakotas (Wind Cave, Badlands, and Theodore Roosevelt), the three in Texas and New Mexico (Big Bend, Carlsbad Caverns, and Guadalupe), the two Hawaiian national parks (Hawaii Volcanoes and Haleakala), the three in the Southeast (Great Smoky Mountains, Shenandoah, and Blue Ridge Parkway), and lots more appealing combinations. Just be sure to budget enough time in each park to fully appreciate them.

Consider visiting national parks close to home. Some national parks are remote and require a long drive to reach them, and some even require a long ferry ride or airplane trip. However, many—even some of the larger national parks—are relatively close to population centers, for example: (i) Cuyahoga Valley National Park sits between Cleveland and Akron, Ohio; (ii) Shenandoah National Park is near the Washington, DC, metropolitan area;

© Robert Manning and Elizabeth Perry 2024. *Conversations About Visiting and Managing the National Parks* (R.E. Manning and E.E Perry)
DOI: 10.1079/9781800626768.0035

(iii) Acadia National Park is a short day's drive from the Boston area; (iv) Everglades National Park is just outside Miami; and (v) Mount Rainier National Park is close to the Seattle area. Also, as noted in Conversation 19, many national parks are located in or near urban areas. These are just examples. There are also a number of good guidebooks to the national parks; see Conversation 71 for brief descriptions of some of the best.

36 NPS App

Post

Responding to a question on Reddit about how to plan trips to national parks, *RangerBumble* noted the NPS App as part of the planning mix:

> *NPS launched its own app a few years ago. Each park is slowly adding more content but the maps are great.*

Response

The NPS is working hard to advance its digital and social media presence (see Conversation 34), and the NPS App is a big step forward. Using its trademark adage, "One app, every park at your fingertips", the NPS recently launched its popular app, the official app of the agency and the national parks. The app includes a variety of tools to help visitors plan their trips and explore the more than 400 units of the National Park System. The app is free, available for iOS and Android devices, and can be downloaded to your smartphone or tablet through the App Store and Google Play. The NPS is proud to say that the app has been created by NPS staff—the people who know the national parks best—helping to make the app authoritative and especially useful to visitors.

The app includes a variety of features, including the following:

- *Interactive maps*—All the national parks have detailed maps that lead visitors along park roads and trails, making the app an especially valuable on-the-ground tool. As *RangerBumble* notes and the NPS emphasizes, these maps are the most up-to-date of the resources available and an authoritative source for park road and trail conditions.
- *Places to go and things to do*—The national parks include lots of ways of experiencing

and appreciating them, including scenic drives, hiking, visiting museums, participating in ranger-led programs, and becoming a Junior Ranger. The NPS App helps lead visitors to all of these attractions.

- *Park tours*—The NPS describes this feature as "like having a ranger by your side to guide your trip". These suggested self-guided tours lead visitors to each park's primary destinations and attractions as well places that are off the beaten track.
- *Amenities*—The national parks include lots of visitor facilities and services—transportation, food, lodging, restrooms, shops, and more. The NPS app leads visitors to these essential facilities and services.
- *Accessibility*—Conversation 54 describes the ways in which the NPS makes the parks as accessible as possible to visitors with special needs, and the NPS app describes these facilities and services at each park.
- *Offline use*—Some of the national parks are found in rural or even remote areas with limited Internet access. The NPS App addresses this problem: download it before you arrive at these parks, then use the app while offline.
- *Virtual postcards*—The NPS App's virtual postcards feature allows users to create and share virtual postcards using your own photos of the park (and you!). Virtual postcards can be shared more widely on social media using #FindYourPark and #NationalParkWeek.
- *News, alerts, and events*—National parks tend to be dynamic places (changing weather conditions, new programs, emergency closures, etc.), and it's a good idea to stay in touch via the NPS App.
- *Virtual passport stamps*—Some national park visitors enjoy collecting passport

© Robert Manning and Elizabeth Perry 2024. *Conversations About Visiting and Managing the National Parks* (R.E. Manning and E.E Perry)
DOI: 10.1079/9781800626768.0036

stamps for each park they visit (see the website "Passport to Your National Parks" (America's National Parks, no date) in the References). The NPS App allows visitors to do this virtually.

- *Volunteer opportunities*—Conversation 98 describes the ways visitors can give back to the national parks through a range of volunteer opportunities. The NPS App includes many of these opportunities.

References

America's National Parks (n.d.) Passport to Your National Parks. Available at: https://americasnationalparks.org/passport-to-your-national-parks/ (accessed 5 July 2024).

National Park Service (2021) The NPS App. Available at: https://www.nps.gov/subjects/digital/nps-apps.htm (accessed 5 July 2024).

37 Recreation.gov

Post

The website, Recreation.gov, includes an option for users to make crowdsourcing postings about it. Here are a few:

> *Corie: The website is beautiful and it's so easy to use. We just booked a weekend in Sequoia for the 4th of July and are stoked to go!*

> *Miller: When it's time to get away and reconnect with nature, the reservation process and app make Paradise accessible.*

> *Joe: I was very surprised* [with Recreation.gov]. *This was smoother than most private reservation sites. The government* [is] *better at booking campsites and tickets than most of the private companies.*

Response

Recreation.gov (https://www.recreation.gov (accessed 5 July 2024)) is a powerhouse of a website/app that's indispensable to making campsite reservations, entering lotteries for special permits, and lots of other arrangements associated with visiting the national parks and other federal recreation areas. In fact, the site is the federal government's centralized travel planning and reservation platform, representing 14 federal agencies that offer outdoor recreation and related activities and opportunities. It also offers valuable tips and associated advice for travel planning to national parks and other public lands (see Conversation 4).

Some of the recreation opportunities in the national parks and other public lands are in especially high demand. For example, campsites in Yosemite Valley are limited in number and can't begin to accommodate public demand for them; reservations for these campsites must be made on Recreation.gov. Hiking to Angel's Landing at Zion National Park is one of the most popular hikes in the National Park System, and the hike requires a permit that is managed through a lottery system on Recreation.gov. Tickets are required to enter Independence Hall during most of the year, and these tickets are managed on Recreation.gov. Also entry to some of the most popular national parks require a "timed entry" reservation, and these are only available on Recreation.gov. These are just a few of the examples that require advance arrangements in the national parks and other federal recreation areas.

Recreation.gov is a large and sophisticated website (some first-time users might say complex, perhaps even confusing at times; however, the above postings suggest generally positive experiences). The website offers detailed instructions on how to: (i) create an account; (ii) review reservation policies (refunds, cancellations, etc.); (iii) enter lotteries; (iv) purchase an annual or lifetime pass (see Conversation 66); and (v) access a help center, and much more. Log onto the website, scroll through its features and read those of interest to you, and create a free account if you think you'll find it useful (and increasingly necessary). You should use the website in conjunction with the NPS websites (see Conversations 34 and 35). For example, if you're planning a visit to Great Smoky Mountains National Park, log onto that park's official website and find the facilities and services you're interested in using/visiting (e.g. campgrounds, tours, special permits). Then find these facilities and services on Recreation.gov to see when and how reservations can be made.

Reservations for facilities and services that are in high demand must usually be made well in advance, often 6 months or more. Recreation. gov (and personal experience) suggests the following approach to making these types of reservations (campsites are used in this example):

© Robert Manning and Elizabeth Perry 2024. *Conversations About Visiting and Managing the National Parks* (R.E. Manning and E.E Perry)
DOI: 10.1079/9781800626768.0037

1. Know the on-sale dates. For example, most campsites can be reserved 6 months prior to your arrival date (but double check this on Recreation.gov and the official park website).

2. Log in to your Recreation.gov account and become familiar with how to make a reservation. Enter the dates you're interested in and then check availability at each location. Avoid weekend dates if possible.

3. Be ready on the day and time when reservations are opened. Synchronize your clock to the Recreation.gov clock to be sure you're ready to request your reservation. Most campsites go on sale at 7 a.m. Pacific time (PT)/8 a.m. mountain time (MT)/10 a.m. Eastern time (ET), but not always! Check the campground's "Seasons and Fees" tab for the specific time and date. On the day of the sale, log in well before the sale begins. Bring up the campground page, add your dates, be ready to select an available campsite and "Add to Cart" the moment they are released for sale. Have your credit card ready and your alternate campsites in mind.

4. Don't hesitate. Seconds can make the difference between getting your reservation or not. Refresh your page at exactly the time sites are released for sale. Once you click "Add to Cart", the site is locked in your cart for 15 min to give you time to complete your reservation. If you do not complete the transaction within 15 min, the campsite is released for others to reserve.

5. Explore alternatives. For example, use Recreation.gov to find less-explored, off-the-beaten-path destinations. If you encounter a campground that does not have availability when you want to visit, use Recreation.gov to explore recommended sites nearby that may have space for you during that time frame. Locations often have peak seasons, and weekends tend to book up quickly as well; if you have flexibility in your schedule, you may find that shoulder seasons or weekdays are more readily available.

6. If you were unable to make a reservation, check back on availability periodically to take advantage of cancellations.

Despite the generally positive reviews of Recreation.gov featured at the beginning of this conversation, the site has been subject to criticism too. (Although some of this may be more related to unhappiness about needing to make reservations so far in advance, or disappointment about not being able to make a reservation, or "win the lottery.") The site is managed by a private company that's been contracted by the federal government, and fees to pay for this service are built into the user's transaction cost. Such so-called "junk fees" are subject to considerable criticism. Moreover, preliminary research suggests that the site (and how to use it) is less well known among some minority racial and ethnic groups, and that this has put them at a disadvantage in visiting national parks and other public lands.

Activities

38 Hiking

Post

Starinhon on Tripadvisor posted this photo from their hike through the Virgin River Narrows at Zion National Park, and wrote the review that follows of the hike as well, titled "Absolutely Unique & Unforgettable!!".

From Tripadvisor.

The Narrows, wow! Wow wow wow! I did this hike a day after Angel's Landing, and I was really wiped out, and was having second thoughts. I'm so glad I sucked it up and did it ... We hiked to the end of Wall Street (GASP! Gorgeous!) with the intent to go back to a split in the trail called Orderville Canyon. Sadly, there was a huge boulder with water rushing down that was blocking the way. Some people got up it, but we would've gotten soaked and it was too cold for that! The hike wasn't bad cardio wise, but it's tough on the muscles and feet. I've been on several hikes all over the country, but this one is the most uniquely awesome! BEAUTIFUL!

Response

Yes, Zion's hiking route through the Virgin River Narrows is one of the most iconic in the National Park System, but is just a sample of the many dramatic hikes in the national parks. But please check Zion's official website for details about this epic hike because it requires a permit and there are some very important safety considerations. The good news is that all visitors are welcome to hike the first few miles of the Narrows, and this is a highlight for many visitors.

Humans and the national parks are both made for walking. At the most fundamental level, walking on two feet is a vital attribute of being human, an evolutionary adaptation that sets us apart from all other animals. Walking allowed for adaptation of our forelimbs into hands for toolmaking, and our brains expanded to meet this new-found ability. Moreover, walking is a miracle, a symphony of our skeletal, muscular, and nervous systems that allows us to place one foot in front of the other for miles on end over all sorts of terrain with little conscious thought and without falling (at least not very often!).

In the context of national parks and related conservation areas, walking is usually called hiking (which sounds a little more intimidating than walking, but needn't be), and the national parks offer unusually abundant and rewarding opportunities. The current 63 units of the National Park System that are titled "_____National Park" include an estimated 21,000 miles of trails and the other more than 350 national parks include many thousands more. The National Trails System includes another 88,000 miles of trails. Further trails on other public and private lands open to public use (see Conversation 4) surely total multiples of the mileages noted above. Clearly, there are many lifetimes of hiking to be done.

Walking can also stimulate our thinking as it did for Aristotle and his philosopher colleagues who often walked as they thought and taught in the Lyceum of ancient Athens. More recent examples of the intellectual power of walking include William Wordsworth, Henry David Thoreau, and John Muir, some of the many poets, philosophers, and writers who found

© Robert Manning and Elizabeth Perry 2024. *Conversations About Visiting and Managing the National Parks* (R.E. Manning and E.E Perry)
DOI: 10.1079/9781800626768.0038

inspiration in their frequent walks. Muir, writing near the end of his life, wonderfully used his prolific walking as a metaphor, reflecting that "I only went out for a walk and finally concluded to stay out till sundown, for going out, I found, was really going in" (Wolfe, 1979, p. 439). But it was rough-and-ready environmental philosopher Ed Abbey who wrote more directly:

> You can't see anything from a car; you've got to get out of the goddamn contraption and walk, better yet crawl, on hands and knees, over the sandstone and through the thornbrush and cactus. When traces of blood begin to mark your trail, you'll see something, maybe.
> (Abbey, 1990, p. 25)

Walking can have important political and spiritual dimensions as well. The rich set of ideas associated with walking, along with the very act of walking itself, have advanced an array of political causes. Gandhi's 1930 Salt March across India protested unfair British taxes, Dr. Martin Luther King, Jr.'s 51-mile march from Selma to Montgomery, Alabama, in 1965 protested unjust voting rights, and Cesar Chavez's 340-mile March for Justice in 1966 called for national attention to the mistreatment of farmworkers (the latter two walks are commemorated in the two associated national parks: Selma to Montgomery National Historic Trail and César E. Chávez National Monument, respectively). Walkers need places to walk in, so one of the political causes closest to walkers is conservation. Consequently, they've banded together in powerful social forces (e.g. the Appalachian Mountain Club, the Sierra Club) for conservation and trails. Walking also contributes to sustainability because it has relatively little environmental impact when done responsibly (see Conversations 60 and 85). Spiritual dimensions of walking are most evident in the pilgrimage. Pilgrims have been walking for centuries to holy sites around the world to seek spiritual guidance, be healed, perform penance, fulfill religious obligations, and signal their faith.

Hiking is the most intimate and authentic way to experience and appreciate the national parks. When you travel at the human scale of 2–3 miles an hour, you can appreciate the parks through so many of the senses. See the tracks of elusive mountain lions at Glacier National Park, hear the iconic call of the canyon wren as you hike through Grand Canyon, smell the sweetness of ponderosa pine bark warming in the sun at Yosemite National Park, taste the salt air as you walk the Ocean Path at Acadia National Park, and feel the solid bedrock beneath your feet as you explore the trails of Isle Royale National Park. Hiking also offers a more personal way to appreciate the parks; step out of your vehicle and onto the trail, away from the roads, and leave the crowds behind, confronting only the beauty and history that's been set aside for your benefit, enjoyment, and inspiration.

References

Abbey, E. (1990) *Desert Solitaire: A Season in the Wilderness*. Simon & Schuster, New York.

Manning, R. and Manning, M. (2020) *Walks of Lifetime in America's National Parks*. Falcon, Guilford, Connecticut.

Wolfe, L.M. (ed.) (1979) *John of the Mountains: The Unpublished Journals of John Muir*. University of Wisconsin Press, Madison, Wisconsin.

39 Camping

Post

Tracy B. spent several nights at Grant Village Campground, one of several in Yellowstone National Park. This has been a traditional way for many people to experience the parks. She offered this very positive review on Yelp:

> *Stayed here for a week, and it was beautiful! The first site we were at was a bit cramped and right across from the bathrooms, but everyone around us was really nice and they respected the campsite rules with noise levels and space. The second site we were at was secluded and that was so nice, it truly felt like we were camping! We would definitely stay here again.*

Response

Camping is a common and much-loved way to visit many of the larger national parks, and developed campgrounds are usually available both inside and outside these parks. Backcountry or wilderness camping is offered in many of these national parks. These options are briefly described below.

Campgrounds in the national parks

Most campgrounds in the national parks are operated by the National Park Service (NPS); these campgrounds are often well located (e.g. some are close to attractions while others offer lots of solitude) and they're rustic (they generally don't provide hot water, showers, or electrical and other hook-ups for recreational vehicles). The names and locations of all NPS-managed campgrounds for each park are listed and described on the park's official website; on the website, select "Planning Your Visit" and either "Eating and Sleeping" or "Camping" (not all parks use exactly the same wording, but it will be similar to what we've noted above). You'll also find information on how campsites are allocated (generally first come, first served, or reservation). If campsites can be reserved, you'll also find how far in advance you can make reservations; generally, it's a good idea to make these reservations as far in advance as possible. A centralized reservation website (Recreation.gov) must usually be used to make campsite reservations; there's a toll-free telephone number as well: (877) 444–6777. (See Conversation 37 for more on this centralized website for reservations in the national parks and many other types of public lands.) Campsite fees are generally nominal and there's usually a liberal cancellation policy. If campsites are allocated only on a first-come, first-served basis, then schedule your visit to arrive at the desired campground as early in the day as possible.

NPS has contracted with private companies to manage some of their campgrounds, and these areas often provide more services such as electrical hook-ups for recreational vehicles (of course, these campsites cost more). If there are concession-operated campgrounds in the park, they'll be noted on the park website with a link to the company that manages them. Campsites in these types of campgrounds can (and should) be reserved well in advance.

Campgrounds outside the parks

There are often campgrounds outside the national parks. These campgrounds are usually managed by private companies and information about them can be found using Internet searches and/or apps designed for this purpose (e.g. AllStays Camp & RV; membership organizations such as KOA, Good Sam Club, and AAA).

© Robert Manning and Elizabeth Perry 2024. *Conversations About Visiting and Managing the National Parks* (R.E. Manning and E.E Perry)
DOI: 10.1079/9781800626768.0039

Chambers of Commerce in towns just outside the parks are also good sources of information. There may be campgrounds near national parks that are located in national forests, state parks, and other public lands (see Conversation 4 on other types of public lands). Use the Internet to find maps of public lands near national parks that interest you and then go to the websites for those areas.

Backcountry/wilderness camping

Many of the larger national parks include backcountry or wilderness areas where visitors can camp and backpack (see Conversation 21). "Backcountry" is a general term that refers to the non-developed portions of many parks, while "wilderness" is a more specific word that refers to non-developed portions of many parks that have been designated by Congress as wilderness areas under the provisions of the 1964 Wilderness Act. Many of the larger national parks may include 90% or more of their land as backcountry or wilderness, and much of this land is open to backpacking. Although this kind of hiking and camping is a traditional way of enjoying and appreciating the national parks, it's also subject to special provisions to help ensure protection of these areas, and a permit is usually required. Pertinent information is on park websites. In some especially popular parks, you may need to reserve permits well in advance or even participate in a lottery.

40 Scenic Drives

Post

Reddit user *BeardOfThorburn* commented about scenic drives through Capitol Reef National Park:

> *It's like living inside a car commercial. But then you get pie (really, they make pies here – look it up haha)*

Wikimedia Commons user *Greg W.* shared an image of such a drive through the park:

Capitol Reef NP, Notom Bullfrog Road, Oyster Shell Reef, Wikimedia Commons/*Greg W.*.

Response

Shortly after establishment of the NPS in 1916, a concerted effort was made to make the national parks more accessible to visitors, and roads for the nation's expanding number of cars was an important part of that initiative. Roads through many of the most iconic national parks were designed by landscape architects to carry their passengers to the park's primary features and along the most scenic routes (just the type of routes featured in car commercials, as *BeardOfThorburn* points out!). Engineers constructed many of these roads in the most daring places. Scenic drives through the national parks

remain primary attractions for most visitors. There are even some national parks that were established as parkways, designed specifically for scenic drives.

Let's look at some examples. Perhaps the most dramatic road in the National Park System is Going-to-the-Sun Road in Glacier National Park. This iconic road, one of the most celebrated in the National Park System, stretches more than 50 miles through the heart of the park, connecting the park's east and west entrances. This scenic drive treats visitors to what may be the most spectacular scenery in the Rocky Mountains, including glacier-carved peaks, turquoise alpine lakes, great swaths of mature forests, and some of the park's most popular trailheads. Sometimes simply called the Sun Road, it was constructed in the late 1920s and early 1930s, and is a National Historic Landmark and Historic Civil Engineering Landmark. The highest point along the road is iconic Logan Pass at 6646 ft, where mountain goats can often be seen. A narrated driving tour of the road can be downloaded from the iTunes Store, and public transit options are also available.

Rocky Mountain National Park's Trail Ridge Road is also impressive. This 48-mile road connects Estes Park on the park's east side with Grand Lake on the west, traveling for 11 miles above treeline and reaching a maximum elevation of just over 12,000 ft. As the road was being built in 1931, NPS Director Horace Albright gushed that "You will have the whole sweep of the Rockies before you in all directions" (National Park Service, 2024). In addition to the views, look for elk and bighorn sheep, stop at the visitor center, and make time for some short hikes.

Crater Lake Rim Drive in its namesake national park follows the 33-mile rim of this vast volcanic crater. The road features the lake's striking blue waters and 30 dramatic overlooks. A ranger-guided trolley tour is

© Robert Manning and Elizabeth Perry 2024. *Conversations About Visiting and Managing the National Parks* (R.E. Manning and E.E Perry)
DOI: 10.1079/9781800626768.0040

available in summer, and several trails lead to the surface of the lake (and a boat tour) and other destinations.

The Acadia Loop Road at Acadia National Park is a 27-mile loop around the east side of Mount Desert Island. This lovely route offers lots of scenic views of the park's granite mountains, inland lakes, and dramatic Atlantic Ocean coastline. It offers access to many of the park's major attractions such as Sieur de Monts, Sand Beach, Otter Point, and Jordan Pond House. A spur road leads off the Loop Road to iconic Cadillac Mountain (though a permit may be needed).

As noted above, some national parks were established as scenic drives or parkways, and the Blue Ridge Parkway may be the best example. Popularly known as "America's Favorite Drive", the parkway meanders for 469 miles that feature mountain views, deep forests, and the pastoral landscapes of the Appalachian Highlands. The parkway connects Shenandoah National Park to the north with Great Smoky Mountains National Park to the south and includes several lodging options along the road or a short drive off it.

These are just some of the most famous examples of scenic drives in the National Park System; in reality, most national parks have paved roads (more than 5000 miles in total), and these offer an appealing way to enjoy and appreciate the parks. If a scenic drive through Capitol Reef National Park isn't enticing enough, *BeardOfThorburn* notes that there's also the freshly made pie along the route in Fruita.

Reference

National Park Service (2024) Park Roads, Rocky Mountain National Park. Available at: https://www.nps.gov/romo/planyourvisit/road_status (accessed 23 July 2024).

41 Biking

Post

bicyclebikecycle recently posted the following on Reddit describing his epic bicycle trip to and through many national parks:

> *Hi! I'm currently 11,000 miles into my ride to all of the National Parks in the USA's lower 48 states. I've visited 35/51 parks. Right now I'm headed from Utah into Colorado. I started in Florida, went up to Seattle, down to LA, and over to Moab, UT. I've got a map on my website of an estimated route, and if any of you live along the way and want to meet up and ride. I'd welcome it! I'm doing this ride to advocate for more hiker/biker spots and cyclist friendly policies in our National Parks, and other publicly managed lands. With traffic becoming crazy in some of these places, and fees also getting a little out of control too, NPS needs to be making sure that they encourage and incentivize cycling on/to/through our public lands – not just driving.*

Response

Wow, *bicyclebikecycle*, we're impressed! We agree with you that biking is, indeed, a good way to see and experience a number of national parks; and we think the NPS agrees too, welcoming bikes in lots of national parks as a good way to experience the parks in a more up close and personal way, and as a substitute for more high-impact activities such as driving.

Bikers can generally use most park roads (though you should be very careful where you're sharing the road with cars as it's easy for drivers to be distracted by the scenery, park wildlife, etc.). Bikers can also use some park trails, though most trails are for pedestrians only. You should carefully check the official NPS websites for the national parks you plan to visit to see which roads and trails are open to biking. Concessioners in some parks offer bike rentals. This NPS website maintains a list of parks where bikes and mountain bikes are allowed (Reference at the end of this conversation). Look for parks that offer special opportunities for biking. For example, Acadia National Park includes a 45-mile network of carriage roads that are now used extensively for biking, and the gateway town of Bar Harbor has several bike rental shops. No cars are allowed on Grand Canyon's Hermit's Rest Road during most of the year (visitors use the park's public transit system instead; see Conversation 62), so this makes for a great bike trip as well (bike rentals are available in the park).

Electric bicycles (popularly known as e-bikes) are relatively new and NPS policy toward them is evolving. An important statement of policy was published in the Federal Register and can be found using a link on the website noted in the Reference. However, this is a long and technical document. The website includes a set of NPS responses to frequently asked questions about e-bikes in the national parks and should be consulted. It's also wise to check the website of the national parks in which you plan to use an e-bike to see what recently promulgated rules and regulations might apply.

Reference

National Park Service (2024) Biking. Available at: https://www.nps.gov/subjects/biking/visit.htm (accessed 8 July 2024).

© Robert Manning and Elizabeth Perry 2024. *Conversations About Visiting and Managing the National Parks* (R.E. Manning and E.E Perry)
DOI: 10.1079/9781800626768.0041

42 Horses and Stock

Post

BeachGrandmax4 reviewed an outing at Marsh-Billings-Rockefeller National Historical Park in Woodstock, Vermont, on Tripadvisor, including a horse-drawn carriage experience:

> *We took this tour as a part of the Forest/Woodworking Festival in Woodstock ... the wagon ride through the park [was] led by Jack and Jerry, two Percheron working horses. The park ranger who accompanied us was well informed and eager to answer our questions. It was very interesting to hear the history of the Marsh, Billings and Rockefeller families and the conservation efforts they made over the last century.*

Response

There's a long tradition of horses and other stock use in the National Park System. Many parks were first explored on horseback, and horses (and other equines such as mules, donkeys, and burros) have been used to help with trail building and other projects. Many national parks allow horseback riding, horses and carriages, and other stock use today. Visitors may be allowed to bring their own horses or some national parks have stables inside or near the parks and these may be licensed by the NPS to offer rides to park visitors (like *BeachGrandmax4* describes). However, all parks have rules governing horse and stock use to help ensure protection of the park and visitors, and it's vital to check the official website of each park for up-to-date opportunities and regulations. Here are a few diverse sample parks that offer horseback riding, horses and carriages, and other stock use.

- *Assateague Island National Seashore*—This national park is a lovely barrier island that spans portions of Maryland and Virginia and features a population of wild horses. More technically, these resident horses are feral, descendants of domestic animals that have reverted to a wild state. Many visitors become aware of these wild horses by reading Marguerite Henry's famous children's book, *Misty of Chincoteague*. Visitors must bring their own horses to the park and should read the park's official website carefully about rules and regulations. Two campsites are available for horse camping during selected times of the year.
- *Marsh-Billings-Rockefeller National Historical Park*—As *BeachGrandmax4*'s post relates, this small but interesting national park in Vermont celebrates the life of early conservationist George Perkins Marsh and the environmental legacy of his historic home and surrounding land. In the late 1800s, owner Frederick Billings had 10 miles of carriage roads constructed on the property and these roads and most trails are open to horseback riding and even carriages.
- *Grand Canyon National Park*—This iconic national park in Arizona offers a special kind of equine use: mules that take visitors along some park trails, including iconic rides into the Canyon. Some trips follow the famous Bright Angel Trail to the Colorado River and back. All of these mule trips are offered by the park concessioner. Visitors may also bring their own horses into the park.
- *Acadia National Park*—Much of the land that is now Acadia National Park in Maine was donated by John D. Rockefeller, Jr., who maintained a home on Mount Desert Island. Rockefeller had 50 miles of artfully designed carriage roads constructed on his property and these are now an important component of the park. Commercial carriage rides are offered on

DOI: 10.1079/9781800626768.0042

portions of the carriage roads and are a great way to experience the natural and cultural history of this part of the park. Privately owned horses are also allowed on some segments of the carriage roads and on some trails.

- *Yellowstone National Park*—This big national park that spans portions of Montana, Wyoming, and Idaho, offers plenty of wide-open spaces for horseback trips. The park includes deep canyons, big rivers, expansive forests, large lakes, iconic wildlife, and the world's largest collection of thermal features. Horseback trips are an historic part of this western park and several outfitters are permitted to offer horseback rides that include day and overnight trips; see the park's official website for details.

- *Cuyahoga Valley National Park*—This national park in Ohio is quite close to Cleveland and Akron. Its heart is the Cuyahoga River, which has been revitalized over the past few decades through extensive efforts to improve the river's water quality. Other features of the park include forests, waterfalls, and interesting flora and fauna. The park is one of an increasing number of national parks in or near major urban areas. Horseback riding is allowed on several trails, but there are no outfitters available.

- *Lassen Volcanic National Park*—Located in northern California, this park features an impressive collection of thermal features, as well as lovely forests, streams, lakes, and meadows. More than 100 miles of trails are open to horses and horse camping is allowed too. Several stables outside the park offer guided horseback tours.

- *Shenandoah National Park*—Just 75 miles from Washington, DC, this national park in Virginia features lovely views of the Appalachian Mountains, large expanses of forests, waterfalls, and President Herbert Hoover's rustic retreat known as Rapidan Camp. Nearly 200 miles of trails are open to horseback riding. Visitors are welcome to bring their own horses or take a guided horseback ride conducted by one of the nearby stables.

Reference

National Park Service (2023) Horseback Riding & Stock Use. Available at: www.nps.gov/subjects/stockuse/visit.htm (accessed 8 July 2024).

43 Hunting, Fishing, and Trapping

Post

Firecap13 used a post on Tripadvisor to enthuse about fishing opportunities at Whiskeytown National Recreation Area, which also permits some hunting:

> *Whiskeytown Lake* [Whiskeytown National Recreation Area] *is my favorite lake in Northern California ... The water is clear, the scenery is beautiful, the wildlife is incredible, and the quiet peaceful coves are awesome. I like that they don't allow Jet Skis or Personal Watercraft on the lake, and that most boaters are families with kids or responsible folks ... The fishing is good, with a selection of: Bass, Trout, Kokanee Salmon, Bluegill, and catfish ... $5 for day use and no launch fees, you really can't beat it.*

Response

Hunting, fishing, and trapping are traditional outdoor activities in the US and may be practiced in many national parks. However, as discussed in the Introduction to this book, the NPS is required to protect the natural and cultural resources of the national parks, and this requires consideration of the potential effects of hunting, fishing, and trapping on park wildlife and associated ecosystems. In some cases, these activities are allowed by federal law (e.g. where the enabling legislation establishing a park requires that these activities be allowed), and in other cases these activities may or may not be allowed based on the judgment of the NPS. Currently, hunting is allowed in 76 national parks, trapping is allowed in 31 national parks, and fishing is allowed in 213 national parks. Where allowed, the NPS generally adopts and enforces the same regulations as the affiliated state wildlife agency and federal wildlife and fisheries agencies such as the US Fish and Wildlife Service. For example, adding on to *Firecap13*'s fishing post, hunting of deer, bears, small game, waterfowl, and upland game birds is permitted at Whiskeytown National Recreation Area in California, with the seasons and regulations following those of the California Department of Fish and Wildlife.

Hunting

Of the more than 85 million acres of the National Park System, about 51 million acres (about 60%) are open to hunting, the vast majority of which are in Alaskan national parks. Hunting may be of three varieties. *Subsistence hunting* is practiced by rural Alaskans and Alaska Natives as defined in the Alaska National Interest Lands Conservation Act. *Tribal treaty hunting* is authorized under the terms of a treaty between the US and the government of another country, including tribal nations. *Recreational hunting* refers to all hunting that is not commercial, subsistence, or tribal. Sixty-six national parks allow recreational hunting, 17 allow subsistence hunting, and one allows tribal hunting. Ten national parks allow both recreational and subsistence hunting. A list of national parks that allow hunting can be found at the website National Park Service (2023) in the References at the end of this conversation, but be sure to check the official NPS website of each national park for updated information and rules and regulations.

© Robert Manning and Elizabeth Perry 2024. *Conversations About Visiting and Managing the National Parks* (R.E. Manning and E.E Perry)
DOI: 10.1079/9781800626768.0043

Fishing

Fishing is allowed in all national parks except when specifically prohibited. *Firecap13* seems to have found a favorite spot in Whiskeytown Lake of Whiskeytown National Recreation Area! Of the more than 400 national parks, 213 allow fishing and shellfishing activities (155 of these parks have all waters open and 58 have partial waters open), 22 parks have all waters closed, and 111 don't include waters that support fish or shellfish that are commonly sought. Fishing regulations may vary by four types of fishing: (i) recreational; (ii) subsistence; (iii) tribal; and (iv) commercial (see the types of hunting noted above). A map showing national parks that allow fishing can be found at the website National Park Service (2022) in the References.

Trapping

Trapping is allowed in only 31 national parks, though an additional 18 national parks allow subsistence trapping (see the types of hunting noted above). Most of the parks that allow trapping are in Alaska, so the total area of the National Park System open to trapping is nearly 48 million acres. Regulations may vary depending on whether trapping is subsistence or recreational.

Be sure to consult the official NPS websites of the parks you plan to visit for the latest information on hunting, fishing, and trapping opportunities and current rules and regulations.

References

National Park Service (2022) Fishing in Parks. Available at: https://www.nps.gov/subjects/fishing/fishing-in-parks.htm (accessed 8 July 2024).
National Park Service (2023) Hunting. Available at: https://www.nps.gov/subjects/hunting/visit.htm (accessed 8 July 2024).

44 River Trips

Post

Travis posted the following on Google Reviews about his trip on the Buffalo River, the prime visitor attraction at Buffalo National River (part of the National Park System):

> My daughter and I camped overnight and traveled about 21 miles in our canoe on the river. The water was moving pretty quickly, which offered quite a thrill when the rapids came. This was one of the best experiences we've had together. This is such a beautiful place to bond with your friends and family. We made memories we will never forget. 10\10!

Response

What a nice story, Travis—thanks for your post. Your river trip sounds like the very best way to experience this national park, and a great way to bond with your daughter too. Scenic drives along park roads, camping out under the stars, hiking park trails, and visiting historical and cultural sites are traditional ways of enjoying and appreciating the national parks. But as you point out, Travis, there are other ways as well, including river trips (see Conversations 41–43 and 45–49 for still other ways). Many national parks include long (some of them very long) stretches of rivers, and floating these rivers can be a great way to see the parks from a very different perspective and in an up-close and personal way. These can be day trips or overnight trips of a few days up to 2 weeks or even more. Experienced boaters can do these trips themselves (though you must read the park's website very carefully and check with park rangers to help ensure your safety) or NPS-approved concessioners also offer these types of trips (see Conversation 70). Here are a few examples, and more details on these kinds of opportunities (individual and guided by outfitters) can be found on the official websites of the national parks you plan to visit.

- *Grand Canyon National Park*—Let's start with what may be the holy grail of national park river trips. The legendary Colorado River drains much of the American Southwest, and the 277-mile section of the river that flows through Grand Canyon National Park makes for an epic adventure. This float trip offers an unusual perspective of the Canyon's world-renowned geological history, some of North America's wildest rapids, other-worldly side canyons to explore, ancient Puebloan sites, long stretches of peace and quiet, and star-filled nights of camping on sandy beaches. Trips can be of varying lengths and are offered by licensed outfitters, though private trips are allowed for qualified boaters.

- *Blackstone River Valley National Historical Park*—This national park in Rhode Island and Massachusetts features the historic Blackstone River that famously powered Slater's Mill and helped start America's Industrial Revolution. One of the best ways to enjoy and appreciate the park is to paddle the river in a kayak or canoe. The main stem of the river meanders 46 miles from Worcester, Massachusetts, to Providence, Rhode Island, through urban landscapes, historic villages, farmlands, and forests; part of this portion the river is in the park and part in the larger Blackstone River Valley National Heritage Area (see Conversation 30 about national heritage areas).

- *New River Gorge National Park and Preserve*—The New River is the centerpiece of this 70,000-acre national park in West Virginia. The river flows through the park for 53 miles and offers a diversity of rafting trips. The upper section of the river is ideal for families and those new to rafting, while

© Robert Manning and Elizabeth Perry 2024. *Conversations About Visiting and Managing the National Parks* (R.E. Manning and E.E Perry) DOI: 10.1079/9781800626768.0044

the lower more technical section is challenging. A number of private companies conduct rafting trips.

- *Grand Teton National Park*—Floating the Snake River through Grand Teton National Park is grand, indeed. This is a day trip that offers what may be the very best views of this dramatic mountain range of jagged, snow-capped peaks. Because of the complexities of the river channel, it's best to join one of the local outfitter trips.
- *Big Bend National Park*—A nearly 120-mile stretch of the famous Rio Grande River in Big Bend National Park defines the international border between the US (Texas) and Mexico. The river glides through 1500-ft deep canyons, along colorful mesas, and through its namesake "big bend", making for a diverse and adventurous journey. Day and overnight trips are offered by a number of outfitters, and do-it-yourself trips are also possible.
- *Gates of the Arctic National Park and Preserve*—The mighty Noatak River flows for more than 300 miles through the wilds of Alaska's Gates of the Arctic National Park and Preserve, all of it above the Arctic Circle. This was a traditional travel route used by Alaska Natives. There are few rapids and the scenery is magnificent, including snow-capped peaks and iconic wildlife such as caribou, Dall sheep, and grizzly bears.
- *Canyonlands National Park*—The Green River flows for nearly 60 miles through Utah's Canyonlands National Park, a lovely multi-day journey along the peaceful, meandering river. Environmentalist Ed Abbey called the park "the most weird, wonderful, and magical place on earth" (Abbey, 1990, p. 132). Camp along the river's beaches and benches and sample some of the hikes that lead into the many side canyons. Outfitters offer a range of services or this trip can be a do-it-yourself adventure.

References

Abbey, E. (1990) *Desert Solitaire: A Season in the Wilderness*. Simon & Schuster, New York.

45 Watching Wildlife (Safely!)

Post

This is a frame from a scary video that shows a visitor to Yellowstone National Park foolishly taking a selfie while standing next to a bison.

Dangerous selfie! Woman gets too close to bison at Yellowstone, New York Post: available at: https://www.youtube.com/watch?v= KeYe0ZUySrY (accessed 8 July 2024).

Response

Most visitors to the national parks find it thrilling to see and appreciate wildlife. But watching wildlife includes an obligation to help protect these animals, and to protect yourself as well! Unfortunately—as this video documents—some visitors ignore this responsibility, imperiling themselves and the welfare of park wildlife. Each year, there are a number of stories in the national news media of visitors acting irresponsibly around wildlife with unfortunate consequences to both.

Wildlife may sometimes appear tame, but they're not. Under no circumstances should visitors attempt to pet, hold, or otherwise touch wildlife; juvenile animals may be rejected by their parents if they've been in contact with humans, making them more vulnerable to predators or other threats. If visitors approach wildlife too closely, animals can be injured when trying to escape, especially around roads or other human structures. Wildlife that become used to being around people, especially in campgrounds and picnic areas, are at risk of eating human foods (which can be dangerous to them) and catching diseases from people and their pets. For example, heartworm from dogs and cats can kill wildlife such as foxes, wolves, coyotes, bobcats, and mountain lions. Black-footed ferrets die from the flu if humans are sick and get too close. Wolves can be infected by canine parvovirus from dogs. Also some wildlife may have to be killed if they become habituated to people and pose a danger.

Of course, wildlife poses dangers to people too. Wild animals can be unpredictable and may bolt or charge without warning. It's important that visitors maintain a distance of at least 25 yards from most wildlife and 100 yards from large animals such as bears, wolves, and bison. If wildlife approach you, then you should move away from them. (It's wise to check the official NPS websites of the parks you're visiting to get the latest guidelines.) Wildlife can be dangerous to pets as well. For example, they can be trampled, if they get too close. Some snakes have a poisonous bite, and smaller wildlife such as squirrels and foxes may carry ticks, fleas, or rabies. Pets may look like prey to wildlife and may be attacked, and small pets may carried off by large birds, even when on a leash.

The NPS recommends the following practices for watching wildlife safely:

- *Know before you go*—Read the official NPS websites of the parks you plan to visit, with special attention to wildlife that live there.

DOI: 10.1079/9781800626768.0045

Note the advice about safely watching wildlife.

- *Give animals room*—Many parks suggest a minimum distance that visitors should maintain from park animals. As a general guideline, if animals react to your presence, you're too close. (If you're close enough for a selfie, you're definitely too close!) Use binoculars and a zoom lens on your camera instead of approaching wildlife.
- *Do not disturb*—It's illegal to feed, touch, tease, frighten, or otherwise intentionally disturb park wildlife. Stay on maintained trails to restrict the human presence to small and predictable areas. If dogs are allowed (see Conversation 58), keep them on leash, pick up droppings, and ensure they're vaccinated. Don't use bird or other wildlife calls or other attractants.
- *Keep your eyes on the road*—Cars pose a special danger to wildlife; be sure to obey speed limits and watch for wildlife crossing the road. If you stop to observe wildlife, pull your car well off the road to be courteous to other drivers.
- *Store your food and stash your trash*—Feeding wildlife endangers them and visitors; don't allow wildlife to associate food with visitors by feeding them or improperly storing food. Follow park guidelines about storing food in cars, picnic areas, and campgrounds.
- *See something, say something*—Tell a park ranger if you've come into contact with wildlife and if you've encountered wildlife that are sick, acting strangely, or dead. If you see visitors who aren't following NPS-recommended guidelines, advise them about proper behavior; contact a ranger if necessary.
- *Be responsible*—Staying safe in the national parks and keeping wildlife wild are the responsibilities of all national park visitors.

References

National Park Service (2020) 7 Ways to Safely Watch Wildlife. Available at: www.nps.gov/subjects/watchingwildlife/7ways.htm (accessed 8 July 2024).

46 Off-Road Vehicles

Responding to a post on Reddit about off-road vehicle permits on Cape Cod, *ppomeroy* had the following advice:

> *Most of Cape Cod's beaches are a part of the Cape Cod National Seashore (NPS). While [many] beaches may display state or township ownership or management, they all fall under NPS regulations and jurisdiction. So before you proceed, check with the ranger station to determine which of their beaches allow ORV usage, access points, etc. Most states require a soft-sand kit in case you get stuck and other items on a list.*

Response

Off-road vehicles (ORVs) come in many forms— dune buggies, air boats, dirt bikes, all-terrain vehicles, off-highway vehicles (OHVs), etc. Technically, any motor vehicle that's designed for or capable of cross-country travel on or immediately over land, water, sand, snow, ice, marsh, wetland, or other natural terrain is considered an ORV by the NPS. ORVs are not allowed to travel off-road in most national parks because of their potential environmental impacts and conflicts with other park visitors.

However, some parks do allow ORVs in limited areas and under certain conditions. For example, a permit might be required. It's imperative that you check the official NPS website of the national parks you're interested in visiting to see if ORV use is allowed and under what conditions.

Several national parks in the arid Southwest allow limited ORV use. For example, Canyonlands National Park allows ORVs on the nearly 70 mile White Rim Road, Great Sand Dunes National Park allows ORVs on the 20 mile Medano Pass Road, Joshua Tree National Park allows ORVs on the Geology OHV Tour Road, Death Valley National Park allows ORVs on the Inyo Mine/Echo Pass Road, and Big Bend National Park allows ORVs on the Black Gap 4 × 4 Trail. Yellowstone National Park allows snowmobiles on selected roads. A few national seashores allow ORVs in limited areas. For example, Cape Cod National Seashore and Cape Hatteras National Seashore allow ORVs on selected beaches. We agree with *ppomeroy*'s advice that visitors should take caution to make sure the area they're visiting with their ORV permits such use.

© Robert Manning and Elizabeth Perry 2024. *Conversations About Visiting and Managing the National Parks* (R.E. Manning and E.E Perry)
DOI: 10.1079/9781800626768.0046

47 Immersive Experiences

Post

Agog84 sought an immersive experience at Everglades National Park on the Nine Mile Canoe Trail and included this in a Tripadvisor review:

> *I'm comfortable paddling on my own so my personal reason was to get an Everglades education and immersion. Novice or not to canoes/kayaks, having an expert sharing Everglades insider knowledge is invaluable if it's your first trip to the vast Everglades … I recommend you reserve 7 days in advance for this popular program. Ranger Shawna represents the NPS extremely well! She's knowledgeable and informative combined with friendly and cheerful in the morning. Plus she remained cool and collected when one couple tipped over and she helped get them situated in their canoe again … There was plenty to learn about the different but interrelated ecosystems, the varying plants and trees, including very cool stuff like wacky carnivorous bladderwort, a fern-like aquatic plant with pretty little yellow flowers. In the mangrove tunnels, we had to concentrate on steering through. Another highlight was spotting the alligators: the 1st one was mostly just bubbles, but the 2nd one we got up close and personal before Ranger Shawna requested we give it space to prevent it feeling threatened and provoke it to attack.*

Response

As noted in Conversation 97, the NPS partners with non-profit "friends groups" to help support the parks through fundraising, volunteer projects, research, and other ways. One of these activities is conducting immersive experiences for park visitors that include knowledgeable guides and tours of special park locations. As *Agog84* notes, the in-depth knowledge of their guide provided them with an "Everglades education and immersion". These types of activities range from a few hours to several days and require a fee to be paid to the organization. Immersive experiences are conducted in a limited number of national parks. Here are some enticing examples.

- *Everglades National Park Institute*—This non-profit group is an official partner with Everglades National Park and the Florida National Parks Association. The institute offers a suite of immersive programs for visitors to Everglades National Park. For example (and the subject of *Agog84's* review), the Institute offers a 3-hour canoe trip on the park's Nine Mile Pond where visitors are guided by an Institute naturalist and learn first-hand about the park's sawgrass and mangrove environments. Paddling experience is required.
- *Grand Canyon Conservancy Field Institute*—This non-profit group is an official partner with Grand Canyon National Park and offers a suite of immersive programs in the park. For example, the Institute offers a guided 7-day "Rim-to-Rim Hike" through the Grand Canyon, where visitors see at first hand the park's world-renowned geology and experience the remarkable diversity of the park. This is a physically demanding backpacking trip, but the Institute will help advise participants on how to train and prepare for this adventure.
- *Yosemite Conservancy*—This is a non-profit group dedicated to supporting Yosemite National Park, and it offers a great variety of immersive programs in and around the park. For example, the organization offers a guided multi-day backpacking adventure for women to Glen Aulin and Waterwheel Falls in the High Sierra portion of the park. This is a moderately strenuous trip and some backpacking experience is recommended.

© Robert Manning and Elizabeth Perry 2024. *Conversations About Visiting and Managing the National Parks* (R.E. Manning and E.E Perry)
DOI: 10.1079/9781800626768.0047

- *Yellowstone Forever*—This non-profit organization works with Yellowstone National Park to offer a variety of immersive and educational programs that focus on the park's wildlife, geology, and cultural history. Programs are led by professors, naturalists, scientists, photographers, writers, historians, and artists. For example, the organization offers a wide variety of guided day hikes in the park that are accessible to most park visitors.

Consider joining one of these kinds of immersive activities to get the most out of your national park visits. Explore the official NPS website of the park you're interested in visiting to see if any of these kinds of adventures are offered.

48 Virtual Visits

Post

Carolschmidt333's image shared on Wikimedia Commons of Lyndon B. Johnson's boyhood home in his namesake National Historical Park shows one approach to visiting, via the pathway by the fence in Johnson City, Texas. However, the park has also created extensive opportunities for virtual visits, touring such places in detail online from wherever you find yourself with an Internet connection.

Lyndon B. Johnson National Historical Park, Fredericksburg, Texas, Wikimedia Commons/*Carolschmidt333*.

Response

It's an impossible task for most people to visit all of the more than 400 national parks (though a few obsessive people have!), so it may be useful to visit some virtually via a number of websites, links, and other media. Virtual visits are also a good way to preview some of the national parks to see if you'd like to visit them in person, or to prioritize the list of parks you're considering. Virtual visits can also allow you to "visit" parks during different seasons of the year (see

Yellowstone National Park during the winter, for example). Fortunately, there are several options for doing all this.

First, the NPS's extensive system of websites is often rich in photos, illustrated with images that will help you see and understand these parks even without visiting them in person. Many of these websites include a "gallery" option that's loaded with even more photos, many of them of very high quality and addressing many dimensions of the parks. At the national level, the NPS maintains its NPGallery Digital Asset Management System that's loaded with photos and can be searched by park, state, and keywords (such as "waterfall").

Another option is more elaborate interactive tours that allow users to navigate around park attractions sites such as a trail or historic home. The National Park Foundation (see Conversation 97) offers virtual tours of a number of diverse national parks. Here you'll find virtual tours of Lyndon B. Johnson National Historical Park, Shenandoah National Park, Women's Rights National Historical Park, Hamilton Grange National Memorial, Crater Lake National Park, and New Bedford Whaling National Historical Park. For example, a virtual tour of Lyndon B. Johnson National Historical Park includes richly detailed examinations (and at your own pace) of the Texas White House, Junction school, and boyhood home (pictured here and inspiring this conversation).

The NPS maintains an active presence on social media, including Facebook, Instagram, Twitter, Flickr, and YouTube (see Conversation 34 for more about this). Here, you can take a virtual tour with a park ranger, share photos and stories with other visitors, get trip ideas and suggestions, swap park stories, etc.

And another way to visit the national parks virtually is through the NPS's elaborate system of live webcams—there are hundreds of them at strategic locations throughout the National Park

© Robert Manning and Elizabeth Perry 2024. *Conversations About Visiting and Managing the National Parks* (R.E. Manning and E.E Perry)
DOI: 10.1079/9781800626768.0048

System. For example, the Brooks Falls Bearcam in Alaska's Katmai National Park provides views of the remarkable site where dozens of grizzly bears at a time gather in July and September to catch spawning salmon. The underwater webcam at Channel Islands National Park allows viewers to peer into this biologically diverse ecosystem and identify the area's many species. The Old Faithful Geyser webcam enables viewers to see the next eruption from anywhere in the world; and the Cherry Blossom Cam allows viewers to monitor the status of the iconic cherry blossoms at Washington, DC's National Mall and Memorial Parks.

All of these are good options, but don't forget to visit the parks in person as well!

References

National Park Service (n.d.a) Multimedia Search-Webcams. Available at: https://www.nps.gov/media/multimedia-search.htm#sort=Date_Last_Modified+desc&fq%5B%5D=Type%3A%22Webcam%22 (accessed 8 July 2024).

National Park Service (n.d.b.) NPGallery Digital Asset Management System. Available at: https://npgallery.nps.gov (accessed 8 July 2024).

Watson, R. (2024) Take a Virtual Visit to a National Park. *National Park Foundation*. Available at: www.nationalparks.org/connect/blog/take-virtual-visit-national-park (accessed 8 July 2024).

49 New Recreation

Post

Recreation is ever-evolving and may cause confusion to visitors to national parks about what's allowed and what's not. On Reddit, *wrybreadsf* posed such a question about a particular type of recreation—drones:

> *I'm seeing conflicting information about the legality of flying [drones] over National Parks in the United States when the operator is positioned outside the park. Can someone confirm that it is indeed illegal to fly over the park even if the operator is outside the park? Or am I wrong about that?*

Response

There's always something new about how to have fun, and drones are an example. But are these types of recreation allowed in the national parks? As *wrybreadsf* mentions, drones aren't welcomed everywhere, and we're sorry, *wrybreadsf*, that drones may not be flown over national parks. (There may be exceptions for search and rescue, research, and other special circumstances.) In fact, all types of new recreation cause pause in determining what may or may not fit within the purpose and regulations of an area. National parks are a good example, as management objectives for these areas must balance enjoyment and protection (see Conversation 73), which then translates into the regulations about what recreational activities are or are not permitted. National parks have a variety of purposes, so while there are some blanket regulations across the National Park System (as with drones), some parks that prioritize wilderness and preservation may have a different (stricter) set of allowances than those that prioritize recreation. Of course, because these activities may be avenues to engagement

with new visitors and future park stewards, it's an especially delicate consideration for park policy and staff.

Some activities in particular could spark debate about whether or not they are allowed in the national parks, especially as the popularity of these places may encourage a lot of use. Activities that could damage the natural or cultural resources found on a site, or the sensitive habitats and geological formations, would generally be scrutinized further. For example, though slacklining is increasing in popularity, securing these lines to sensitive plant species or rare features could damage the environment and thus the park may limit visitors' slacklining. Geocaching may encourage visitors to go into sensitive areas and also to leave items (against Leave No Trace principles; see Conversation 60), and so this is generally not allowed either. If activities could substantially disrupt the experience of other visitors, then these activities might also be regulated or prohibited. Examples might be anything loud, dangerous, or intrusive for a setting, such as motorized watercraft/ activities on a waterbody traditionally used only for paddling, or using drones within the park and perhaps harassing visitors or wildlife with these flights. Many of these types of situations raise concern over conflict among park visitors (see Conversation 88). Where there are partial allowances, you may find that parks use zoning, permitting, and seasonal restrictions to manage the outdoor recreation allowed (see Conversation 89).

However, there are plenty of new pursuits that are allowed. Technology concerned with augmented reality or fitness trackers are certainly interesting ways to encourage recreation and can add to an experience. Paddleboarding is a great way to get out onto the waters where canoes and kayaks once dominated. Using telescopes and astronomy apps can open curiosities

© Robert Manning and Elizabeth Perry 2024. *Conversations About Visiting and Managing the National Parks* (R.E. Manning and E.E Perry)
DOI: 10.1079/9781800626768.0049

to the night sky. Trail running adds another way to experience the landscape alongside walking and hiking.

Given the diversity of the National Park System, it's not unusual that some recreation activities are allowed in some national parks, but not others. For example, Conversation 41 discusses biking in national parks. There are places in the National Park System where road bicycles, mountain bikes, and the electronic versions of both may be allowed, but also places where they shouldn't be taken, and this situation can be dynamic as new forms of recreation emerge. For example, the carriage roads at Acadia National Park are wonderful places to bring your bike, and as technology continues to advance, Class 1 e-bikes are now allowed on the carriage roads (though a speed limit must be observed).

As always, the best way to find out about whether the recreation you enjoy or think you'd like to try is allowed in a particular national park is to visit the park's website or contact the park directly. If your activity isn't allowed, park staff may be able to point you toward nearby places where such activities are welcomed.

Reference

National Park Service (2017) Unmanned Aircraft in the National Parks. Available at: https://www.nps.gov/articles/unmanned-aircraft-in-the-national-parks.htm (accessed 8 July 2024).

Learning/Education

50 Visitor Centers

Post

Shane P. shared this posting on X about a recent visit to Gettysburg National Military Park, noting in particular the "energy" he felt at the park's powerful Museum and Visitor Center:

> *Got to visit the Gettysburg National Military Park Museum* [and Visitor Center] *briefly this past weekend. What an important historical place with an energy that is palpable.*

Response

Planning your national park visits is an important, educational, and exciting way to prepare for your visit, as discussed in Conversation 33. However, once you arrive in the parks, make your first stop at the park's visitor center, usually located near the park entrance. Nearly all national parks include visitor centers, and some of the large ones have several spread over the park's geography. These are free and welcoming places where you can learn more about the parks. For example, visitor centers almost always have educational displays and exhibits about the park's natural and cultural history, important advice about how to stay safe in the national parks (see Conversation 63), and how to respect and protect park resources (see Conversations 59 and 60), as well as informational brochures and maps. Some, like the Gettysburg National Military Park Museum and Visitor Center that *Shane P.* visited, can evoke strong emotions through the use of interpretive design. Most are also staffed by park rangers and volunteers who can help you plan your visit and answer any questions you may have. Many also include a documentary film about the park, a small book and retail store, and free restrooms (another reason to make visitor centers your first stop!).

Examples of iconic and popular visitor centers include the following.

The South Rim Visitor Center at Grand Canyon National Park includes a large open-air space with helpful and educational displays on the park's world-famous geology, its vital cultural history, and suggestions for visiting the park. An associated indoor space includes interactive exhibits, a film, and an information desk staffed by park rangers and volunteers. Directly across the pedestrian plaza you'll find a large book and gift store, a small cafe, bike rentals, and the hub of the park's innovative public transit system. A short walk takes you to Mather Point, one of the best views of the Canyon.

The Old Faithful Visitor Education Center at Yellowstone National Park is strategically located close to world-renowned Old Faithful Geyser; in fact, you can even watch the geyser's eruption from the center's tall glass wall at the front of the building. The center's educational displays focus on: (i) the park's hydrothermal features, including its geysers, hot springs, mudpots, and fumaroles; (ii) the volcano beneath Yellowstone; (iii) the living things that exist in this extreme environment; and (iv) the ongoing program of research in the park. Children enjoy the Young Scientist exhibit room, and evening ranger-led programs are offered. The visitor center includes an information desk, predictions for the time of the next eruption of Old Faithful and other geysers, books and souvenirs, and films shown in the theater. The building is Leadership in Energy and Environmental Design (LEED) certified to minimize its impact on the surrounding environment.

Gettysburg National Military Park's Museum and Visitor Center (that *Shane P.* found so energizing) is a large building that helps visitors learn how to best enjoy and appreciate this important historical park. The site includes a National Park Service (NPS) Information Desk,

© Robert Manning and Elizabeth Perry 2024. *Conversations About Visiting and Managing the National Parks* (R.E. Manning and E.E Perry)
DOI: 10.1079/9781800626768.0050

museum, film, and cyclorama painting. The information desk is staffed by NPS rangers who can orient visitors to the large visitor center and museum and describe options for touring the battlefield and ranger-led programs. The Gettysburg Museum of the American Civil War features 22,000 ft^2 of exhibit space that features items from the one of the largest collections of Civil War relics, interactive exhibits, and multimedia presentations that address the Civil War, including the tragic Battle of Gettysburg.

The massive Battlefield of Gettysburg cyclorama painting (measuring 377 ft in circumference and 42 ft high) is featured in another part of the building. The building also offers the dramatic interpretive film, *A New Birth of Freedom*, food service, a bookstore, and the McKenna Foundation Resource Room that provides free access to research materials. The Museum and Visitor Center is privately owned and operated by the Gettysburg Foundation, in partnership with the NPS.

51 Museums

Post

Raisal B. offered this five-star Google Review of the Ellis Island National Museum:

The Ellis Island National Museum offers a captivating journey through the history of immigration in the United States. With interactive exhibits and poignant displays, visitors can trace the experiences of millions who sought opportunity and refuge on American shores. From arrival processes to personal stories, the museum provides a profound insight into the diverse tapestry of America's immigrant heritage. A must-visit for those seeking to understand the roots of American identity.

Response

Many of the more than 400 units of the National Park System include museums; some of the larger parks have several. Here, you'll find what some call the "treasures of the nation", extensive collections that offer first-hand illustrations of America's natural and cultural history. The Ellis Island National Museum certainly fits this description, as *Raisal B.* notes in his posting. In fact, the National Park System includes the largest network of museums in the nation, perhaps the world. With the exception of the museums collectively known as Smithsonian, the museums of the national parks hold the largest collection of objects, specimens, archival records, and photographs documenting the history, culture, and natural resources of the US, a collection of more than 100 million museum objects and archival documents located across the many national parks. These museums help tell the stories of the American land, its diverse cultures, and significant events and innovative ideas that inspire the world. Moreover, these collections are largely *in situ*, found in the locations where these natural objects were originally collected and cultural objects were made and used.

NPS museums are nearly as old as the parks themselves. Shortly after Yosemite National Park was established in 1890, park staff began collecting, labeling, and displaying local flora as a way for visitors to learn first-hand about what they were seeing. The park established a purpose-built museum in 1926 that addressed the natural and cultural history of the area. The first director of the NPS, Steven Mather, envisioned that all the parks would have museums, a goal that was endorsed by the Secretary of the Interior in 1918 when he wrote that "The educational, as well as the recreational, use of the national parks should be encouraged in every practicable way", continuing "Museums containing specimens of wild flowers, shrubs, and trees and mounted animals, birds, and fish native to parks, and other exhibits of this character, will be established" (National Park Service, 2004). Now, many national parks exhibit museum collections that include natural history specimens, Indigenous cultural objects, historic furnishings, historic photographs, important documents, and artifacts of everyday life that are manifestations of our nation's life and history.

The following are some representative examples of museums in the National Park System:

- *Yavapai Museum of Geology, Grand Canyon National Park*—Perched directly on the South Rim of the Grand Canyon, the museum's panoramic windows offer what may be the very best view of the park's world-renowned geology. Paired with the museum's three-dimensional exhibits, beautifully crafted artwork and photographs, and large-scale relief map, visitors can learn to identify the park's rock

© Robert Manning and Elizabeth Perry 2024. *Conversations About Visiting and Managing the National Parks* (R.E. Manning and E.E Perry)
DOI: 10.1079/9781800626768.0051

layers and understand the park's geological history.

- *Ellis Island National Museum of Immigration, Statue of Liberty National Monument*—Millions of immigrants entered the US through New York's Ellis Island from 1892 to 1924. Today, over 100 million Americans can trace their ancestry to these immigrants who helped shape the nation. Part of Statue of Liberty National Monument, the museum allows visitors to search the extraordinary collection of arrival records to discover more about their ancestry and to learn about the experiences of immigrants who passed through the Golden Door. As *Raisal B.*'s post notes, this museum relates the story of immigration, which is a story of America.
- *Gettysburg Museum of the American Civil War, Gettysburg National Military Park*—This 22,000 ft² of exhibit space features relics of the Battle of Gettysburg, the personal possessions of soldiers who served in the Civil War, interactive exhibits, and multimedia presentations that cover the conflict from beginning to end. The museum includes the award-winning film, *A New Birth of Freedom*, and the monumental Gettysburg cyclorama oil painting, along with light and sound effects, that immerse visitors in the fury of Pickett's Charge during the third day of the Battle of Gettysburg.

- *Visitor and Research Center, Mesa Verde National Park*—This state-of-the-art, LEED-certified building is located just inside the park entrance and serves as the park's primary visitor center and also houses the park's research and storage facility for its archives and museum collection of over three million objects. Visiting this facility will help visitors appreciate the rich Ancestral Puebloan culture and daily life that was practiced in the park's iconic cliff dwellings.

Of course, it's challenging to visit all of the museums that might be of interest, so many collections may be accessed online as part of the NPS's Museum Management Program. Virtual park museum exhibits include American history and prehistory, ancient pottery, Civil War uniforms, presidents and first ladies, Revolutionary War to World War II, dinosaurs, decorative arts, and much more. The Web catalog of museum collections is a searchable online database that provides access to park collections and images (see National Park Service (n.d. a) in the References). Impressive virtual tours of NPS museum collections are also available via Google Arts & Culture (listed here in the References).

References

Google Arts & Culture (n.d.) The Hidden Worlds of the National Parks. Available at: https://artsandculture .google.com/project/national-park-service (accessed 9 July 2024).

Maounis, J. (2016) Treasures of the nation. In: Manning, R., Diamant, R., Mitchell, N. and Harmon, D. (eds) *A Thinking Person's Guide to America's National Parks*. Braziller Publishers, New York, pp. 175–184.

National Park Service (n.d. a) Museum Collections. Available at: https://museum.nps.gov/ParkIndex.asp x (accessed 9 July 2024).

National Park Service (n.d. b) Museum Management Program. Available at: https://www.nps.gov/museu m/index.html (accessed 9 July 2024).

National Park Service (2004) National Park Service historical handbook series. Available at: https://www. nps.gov/parkhistory/online_books/hh/index.htm (accessed 23 July 2024).

National Park Service (2020) Museum Management Program. Available at: https://www.nps.gov/orgs/14 54/index.htm (accessed 9 July 2024).

52 Interpretation

Post

Interpretation at national parks often involves NPS interpretive rangers showing visitors interesting areas and artifacts in parks; "rangers pointing at things" has become a lighthearted term for these types of interactions. In this photo posted on Wikimedia Commons, rangers from Glen Canyon National Recreation Area point at an eclipse.

Rangers pointing at an eclipse, Wikimedia Commons/NPGallery.

Response

"Interpretation" is an important word in the parlance of the national parks and the NPS but it has a specialized meaning in this context. To most of us, the word interpretation means translating one language into another. In a sense, that's what it means in the national parks: translating technical information about the parks—their underlying geology, flora and fauna, ecological processes and relationships, as well as their human and cultural history—into terms that can easily be understood and appreciated by park visitors.

But it's more than this: it's an important part of carrying out the mission of the NPS. The Congressional legislation establishing the agency in 1916 (often called the "Organic Act"—see Conversation 6) directed the agency: "to conserve the scenery and the natural and historic objects and the wildlife therein and to provide for the enjoyment of the same in such manner and by such means as will leave them unimpaired for the enjoyment of future generations" (United States Government, 2019, p. 1). The underlying premise of interpretation is that visitors are more likely to appreciate and help preserve the parks if they understand the natural and cultural resources the parks have been established to protect.

Interpretation generally takes two forms in the national parks: (i) personally delivered programs; and (ii) a variety of media. Most visitors are familiar with programs delivered by NPS rangers. Classic examples include guided walks and campfire talks (with plenty of "pointing", as the image above lightheartedly demonstrates) but these programs can take many forms. Even the more informal interactions between rangers and visitors at visitor centers and elsewhere in the parks can be good examples of interpretation. All national parks include a variety of interpretive media—the classic free park map/guide available for all national parks, the free newspaper available in most national parks, the information/education panels posted throughout most national parks, and a host of electronic media such as the NPS's extensive network of websites and its growing presence on social media (see Conversation 34).

The history of interpretation in the national parks can be traced all the way back to John Muir, often considered the founding father of the national parks. Muir kept a journal of his explorations throughout the Sierra Nevada Mountains of California in the late 19th century. In an entry in 1896, he wrote "I'll interpret the

© Robert Manning and Elizabeth Perry 2024. *Conversations About Visiting and Managing the National Parks* (R.E. Manning and E.E Perry)
DOI: 10.1079/9781800626768.0052

rocks, learn the language of flood, storm and the avalanche. I'll acquaint myself with the glaciers and wild gardens, and get as near the heart of the world as I can" (Wolfe, 1945, p. 144). By learning about the natural world, Muir fashioned this knowledge into engaging letters, newspaper articles, books, and speeches to help advance the cause of national parks. Author Freeman Tilden was also influential in shaping the program of interpretation in the national parks, writing a foundational book on the topic titled *Interpreting Our Heritage* (Tilden, 2008). His legacy is captured in his dictum, "Through interpretation, understanding; through understanding, appreciation; through appreciation, protection" (p. 38). Tilden defined interpretation as "an educational activity that aims to reveal meanings and relationships through the use of original objects, by first-hand experience ... rather than simply communicate factual information" (p. 33).

NPS interpreters are careful to tell the stories of America that are represented in the national parks from multiple points of view and to stimulate inquiry and related civic dialogue. Many national parks address important American places and history that can be viewed from a variety of perspectives; examples include: (i) the importance of environmental protection; (ii) the construction (and deconstruction) of dams on free-flowing rivers; (iii) the role of climate change on park landscapes; and (iv) the Civil Rights Movement. Consideration of these places and issues demand to be heard from multiple voices (see Conversation 15 for more about this).

A bedrock principle of interpretation is to establish connections between the national parks and visitors. The NPS defines interpretation as "a catalyst in creating an opportunity for the audience to form their own intellectual and emotional connections with the meanings and significance inherent in the resource" (Bacher *et al.*, 2007, p. 5), and the National Association for Interpretation (2024) defines it as a "communication process that forges emotional and intellectual connections between the interests of the audience and the meanings inherent in the resource." Building these connections between visitors and park resources is designed to develop public support for the national parks. An appropriate aphorism is

that caring *about* something is the first step toward caring *for* it.

In addition to the interpretive programs conducted in the national parks, interpretation has been extended well beyond park boundaries. For example, NPS interpreters have developed a host of educational materials used by many schools and teachers. These materials capitalize on the principles of "place-based" education and "high-impact" educational activities. In fact, the national parks are increasingly considered "America's classroom" (see Conversation 13). "A Park for Every Classroom" program develops materials and resources for schoolteachers that enable the parks to become real-world extensions of the classroom. Virtual visits to selected national parks serve as powerful teaching and learning resources. For example, real-time and interactive visits with ranger/divers at Channel Islands National Park allow students to learn about vital ocean resources, including the park's many marine mammals. Electronic field trips and lesson plans can be helpful to teachers and students. Find helpful materials and advice on the NPS network of websites; each park has "Nature and Science" or "History and Culture" links (depending on the types of resources included in the park), a "For Teachers" link, and a national park system-wide link. See Conversation 13 on America's Classroom for more about all this.

Generally, there are two types of park rangers—interpretive rangers and law enforcement rangers. The former develop and deliver interpretive programming in the national parks, while the latter help ensure that park rules and regulations are respected and enforced. Interpretive rangers bring three kinds of knowledge and skills to their work: (i) they must have substantive knowledge about the natural and cultural resources that are protected in the parks they serve; (ii) they must have a well-developed sense of the audiences they are addressing; and (iii) they must have strong oral and written communication skills.

Be sure to participate in as much of the variety of interpretive materials and programs delivered in the national parks as possible. When planning your visits, look carefully at the official NPS website for each park, paying special attention to the "Learn About the Park" and "Calendar" (a schedule of interpretive and other programs) options, and plan to stop at the park visitor center. If you are a teacher, consider the educational and interpretive materials that have been developed by the NPS. There's plenty to discover (and pointing is optional).

References

Bacher, K., Baltrus, A., Barrie, B., Bliss, K., Cardea, D. *et al.* (2007) *Foundations of Interpretation: Curriculum Content Narrative*. National Park Service. Available at: https://www.nps.gov/idp/interp/1 01/foundationscurriculum.pdf (accessed 23 July 2024).

Hudspeth, T., Camp, M. and Cirillo, J. (2016) Lifelong learning. In: Manning, R., Diamant, R., Mitchell, N. and Harmon, D. (eds) *A Thinking Person's Guide to America's National Parks*. Braziller Publishers, New York, pp. 57–68.

Manning, R. (2016) How America's best idea can be colleges' best opportunity. *Chronicle of Higher Education*, April 13. Available at: https://www.chronicle.com/article/how-americas-best-idea-can-b e-colleges-best-opportunity/ (accessed 8 July 2024).

National Association for Interpretation (2024) What is Interpretation? Available at: https://nai-us.org/inter p/nai/_About/what_is_interp.aspx (accessed 23 July 2024).

National Park Service (2007) Foundations of Interpretation Curriculum Content Narrative. National Park Service Interpretive Development Program. Available at: https://www.nps.gov/idp/interp/101/found ationscurriculum.pdf (accessed 8 July 2024).

National Park Service (2024) Educators. Available at: www.nps.gov/learn (accessed 9 July 2024).

Tilden, F. (2008) *Interpreting Our Heritage*, 4th edn. University of North Carolina Press, Chapel Hill, North Carolina.

United States Government (2019) National Park Service Organic Act. An Act to establish a National Park Service, and for other purposes. Public Law (United States) 64-235, H.R. 15522, 39 Statute 535, enacted August 25, 1916. Available at: https://www.govinfo.gov/content/pkg/COMPS-1725/pdf/CO MPS-1725.pdf (accessed 18 July 2024).

Wolfe, L.M. (1945) *Son of the Wilderness: The Life of John Muir. Quoting Muir's Journals, c. March, 1871*. University of Wisconsin Press, Madison, Wisconsin.

53 Junior Ranger Program

Post

Nico A. shared his family's love of the Junior Ranger Program on LinkedIn, hitting on many ideals of the national parks:

> *Our family loves the National Park Junior Ranger Program! It's an incredible educational opportunity for young adventurers to engage in hands-on activities, interactive learning, and exploring the great outdoors. This program inspires a deep appreciation for nature and wildlife while instilling a sense of responsibility and stewardship. Through connecting with the natural world and learning about conservation, these young guardians of the wilderness develop a profound understanding of preserving our national treasures for future generations. The Junior Ranger Program isn't just about earning a badge; it's a path to a lifelong connection with nature and a commitment to environmental stewardship.*

Response

Explore. Learn. Protect. This is the motto of the iconic NPS Junior Ranger Program, a powerful message to impart to your children and grandchildren, and a nice way for them to join the NPS "family" as Junior Rangers. This is an activity-based program conducted in almost all of the national parks. Participants get a free Junior Ranger activity booklet, complete the activities described in the booklet during their visit, share what they've learned with a park ranger, and receive an official Junior Ranger patch and certificate. Participants are typically between ages 5 and 13 (though adults are welcome to participate, too!). As *Nico A.* so aptly notes, the engaging activities are hopefully about more than just collecting badges, but actually inspiring a new generation of park guardians and environmental stewards.

Variations on the classic Junior Ranger Program include National Theme Junior Ranger Booklets and the Junior Ranger Online program. The former includes a set of booklets addressing topics important to many national parks. Examples include *Park Explorer*, *Wildland Firefighter*, *Railroad Explorer*, *Spaceflight Explorer*, *Angler*, *Cave Scientist*, *Archeologist*, *Paleontologist*, and *Underground Railroad Explorer*. Some programs offer online activities, a downloadable booklet, and completion awards. The Junior Ranger Online program offers interactive and printable activities. Participants can view parks online in real time and do scavenger hunts, word games, and more. The link below contains details on these popular programs. (See Conversation 57 for more about children and grandchildren in the national parks.)

Reference

National Park Service (2024) Become a Junior Ranger. Available at: www.nps.gov/kids/become-a-junior-ranger.htm (accessed 9 July 2024).

© Robert Manning and Elizabeth Perry 2024. *Conversations About Visiting and Managing the National Parks* (R.E. Manning and E.E Perry)
DOI: 10.1079/9781800626768.0053

Tips

54 Accessibility

Post

Tamara posted the following on Facebook about the accessibility of national parks, an issue that the National Park Service (NPS) is working hard to address:

> *I LOVE that* [park staff at Denali National Park] *created a Jr. Ranger pledge in American Sign Language!! So often services for the deaf get overlooked or minimized. What a great way to show inclusion!*

Response

We're pleased that your visit to Denali National Park was so successful, and thanks for your post about the important issue of universal accessibility to the national parks. The Introduction to this book recounts the foundational democratic ideal of the national parks: these are the places that tell the stories of America's natural and cultural history, and they've been set aside for the benefit and enjoyment of everyone. The NPS is committed to ensuring that people with disabilities have equal opportunities to visit and enjoy these important places and to take advantage of associated facilities, programs, services, and activities. In its groundbreaking report on disability and the national parks, *All In! Accessibility in the National Park Service 2015–2020*, the NPS wrote:

> National parks that seek continued relevance and success in the 21st century must swiftly improve institutional capacity to prioritize accessibility and expand access to parks. At a very foundational level for parks, this means all people are entitled to the same rights and services.
>
> (National Park Service, 2014, p. 6)

Examples of the ways in which this goal is being furthered include: (i) Braille alternatives to print material; (ii) sign language interpretation of ranger-guided walks and tours; (iii) accessible camping sites and trails; and (iv) ramps and elevators that make park buildings more fully accessible.

In fact, there's been a long association between national parks and disability-related places and people. For example, Boston Harbor Islands National Recreation Area once housed a school for children with behavioral issues in the 18th and 19th centuries, Catoctin Mountain Park accommodated physically disabled children in its camp program, and Harriet Tubman National Historical Park and Harriet Tubman Underground Railroad National Historical Park celebrate Tubman's leadership of the Underground Railroad and tell the story of Tubman's disabilities. The National Park Service's Disability History series highlights many disability-related stories associated with the national parks.

Accessibility issues in the parks are typically addressed in the following categories.

Mobility devices

The Americans with Disabilities Act (ADA) defines a wheelchair as "a manually-operated or power-driven device designed primarily for use by an individual with a mobility disability for the main purpose of indoor or of both indoor and outdoor locomotion" (US Department of Justice Civil Rights Division, 2020). Devices that meet this definition are allowed anywhere foot travel is allowed in national parks, including wilderness areas (see Conversation 21). However, mobility devices powered by batteries, fuel, or other engines, that are not primarily designed for individuals with mobility disabilities, but that

DOI: 10.1079/9781800626768.0054

are used by such individuals for the purpose of locomotion, are classified as Other Powered-Driven Mobility Devices and are not allowed in national parks. Examples include golf cars/carts, electronic personal assistance mobility devices (such as the Segway® Personal Transporter), or any mobility device that doesn't meet the definition of a wheelchair and is designed to operate in areas without defined pedestrian routes. The NPS often provides special facilities designed to accommodate wheelchairs, such as convenient parking, ramps, automatic-opening doors, and elevators.

Deaf/hearing loss

Many parks offer special assistance related to hearing disabilities, but these may vary substantially by park. Prominent examples of assistance programs include portable assistance listening devices for ranger-led programs, real-time captioning of live events in-person or digitally, provision of an American Sign Language interpreter for in-person programs, and warnings/notifications about safety-related issues, parking-related concerns, and campgrounds/campsites accessibility.

Blind/low vision

Many parks offer special assistance associated with vision-related disabilities. Prominent examples include programs that offer tactile information, maps, and models, where and how to access audio and alternative descriptions of parks and related programs, advice regarding special safety concerns, and supplemental accessibility assistance with buildings and other facilities.

Intellectual

Many parks offer special assistance to visitors with intellectual disabilities. Examples include notification of safety-related concerns, general descriptions of park films, exhibits, and programs, availability of sensory-friendly devices (e.g. noise-reducing headphones, sunglasses, ear plugs), and recommended quiet places.

Service animals

Dogs classified as service animals are trained to perform specific tasks that assist a person with a disability. Examples of such tasks include guiding people who are blind, alerting people who are deaf, pulling a wheelchair, alerting and protecting a person who is having a seizure, reminding a person with mental health concerns to take prescribed medications, and calming a person with Post-traumatic stress disorder (PTSD) during an anxiety attack. Service dogs are permitted anywhere that visitors can go in national parks. Service animals are working animals, not pets, and the work or task a dog has been trained to provide must be directly related to a person's disability. Emotional support, therapy, and companion animals are considered pets, not service animals under ADA provisions, because they have not been trained to provide a task directly related to a disability. Service dogs in training are not service animals under ADA and are also considered pets. (See Conversation 58 on dogs in national parks.)

As Conversation 70 describes, many parks' commercial facilities and services (e.g. lodgings, food service) are operated by private companies licensed by the NPS, and are generally referred to as "concessions". The operators of these concession facilities and services are required to address accessibility issues (see in the References at the end of this conversation).

The NPS also participates in the Access Pass, a free, lifetime pass to more than 2000 recreation sites managed by five federal agencies (see Conversation 66 on entrance passes). The pass is available to US citizens or permanent residents who have been medically determined to have a permanent disability (which doesn't have to be a 100% disability).

Individuals who think they've been discriminated against or unreasonably denied access to national parks may file a complaint to the Director of the National Park Service Office of Equal Opportunity Programs (see National Park Service (2024a) in the References for details).

References

National Park Service (n.d.) Series: Disability History: An Overview. Available at: https://www.nps.gov/articles/series.htm?id=88713887-1DD8-B71B-0B40487E6097176E (accessed 9 July 2024).

National Park Service (2014) *All In! Accessibility in the National Park Service 2015-2020*. National Park Service, US Department of the Interior. Available at: https://www.nps.gov/aboutus/upload/All_In_Accessibility_in_the_NPS_2015-2020_FINAL.pdf (accessed 9 July 2024).

National Park Service (2023) Concessions Accessibility. Available at: https://www.nps.gov/subjects/concessions/access.htm (accessed 9 July 2024).

National Park Service (2024a) Accessibility. Available at: https://www.nps.gov/aboutus/accessibility.htm (accessed 9 July 2024).

National Park Service (2024b) Disability History Series Introduction. Available at: https://www.nps.gov/articles/disability-history-series-introduction.htm (accessed 9 July 2024).

US Department of Justice Civil Rights Division (2020) ADA (Americans with Disabilities Act) Requirements: Wheelchairs, Mobility Aids, and Other Power-driven Mobility Devices. Available at: https://www.ada.gov/resources/opdmds (accessed 23 July 2024).

55 Avoiding the Crowds

Post

rsnorunt posted a message on Reddit asking for advice about an upcoming trip to Glacier National Park, one of the most popular national parks. Lots of people replied with good ideas, including this posting by *Huckleberry-Hiker*:

> *Start your days early to ensure you'll find a parking spot, or use the shuttle bus for hikes on the Going to the Sun Road.*

Response

Thanks to *Huckleberry-Hiker* for raising this issue and for offering such good ideas! In the following, we suggest these and more ideas that have served us well, including starting your days in the park early to help ensure the availability of a parking spot at the destinations you'd like to visit and, maybe even better, take shuttle buses that are offered in an increasing number of national parks to avoid the whole issue of finding parking spots (see Conversations 62 and 92 on public transit in the national parks). Read on for more ideas.

Yes, the national parks can be crowded, at least in some places and at some times. This is the inevitable consequence of their foundational importance in American society, the suite of outdoor recreation opportunities they offer, and their often stunning beauty; the hundreds of millions of annual visits to the national parks should be celebrated. (See Conversation 3 for more information on the number and distribution of visits to the national parks). However, from a pragmatic standpoint, there are several effective strategies and tactics that can be employed to deal with crowding and even find precious moments of solitude.

Visit less well-known national parks

While every national-park goer needs to visit Yellowstone, Yosemite, and Grand Canyon at some point, consider visiting some of the less well-known parks as well; examples include Great Sand Dunes National Park and Preserve (Colorado), Guadalupe Mountains National Park (Texas), North Cascades National Park (Washington State), and Capitol Reef National Park (Utah). Also don't forget that the 63 units of the National Park System that are titled "National Park" (e.g. Yellowstone National Park) represent only a fraction of the more than 400 parks of the National Park System (see Conversation 1 for more about this). All of the more than 400 national parks are important manifestations of the nation's natural and cultural history and are well worth visiting, and many are comparatively underutilized; find the names and locations of all of the more than 400 national parks on the NPS network of websites as described in Conversation 35.

Visit national parks in the off-season

In the analogous temporal dimension, consider visiting the national parks in the off-season, though these shoulder seasons are growing shorter as more people are adopting this strategy and parks' climates are changing. Many parks accommodate the majority of their visits in the three summer months, leaving the rest of the year relatively fallow. The waterfalls of Yosemite are typically at their peak in May, fall foliage at Acadia is at its most colorful in October, and wildflowers at Grand Canyon are usually most prolific in April. Use these shoulder seasons in these and other parks to your advantage. Moreover, many of the predominantly

DOI: 10.1079/9781800626768.0055

historical/cultural national parks can be visited year-round.

Visit other parks and public lands

As discussed in Conversation 4, national parks are only one type of parks and public lands in the US. Others include national forests, national wildlife refuges, lands administered by the Bureau of Land Management, state parks, and local parks. Consider visiting these areas in addition to national parks.

Get out of your car and walk

Walking is the most intimate way to enjoy and appreciate the national parks (see Conversation 38 for more about this). It seems to be the natural law of the parks that the number of people you see decreases exponentially with each mile from the trailhead.

Use public transit when available

Traffic congestion and lack of parking plague some national parks and the NPS is responding with public transit systems, usually shuttle buses; poster children include Zion, Rocky Mountain, Yosemite, Acadia, Denali, Grand Canyon, and a growing list of other national parks. Use these (often free) transit systems to avoid the traffic and parking headaches that too many of us face in our everyday lives. (See more about public transit in the national parks in Conversations 62 and 92.)

Rise early and/or stay late

When in the parks, get to attraction sites and trailheads early in the day and consider hikes later in the day; parking spaces are more readily available at these times and you'll experience the parks at the "golden hours" when the light is at its finest—soft and rich—for viewing and photographing and when wildlife is more likely to be seen and heard.

Purchase park passes and other goods before entering a park

Some national parks require an entrance fee/pass (see more about this in Conversations 65 and 66). There are several types of passes, including a week-long or annual pass to individual parks, an annual pass to all areas of the National Park System, and special passes for active duty military personnel (free), seniors, volunteers (free), and disabled visitors (free). Of course, you can obtain passes at the parks you visit, but this may require waiting in line at the park entrance station or visitor center. You can obtain passes in advance at several websites, including www.nps.gov/planyourvisit/passes.htm, https://www.recreation.gov, and https://store.usgs.gov/recreational-passes (all accessed 9 July 2024). You can also save time (and usually money) by purchasing the goods you'll need (e.g. food, fuel, camping supplies) for your visit before you enter the park. Many of these items are often available in the parks, but only at a few locations, and you may have to wait behind other visitors to make your purchases (wouldn't you rather be on the trail?) and pay relatively high prices.

Welcome other visitors

Finally, welcome other visitors to the national parks; it's a wonderful thing that so many like-minded people are interested in the parks. Moreover, the national parks have become such an important component of our society at least partly because so many people visit and appreciate them. Yes, large numbers of visitors can sometimes cause crowding and congestion, but here in this conversation we offer a number of ways to overcome this. A wise NPS ranger once said that appreciation of the parks leads to their protection, and the parks need all the stakeholders they can get. Be especially welcoming of visitors from historically underrepresented groups (see Conversation 93 for more about this issue).

Reference

Manning, R. and Manning, M. (2020) *Walks of a Lifetime in America's National Parks*. Falcon, Guilford, Connecticut.

56 Be an Artist-in-Residence

Post

Ben Cosgrove (https://www.bencosgrove.com/ (accessed 9 July 2024)) has been an artist-in-residence with the National Parks Arts Foundation at a number of national parks. His record, *Bearings*, is partially inspired by his residency at Hawaii Volcanoes National Park. On *Big Blend Radio*'s YouTube page, they describe this work as follows:

> *Cosgrove relied on a novel and improvisation-focused compositional style that aimed to reflect the real experience of learning topographical space through movement.*

Response

In the second half of the 19th century, a number of American artists began painting the American landscape as a way to celebrate its vast and wild character. Prominent among these artists was Thomas Moran who accompanied the Congressionally funded 1871 Hayden Expedition to explore the area that would become Yellowstone National Park. In fact, Moran's paintings of the area—particularly his monumental 7 ft by 12 ft oil painting, *Grand Canyon of the Yellowstone*, that was hung in the Capitol Building—were instrumental in convincing Congress to establish Yellowstone National Park in 1872, the first national park in America and the world.

Ever since, the national parks have inspired artists who work in a variety of media. In fact, some national parks have been established to celebrate artistic expression; examples include Saint-Gaudens National Historical Park and Wolf Trap National Park for the Performing Arts. This artistic heritage is celebrated in the NPS's Artist-in-Residence Program. More than 50 national parks participate in this program, offering artists an opportunity to honor and interpret the parks by creating works of art in a great variety of natural and cultural settings. This program addresses visual arts, writing, music, and other creative media. Artists spend an extended period in the park—up to a month or more—and most residencies include lodging. Coverage of Cosgrove's album, the inspiration for this post, notes that he has participated in multiple residencies in national parks, steeping himself in musical inspiration from these landscapes and experiences. Year-round "resident artist" opportunities are also available at some parks for participants who have a home or seasonal residence within commuting distance of the park. Artists-in-residence are usually asked to participate in park programs by sharing their art with the public and donating an art piece to the park collection.

Reference

National Park Service (2022) Arts in the Parks. Available at: https://www.nps.gov/subjects/arts/index.htm (accessed 9 July 2024).

© Robert Manning and Elizabeth Perry 2024. *Conversations About Visiting and Managing the National Parks* (R.E. Manning and E.E Perry)
DOI: 10.1079/9781800626768.0056

57 Children and Grandchildren

Post

leemcat posted the following question on Tripadvisor:

> *Are there paved walking trails or wooden trails that can accommodate strollers and pushing an infant and toddler around? Or are all walking trails natural terrain?*

Response

Great question, *leemcat*. The short answer is that this varies among the national parks. Many of the larger national parks have short nature trails that are well maintained and may even be surfaced with asphalt or wood, and many of the national parks closer to population centers are likely to have paved trails. Your comment raises the larger issue of children and grandchildren in the national parks and there's lots of good news about this.

Parents and grandparents have been introducing their children to America's national parks for generations. There are more than 400 national parks to choose from, ranging from large natural parks like Yellowstone and Grand Canyon, to historic sites like Statue of Liberty and Independence Hall, and all tell the important stories of America. At natural parks, you can hike, bike, ride horses, swim, raft, take scenic drives, and camp under the stars (though more conventional lodging is also often available). At historic parks, you can see our country through the eyes of a founding father (or mother!), live the life of a Revolutionary War soldier with booming cannons and muskets, and walk with a hero of the Civil Rights Movement. Create lasting memories for your children and grandchildren (and you) in the national parks by following these guidelines.

Start by finding the parks that interest you the most or those close to home. Log onto the NPS website (www.nps.gov (accessed 7 July 2024)), click on the "Find a Park" option, and search by state or use the handy national map. (See Conversations 33 and 35 for more on planning a national park visit.) It's a good idea to involve the children in the planning process, as everyone can learn a lot about the natural and cultural history of the nation simply by looking at the brief descriptions of parks on the NPS "Find a Park" website. Then look more carefully at the official NPS website for each park you're interested in visiting for information on places to go, things to see and do, and logistics, including camping/lodging if you're staying overnight. (See Conversations 39 and 67–69 for information on camping and lodgings, respectively.) Most websites have a "For Kids" section. Scrolling through the photo-rich websites with the kids will get all of you excited. Some of the national parks are very popular, so plan and make reservations as early as possible. See the website "Advice from a Ranger: Visiting National Parks with Kids" (National Park Service, 2020) in the References at the end of this conversation.

Are any of your children/grandchildren in the fourth grade? If so, they (and you!) can get a free year-long Every Kid Outdoors pass to all the national parks. See the website links provided in the References for this pass and other types of money-saving passes. (Conversations 65 and 66 provide more information on entrance fees and passes.) Take advantage of the iconic NPS Junior Ranger Program, offered nearly everywhere in the National Park System. Using the Junior Ranger booklet available at park visitor centers or downloadable from park websites, kids complete a series of activities during their visit, share their answers to questions with a park ranger, take an oath to help protect the parks, and receive an official Junior Ranger badge and certificate, a highlight for many children (see Conversation

© Robert Manning and Elizabeth Perry 2024. *Conversations About Visiting and Managing the National Parks* (R.E. Manning and E.E Perry) DOI: 10.1079/9781800626768.0057

53 for more about the Junior Ranger Program). Junior rangers are typically between the ages of 5 and 13, though parents and grandparents can (and do!) participate as well.

Most parks have trails and many include short nature or history trails that have accompanying educational booklets and signs along the way that allow visitors to learn about the park's natural and human history. Start with short trails that have kid-centric attractions such as lakes and rocks to climb on. Most national parks have visitor centers that offer interactive displays about the park and a video, and these facilities are staffed with park rangers and other knowledgeable staff who can answer questions and help you plan your visit, including suggestions about which trails are most appropriate for children. This is a good way to start your visit to all the parks (see Conversation 50 for more about park visitor centers).

Consider joining NPS rangers on their iconic guided walks, campfire talks, and other activities; most programs are free of charge. See the official website of the parks and check at visitor centers for a schedule of activities.

Food and other services are sometimes available in the parks, but these facilities can be crowded and expensive. Bring food (including lots of snacks) and drinks with you and enjoy the many world-class opportunities for picnics. Other things to pack include sunscreen, lots of water, insect repellant, hats, sunglasses, hand sanitizer, and a blanket for picnics; bring lightweight daypacks for everyone to carry this gear. At the larger parks, be sure to fill your car's gas tank or charge the car's batteries before you enter the park.

Although there's a lot to do with children in most national parks, build in some leisure time on your visit; children (and parents/ grandparents!) can get tired and lose their focus. Some free time is often welcome and can allow children the opportunity for spontaneous activities. Take lots of photos, allowing the kids to take some of their own. When you get home, make a photo album that will be a family treasure for years. Consider participating in the National Parks Passport program. Passport booklets can be purchased online and at park visitor centers, and kids can get the booklet stamped at all national parks. Try to get into the parks early each day before the crowds build up and parking becomes scarce, then end your day early so everyone can rest.

Reference

America's National Parks (n.d.) Passport to Your National Parks. Available at: americasnationalparks.org/passport-to-your-national-parks (accessed 5 July 2024).

National Park Service (2020) Advice from a Ranger: Visiting National Parks with Kids. Available at: https://www.nps.gov/articles/visiting-national-parks-with-kids.htm (accessed 10 July 2024).

National Park Service (2024) Plan Your Visit. Available at: https://www.nps.gov/planyourvisit/index.htm (accessed 10 July 2024).

United States Government (n.d) Every Kid Outdoors. Available at: https://everykidoutdoors.gov/index.htm (accessed 10 July 2024).

58 Dogs in the National Parks

Post

FluffyMcFlurry posted the following comment on Reddit about the often contentious issue of dogs in the national parks:

> I know dogs are not allowed on any trails in the park. I have a service dog and the ranger said we could go on a trail with my service dog. I know I technically could take my dog anywhere since he's a service dog, but I really don't want to abuse that.

Response

Thanks for raising this issue, *FluffyMcFlurry*—it's an important one that sometimes causes some heartburn among national park visitors. It's only natural that many visitors would like to bring their dogs with them when they visit the national parks. Many national parks welcome our furry family members; your dog can even become a BARK Ranger! But you must be a responsible pet owner and be aware of NPS policy about dogs (which can vary among parks; it's a good idea to check the official website of the parks you plan to visit).

Dogs have a happy history in the national parks. For example, consider Gracie, a border collie "employed" at Glacier National Park. She learned to move wildlife—bighorn sheep and mountain goats in particular—away from the popular Logan Pass area, reducing the problem of wildlife getting too close to people (or is it the reverse?). The sled dogs of Denali National Park are also hard working: in summer they offer popular daily demonstrations to visitors and in the winter they're invaluable for backcountry travel by park rangers. Also, of course, we all recognize the value of dogs that assist in search and rescue missions.

But just as there are rules that apply to people in the national parks, there are also rules for dogs, and because the National Park System is so diverse, it's not surprising that regulations about pets vary among parks. Most parks allow dogs to travel with visitors in their cars, and many allow dogs on leash (no more than 6 ft) and under control in developed areas such as campgrounds, some lodgings, and on some trails. Other common rules include prohibition of dogs in public buildings, on many public transit vehicles (such as shuttle buses), and at swimming beaches. There are also limits on noise that bothers other visitors or disturbs wildlife. A few national parks allow only service dogs.

It's easy to check with individual national parks before you plan your visit. Using your favorite search engine, simply enter the name of the park you're thinking of visiting, followed by "nps"; this will take you to the official NPS website for the park. Once at the park website, select "Pets" from the menu or enter "pets" in the search option. Let's take an example. The website for Petrified Forest National Park (Arizona) indicates that this is especially pet friendly, allowing dogs in most of the park (though they must be on leash). If you have questions that aren't covered on the website, all national parks have a "Contact Us" button at the bottom of their front page; using this option will usually result in a response within a few days (see Conversation 64 for more about this). (The phone option is less useful, as the NPS is so thinly staffed that it's often difficult to reach someone.) General NPS policy on dogs can be found at the at the end of this conversation.

Not only can your dog enjoy visiting most national parks with you, Fido can become a BARK Ranger, which affords special privileges; some parks offer BARK Ranger days and hikes. A dog (with your help) can be sworn in as a BARK Ranger and can even sport a special collar tag (available for a small fee) attesting to this status. The self-guided program to become

© Robert Manning and Elizabeth Perry 2024. *Conversations About Visiting and Managing the National Parks* (R.E. Manning and E.E Perry)
DOI: 10.1079/9781800626768.0058

a BARK Ranger involves the owner signing a pledge to:

- **B** – Bag your dog's waste and properly dispose of it.
- **A**– Always leash your pet on a leash of 6 ft or less and have the dog under control.
- **R** – Respect wildlife.
- **K** – Know where you can go.

The BARK Ranger program, begun in 2015 in Olympic National Park, has been widely adopted throughout the National Park System. There are even programs in some parks where BARK Ranger owners can become Volunteers-in-Parks (VIPs) and go "on patrol" in the park with their BARK Ranger dogs, helping to ensure that all dogs and owners are having a good experience and following applicable rules.

Rules on dogs in national parks are designed to keep your pet safe. Dogs can be endangered in new and potentially dog-unfriendly environments. Examples of threats include large predators such as grizzly bears and wolves in Yellowstone National Park, geyser basins with thin crusts at Lassen Volcanic National Park, and hot lava at Hawaii Volcanoes National Park. Even common wildlife such as porcupines and skunks can pose a risk to your canine companion.

Given the National Park System's diversity, dog owners need to be careful that their pets are prepared for sometimes extreme weather, steep climbs, rough trails, and other challenging conditions. For example, summer temperatures in some parks can approach and even reach well into the triple digits. Dogs cool themselves through panting rather than sweating, and this makes them more susceptible to overheating and even heatstroke (which can come on quickly). Take plenty of water for your dog, plan hikes in the cool of the morning, rest in shady areas, and avoid the hot summer months. It may be wise to check with your vet to see if your dog is fit enough to handle a demanding hike. NPS rangers report that calls for dog rescues are not unusual.

Restrictions on dogs are also designed to protect the parks. For example, the presence of dogs and the scent they leave behind can affect the natural behavior of wildlife, and there is the potential threat of passing animal diseases from pets to wildlife. It's believed that the canine parvovirus was transmitted to wolves at Isle Royale National Park from a pet dog and the infected wolf population declined precipitously. Heartworms from dogs can kill foxes, coyotes, bobcats, and mountain lions. Of course, dogs shouldn't chase or otherwise harass wildlife. Leashing dogs is also respectful of other park visitors.

Some parks have kennels in or adjacent to them so your pet can be comfortable (even pampered!), should you want to do an activity that isn't suitable for your furry friend.

What about service animals? Service animals are defined by the NPS as:

> a dog that has been individually trained to do work or perform tasks for the benefit of an individual with a disability, including a physical, sensory, psychiatric, intellectual, or other mental disability. The tasks performed by the animal must be directly related to the person's disability.
>
> (National Park Service, 2023)

Service dogs are not considered pets and can generally go anywhere visitors are allowed. Therapy dogs are classified as pets and are eligible to become BARK Rangers, but all other restrictions on dogs apply. See Conversation 54 for more on the accessibility of national parks.

There's room in most national parks for both visitors and their dogs. But dog owners need to be responsible: know the rules that apply to dogs and make sure to follow them, protecting pets, people, and the parks.

Reference

National Park Service (2023) Pets. Available at: www.nps.gov/subjects/pets/index.htm (accessed 10 July 2024).

59 Responsible Recreation

Post

Taking part in recreational activities responsibly includes disposing of waste and trash properly. Posting this image to Wikimedia Commons, user *Killarnee* shows a ranger at Joshua Tree National Park frowning with a large piece of litter, perhaps a mylar balloon.

Mylar balloon litter, Wikimedia Commons/Joshua Tree National Park.

Response

National parks have been established to help protect many of the nation's most important natural and cultural resources. So it's important that visitors help the NPS do this by taking part in recreation responsibly and limiting their potential impacts. Impacts certainly include very visible ones, like the litter in the image above. In addition, visiting the parks safely requires visitors to be aware of potential hazards such as extreme weather and wild animals; it's imperative that visitors prepare for these potential hazards by enjoying their recreation responsibly. Taking part in recreation responsibly also helps to keep NPS rangers and other employees safe by limiting the need for emergency assistance and search and rescue services.

The NPS maintains a helpful website (see National Park Service (2024) in the References at the end of this conversation) that offers advice on how to take part in recreation responsibly. For example, the following five principles can help visitors plan and conduct their trips in ways that protect park resources and contribute to the safety and quality of recreation:

1. Know before you go—Read about the parks you plan to visit on their official NPS websites. Here you'll find out about places to visit and things to do, but also how to prepare yourself for potential hazards that might apply such as extreme weather, emergency closures, fire restrictions, and rules and regulations.
2. Plan and prepare—Reservations and/or permits may be required to visit particular sites and participate in some activities. Moreover, special equipment and expertise may be needed to participate in selected activities.
3. Build an inclusive outdoors and respect others—Be sure to welcome other visitors to the park and help improve the quality of the park experience for everyone.
4. Leave no trace—Conduct yourself in ways that limit your impacts on park resources and the quality of the visitor experience for others. The non-profit group, Leave No Trace, has developed seven principles to guide use of the national parks and other public lands (see Conversation 60).
5. Make it better—All visitors to the national parks have a responsibility to sustain the parks, including the natural and cultural resources they protect and the quality of the visitor experience for all.

This website also includes more detailed guidelines and suggestions for enjoying recreation responsibly for a variety of specific recreation activities. Other important resources for

DOI: 10.1079/9781800626768.0059

helping visitors take part responsibly include the NPS Trip Planning Guide (National Park Service, 2023) and the Recreate Responsibly website noted below (Recreate Responsibly, 2022).

References

National Park Service (2023) Trip Planning Guide. Available at: www.nps.gov/subjects/healthandsafety /trip-planning-guide.htm (accessed 10 July 2024).

National Park Service (2024) Recreate Responsibly. Available at: https://www.nps.gov/planyourvisit/recreate -responsibly.htm (accessed 10 July 2024).

Recreate Responsibly (2022) To recreate responsibly is to care for one another and the places we play. Available at: www.recreateresponsibly.org/ (accessed 10 July 2024).

60 Leave No Trace

Post

In response to an article in the New York Times ("How to go camping: A beginner's guide"; Glusac, 2023), reader *Mark* commented:

> *Leave no trace!! It is so important. It boggles my mind that people actually think it is OK to litter. [There] is a lack of understanding of the bigger concept: if everyone who visited even littered just a little bit, it all adds up.*

Response

Nearly all of the National Park System is open and welcoming to outdoor recreation—walking/hiking, camping, birding, photography, etc. But recreation can have impacts to the environment, such as littering, soil compaction, destruction of groundcover vegetation, disturbance of wildlife, water pollution. As *Mark* notes, littering adds up. So too do these other impacts on the environment, as altering soil, vegetation, wildlife, and water has cumulative effects. The presence of other people can also impact the quality of the recreation experience for others through the environmental impacts that have accumulated and through inappropriate behavior, such as not following park rules, boisterous behavior, and other issues (see Conversations 85 and 86 for more about this). While the impact of a single individual or small group might be minimal, these impacts can be substantial when magnified by the hundreds of millions of annual visits to the parks (see Conversation 3 about visitation).

The non-profit organization, Leave No Trace, Inc. (often abbreviated LNT), has become instrumental in addressing recreation-related impacts in the national parks and elsewhere. The organization was formed in 1987 and now works with the NPS, the US Fish and Wildlife Service, the Bureau of Land Management, the US Forest Service, and other agencies and organizations to develop and advance science-based guidance on minimum-impact outdoor recreation practices and behaviors. The Leave No Trace educational program reaches more than 15 million Americans each year. The heart of the program is their Seven Principles of Leave No Trace, briefly described as follows.

Principle 1: Plan ahead and prepare

Lack of planning can lead to damage to natural and cultural resources and the quality of recreation experience. Points to remember include: (i) know rules and special concerns for the area you'll visit; (ii) prepare for extreme weather, hazards, and emergencies; (iii) schedule your trip to avoid times of high use; (iv) visit in small groups (split larger groups into several smaller ones if needed); (v) repackage food to minimize waste; and (vi) use a map and compass/GPS (Global Positioning System) to eliminate use of rock cairns, flagging, or marking paint.

Principle 2: Travel and camp on durable surfaces

Walking/hiking and camping are two of the primary activities that can result in damage to fragile soils, vegetation, and wildlife. Points to remember include: (i) durable surfaces include established trails, campsites, rock, gravel, dry grasses, and snow; (ii) protect riparian areas by camping at least 200 ft from lakes and streams; (iii) in popular areas, concentrate use on existing trails and campsites; (iv) walk single file in the middle of the trail, even when the ground is wet or muddy; (v) keep campsites small and focus activity in areas where vegetation is absent; (vi) in undisturbed areas, disperse use to prevent

© Robert Manning and Elizabeth Perry 2024. *Conversations About Visiting and Managing the National Parks* (R.E. Manning and E.E Perry) DOI: 10.1079/9781800626768.0060

creation of new campsites and trails; and (vii) avoid places where impacts are just beginning.

Principle 3: Dispose of waste properly

The waste humans create can have severe impacts if not disposed of properly. Points to remember include: (i) pack out what you pack in, including all trash, leftover food, and litter (remember to inspect your campsite and rest areas for trash and spilled food)—burning trash is never recommended; (ii) deposit solid human waste in catholes dug 6–8 inches deep at least 200 ft from water, camp, and trails; cover and disguise the cathole when finished; (iii) bury toilet paper deep in a cathole or pack the toilet paper out along with other hygiene products; and (iv) to wash yourself or your dishes, carry water 200 ft away from streams or lakes, use small amounts of biodegradable soap, and scatter strained dishwater.

Principle 4: Leave what you find

The items we find in nature have a role to play, either in the ecosystem or the cultural story of the landscape; leaving what we find in place helps to preserve these natural and cultural resources. Points to remember include: (i) preserve the past—observe cultural or historic structures and artifacts, but do not touch them; (ii) leave rocks, plants, and other natural objects as you find them; (iii) avoid introducing or transporting non-native species; and (iv) don't build structures, furniture, or dig trenches.

Principle 5: Minimize campfire impacts

The natural appearance of many areas has been degraded by overuse of campfires and increasing demand for firewood; moreover, wildfires threaten outdoor spaces and many are caused by humans. Points to remember include: (i) campfires can cause lasting impacts to the environment—use a lightweight stove for cooking and enjoy a candle lantern for light;

(ii) use established fire rings, pans, or mound fires where fires are permitted; (iii) keep fires small—use only sticks from the ground that can be broken by hand; and (iv) burn all wood and coals to ash, put out campfires completely, then scatter cool ashes.

Principle 6: Respect wildlife

Whenever you're in an outdoor space, you're in the natural habitat of many wild animals and you should work to minimize your impact on them. Points to remember include: (i) observe wildlife from a distance—don't follow or approach them; (ii) never feed animals—feeding wildlife damages their health, alters natural behaviors, and exposes them to predators and other dangers; (iii) control pets at all times, or leave them at home; and (iv) avoid wildlife during sensitive times: mating, nesting, raising young, and winter.

Principle 7: Be considerate of others

One of the most important components of outdoor ethics is to maintain courtesy toward others, as it helps everyone enjoy their outdoor experience. Points to remember include: (i) respect others and protect the quality of their experience; (ii) be courteous, including yielding to other users on the trail; (iii) greet horseback riders and ask which side of the trail to move to when passing; (iv) take breaks and camp away from trails and others; and (v) let nature's sounds prevail by avoiding loud voices and noises.

Resolve to be part of the solution rather than part of the problem when it comes to protecting the national parks and other valuable public lands, and lead by example for your community, family, friends, and other park visitors. LNT's seven principles help make it easy. Free online courses and other educational materials about Leave No Trace are readily available via the links listed in the References.

References

Glusac, E. (2023) How to go camping: A beginner's guide. *New York Times*, August 29 2023. Available at: https://www.nytimes.com/2023/08/29/travel/tips-for-beginning-campers.html (accessed 23 July 2024).

Leave No Trace (2024a). Available at: https://lnt.org/ (accessed 10 July 2024).

Leave No Trace (2024b) Training for All. Available at: https://lnt.org/get-involved/training-courses/ (accessed 10 July 2024).

National Park Service (2024) Leave No Trace Seven Principles. Available at: https://www.nps.gov/articles/leave-no-trace-seven-principles.htm (accessed 10 July 2024).

61 Rules and Regulations

Post

Responding on X to a news story from Yellowstone National Park about a visitor being sanctioned for walking on thermal areas (an illegal activity), *Ron* wondered why such transgressions occur:

> *The rules at national parks are there for a reason, yet so many people continue to break them. I can't tell you how often I see people wander off a trail when posted signs clearly tell visitors to stay on trails and walkways.*

Response

Ron, we wish signage was fully effective in keeping people safe in the parks and abiding by park rules, but alas. As described in Conversation 6, the NPS has been charged by Congress to protect the national parks and to make them available to the public for enjoyment and appreciation. This requires that reasonable rules and regulations on public use of the parks be formulated, that these rules be communicated to visitors, and that rules and regulations be enforced when and where necessary. These rules and regulations have the force and effect of law, and violations are punishable by fines, imprisonment, or both.

Park rules and regulations often vary by park and can be found on the official NPS website for each park. Visitors should consult them as they're planning their trips. These rules and regulations are also often posted at park visitor centers, included in most park literature, and posted on signs placed around the parks. Most of these rules and regulations are straightforward

in their intent to protect park resources and visitor safety. For example, the following activities are prohibited at Yellowstone National Park, where the transgressions occurred that *Ron* and the news story noted:

- willfully remaining near or approaching wildlife, including nesting birds, within any distance that disturbs or displaces the animal;
- hunting or feeding wildlife;
- traveling off boardwalks or designated trails in hydrothermal areas;
- throwing anything into thermal features;
- swimming in hot springs;
- removing or possessing natural or cultural resources (such as wildflowers, antlers, rocks, and arrowheads);
- leaving detachable side mirrors attached when not pulling trailers;
- traveling off-road by vehicle or bicycle;
- camping outside of designated areas;
- spotlighting wildlife (viewing with lights);
- imitating elk calls or using buglers imitating wolf howls;
- using electronic equipment capable of tracking wildlife;
- launching, landing, or operating unmanned aircraft (drones) on land or water; and
- smoking in geyser basins or on trails; there is no smoking in buildings or within 25 ft of building entrances.

To help protect park resources and the quality of visitor experiences, visitors should also be familiar with Leave No Trace guidelines described in Conversation 60.

© Robert Manning and Elizabeth Perry 2024. *Conversations About Visiting and Managing the National Parks* (R.E. Manning and E.E Perry)
DOI: 10.1079/9781800626768.0061

62 Take the Bus in the National Parks

Post

A Reddit subscriber asked about traffic congestion in the national parks and how to avoid it. *aet39456inabox* responded with the following strongly felt posting:

> *Getting to national parks by car **should** be difficult and fewer cars is in the best interests of conservation and climate. Yosemite and other national parks are not just another playground—they are critical ecosystems and all visitors (regardless of socioeconomic class) should minimize their footprints in these spaces.*

Response

Conversation 3 discussed the rising number of visits to the national parks—recently surpassing 300 million annually. This has created problems with crowding in some of the parks, at least at some times, and this is often manifested in traffic congestion on park roads and a chronic shortage of parking at park attractions and trailheads. But there's a transportation revolution happening in many parks: sophisticated and convenient shuttle bus systems are being established that reduce congestion and stress and improve the quality of the visitor experience. Moreover, these public transit systems help address the environmental degradation caused by automobiles, including air pollution, carbon emissions that contribute to climate change, excessive noise, and collisions with park wildlife. Consider taking the bus in the parks that have established transit systems (some parks require them). The following are good examples that are helping to lead the National Park System.

Grand Canyon National Park

World-famous Grand Canyon National Park is a pioneer, having provided a shuttle bus service for 40 years, expanding into the impressive prototype of today's national park. The park's large and contemporary visitor center on the popular South Rim serves as the hub for a fleet of buses on five interconnecting routes that serve all major visitor attractions. The buses run on compressed natural gas, reducing harmful emissions and noise. Buses run every 15–30 min, can accommodate bikes, and are wheelchair accessible (sorry, no dogs allowed). They are free (actually, visitors are helping to pay for this service through the entrance fees they pay).

Zion National Park

Lovely Zion Canyon is the scenic heart of this popular national park, a place all visitors should see and experience. But its two-lane dead-end road became increasingly congested and noisy. Rather than expanding the road and parking lots, the NPS established a state-of-the-art shuttle bus system that carries visitors in and out of the canyon from the visitor center just inside the park (Zion Canyon Line) and even from the adjacent town of Springdale where many visitors stay (Springdale Line). The road into the canyon is now closed to cars for most of the year, adding a sense of quiet and peacefulness. Shuttle buses are wheelchair accessible, operate frequently between early March and mid-November, and even include informative narration; and they're free! Sorry, no dogs allowed.

© Robert Manning and Elizabeth Perry 2024. *Conversations About Visiting and Managing the National Parks* (R.E. Manning and E.E Perry)
DOI: 10.1079/9781800626768.0062

Acadia National Park

Acadia National Park shares Maine's Mount Desert Island with several local communities, and the free Island Explorer shuttle bus system offers transportation throughout much of the region. The park's fleet of clean-fuel, propane-powered buses connects major attractions—including the visitor center, campgrounds, carriage road entrances, scenic vistas, and trailheads—with local communities, even including the local airport. Buses are wheelchair accessible, bike racks are available, and "good" dogs are welcome. Buses travel nine routes. Download the myStop App for real-time interactive location and schedule information. The Island Explorer operates from late June to the end of August, with some routes continuing to early October.

Rocky Mountain National Park

Some of America's most dramatic mountains make up the heart of Rocky Mountain National Park (affectionately known as "Rocky"). To help address growing visitor demand, Rocky's shuttle bus system services trailheads and other attractions in the spectacular Bear Lake and Moraine Park areas. A large park-and-ride facility offers parking, and here visitors can choose to take the Bear Lake Route or the Moraine Park Route; both offer outstanding hiking opportunities. Parking is limited in both of these regions, so the shuttle bus system assures visitor access. There's also a Hiker Shuttle Route that takes visitors from the adjacent town of Estes Park to the park-and-ride facility. The buses operate from late May to mid-October, and tickets can be reserved at https:www.recreation.gov (accessed 10 July 2024) (see Conversation 37). Most buses are wheelchair accessible, but dogs aren't allowed; rides cost $2.00 for a group of up to four.

Denali National Park and Preserve

Alaska's vast Denali National Park and Preserve is more than 6 million acres, larger than some states. To help keep this wilderness park wild, a large and diverse bus system takes visitors deep into the park on the 92-mile Denali Park Road, the primary road in the park; the road generally parallels the magnificent Alaska Range. Private cars are not allowed beyond the first 15 miles. Visitors can choose among two types of buses and several routes. The familiar green "transit buses" are not narrated and travel different distances into the park, all the way to the end of the road at Kantishna, if desired; these buses are ideal for hikers and cost depends on the length of the trip. Tour buses are narrated, travel shorter distances, and are more expensive. All bus riders enjoy the park's varied landscapes, views of 20,310-ft Denali (when not shrouded in the clouds), and world-class wildlife. The buses run from late May through early September, but only some buses can accommodate wheelchairs, and dogs aren't allowed.

Buses and other forms of public transit are changing the way visitors experience an increasing number of national parks, and all for the better, lessening the environmental and social impacts of automobiles and enhancing the quality of the visitor experience. (See Conversation 92 on sustainable transportation in the national parks.) The five parks described above are just examples. Always check the official NPS website of the parks you're visiting to get the most up-to-date information. Enjoy the ride!

63 Visitor Safety

Post

Justin on LinkedIn shared a strategy to enjoy his much-anticipated vacation hikes in national parks: train with shorter hikes in nearby national parks!

> *This weekend my wife and I did an urban hike in Atlanta, including meandering past our closest NPS site: the Martin Luther King Jr. National Historic Park. We* [enjoyed] *spending the day together, but we also wanted the time to get our bones warmed up for all the hiking we'll do in a week on our vacation back to Shenandoah National Park in Virginia ...*

Response

The remarkable diversity of the National Park System offers visitors lots of ways to enjoy and appreciate these places. Popular activities include boating, fishing, swimming, biking, camping, driving, walking/hiking, motorcycle riding, photography, wildlife watching, and enjoying the parks after dark. But all of these activities include some potential risks, and visitors should be as prepared as possible to help ensure their safety. The NPS offers detailed safety-related advice about all of these activities at their helpful website (see National Park Service (2024a) in the References at the end of this conversation).

Let's take a look at safety-related advice for walking/hiking as an example. This is one of the most popular activities in the national parks and can be done in nearly all parks, from historic sites to wilderness areas. The NPS suggests preparing for walking/hiking safely by considering the following four topics.

Know your limits

The national parks include a great diversity of walking/hiking opportunities, from a short walk around Gettysburg Battlefield to the epic 2200-mile Appalachian National Scenic Trail, and they can all be enjoyable and satisfying. But be sure to choose a trail that's within your abilities. This could include preparing for more challenging hikes with regular practice, as *Justin* enjoys. Before you set out, ask yourself the following questions:

- What is my experience level with hiking?
- How much equipment, food, and water can I comfortably carry?
- Am I physically fit enough for this trail?
- Have I ever hiked in this type of environment?
- Am I able to handle hiking in higher elevations (where there is less oxygen in the air)?
- Should I hike with others (as a safety measure)?

Plan your hike

Consult the official NPS website for the parks you're considering visiting and descriptions of trails and hiking. Many national parks are the subjects of detailed hiking guidebooks, and these can be very helpful too, as can NPS rangers at the parks you're visiting. Important considerations in choosing what hikes to do include:

- Pick a trail that's within the abilities of you and your group.
- Leave a trip plan (where and when you're going) with a trusted friend or family member.

© Robert Manning and Elizabeth Perry 2024. *Conversations About Visiting and Managing the National Parks* (R.E. Manning and E.E Perry) DOI: 10.1079/9781800626768.0063

- Have an emergency plan for problems such as getting lost or injured; consider taking a wilderness first aid and backcountry navigation class.
- Have a way to communicate by carrying a cellphone and an emergency locator beacon where cellphone service is unavailable.
- Be prepared for difficult weather with rain gear and warm clothing.
- Have a Plan B ready if weather or other issues are potentially threatening; the national parks offer many ways to enjoy them.
- Check "Park Alerts" on the official NPS website for the park you're visiting; trails are occasionally closed at short notice due to wildfires, bear sightings, etc.
- Acclimate to the altitude; some trails are at high elevations that require a day or two to acclimate.

What to bring

Many hikes in the national parks require a variety of supplies and equipment, often called the "Ten Essentials"; see a listing and description of these items at the website National Park Service (2024b) in the References. Other items to consider include comfortable but sturdy shoes/boots, wool socks, bug spray, moleskin or other treatment for blisters, and a water filtration/purification option.

Hike smart

The NPS offers the following tips for "hiking smart":

- Ask a ranger for the latest conditions and advice before setting out.
- Let the slowest hiker in your group set the pace.
- Keep track of your time and distance.
- Yield to uphill hikers.
- Take frequent breaks.
- Eat snacks and drink water.
- Take your time and watch your step.
- Stay away from fast-flowing waters and slippery slopes.
- Consult local tide tables on coastal trails.
- Check clothing and body for ticks.
- Beware of wildlife (see Conversation 45 for more about this).

A big part of enjoying the national parks is staying safe; take the time to learn about safety issues.

References

National Park Service (2024a) Be Prepared for Your Activity in the Park! Available at: www.nps.gov/subjects/healthandsafety/prepare-for-your-activity.htm (accessed 10 July 2024).
National Park Service (2024b) Ten Essentials. Available at: www.nps.gov/articles/10essentials.htm (accessed 10 July 2024).

64 Contacting the NPS

Post

Responding to a Facebook post about Rocky Mountain National Park always "picking up the phone", *Stephanie* shared:

> *I've always had great luck speaking to people at all the national parks I've called. Always professional and share so much great information. We still have Rocky Mountain National Park on our list to visit.*

Response

This book provides much of the information you'll need to plan your visits to the national parks. However, the National Park System is highly diverse and you may want to contact parks directly for additional information or clarification. You'll find a phone number for each park near the bottom of the first page of its official NPS website. Because the NPS is staffed very thinly, you'll probably be connected to a phone tree, and you may have to leave a message; but sometimes there's a way to be connected to a staff member who will be able to answer your questions. It seems *Stephanie* has had good luck in that regard, and volunteers staff the Rocky Mountain National Park phone line during business hours in an effort to make sure that everyone gets connected to a person knowledgeable about the park. Another good option is to use the electronic "Contact Us" button near the bottom of the first page of the park's website. This will allow you to email your questions; experience suggests that you'll probably receive a personal reply within a few days. While you're at it, consider requesting a free park map and newspaper through this email option (though this type of information is probably online at the park's official website as well).

© Robert Manning and Elizabeth Perry 2024. *Conversations About Visiting and Managing the National Parks* (R.E. Manning and E.E Perry)
DOI: 10.1079/9781800626768.0064

Logistics

65 Entrance Fees

Post

A Yelp review comment by *Darlene* expressed some unhappiness with the entrance fee at Yosemite National Park:

> *Additionally, once you arrive at Yosemite, you have to pay a $35 entrance fee.*

Response

Darlene raises the challenging issue of fees to visit the national parks, a topic that causes heartburn among some visitors. After all, don't we already pay for the national parks through our taxes? Well, yes we do, sort of. But unfortunately, Congress allocates only a very small portion of the federal budget—less than 1/15th of 1% each year—to the National Park Service (NPS), and that's simply not enough to keep up with the rapidly increasing demand to visit the parks. For example, there's a backlog of maintenance projects in the parks that's estimated at more than $20 billion, and the number of park rangers has been steadily declining.

Fees to use the national parks are disagreeable among some visitors, but they're also troublesome from a philosophical standpoint; at their most foundational level, national parks are a democratic institution, explicitly established to be accessible and welcoming to all people regardless of social status, including income. From the very beginning of the national parks in the 19th century, Congress has been reluctant to allow or raise entrance fees and associated charges such as fees for camping; even now, they require such fees to be nominal so as not to price anyone out of the parks. Moreover, the vast majority of the more than 400 parks that comprise the National Park System are free.

For the approximately 100 national parks that charge an entrance fee, the fees can apply to cars, motorcycles, or individuals, and range from $5 to $35. (See the link in the Reference at the end of this conversation for a list of the national parks that charge entrance fees and how they're charged.) The $35 entrance fee charged to *Darlene* at Yosemite is the maximum currently allowed. However, it's important to note that this fee entitles her and accompanying family/friends in her car, to a full week in the park. Moreover there are several types of passes that can be purchased—annual passes to individual parks or all parks, discounted or even free passes for seniors, disabled visitors, volunteers, active duty military personnel—that make multiple visits more economical (or even free). (See Conversation 66 about entrance passes.) Free entry is offered to all visitors on selected days each year, usually January 15 (birthday of Martin Luther King, Jr.), April 20 (first day of National Park Week), June 19 (Juneteenth National Independence Day), August 4 (Anniversary of the Great American Outdoors Act), September 28 (National Public Lands Day), and November 11 (Veterans Day).

When and where visitors are required to pay a fee to enter a park and/or other fees, they should be comforted by the fact that all of this money goes directly to the National Park Service (NPS). It is used to: (i) enhance visitor safety and enjoyment; (ii) repair, maintain, and enhance visitor facilities and services; (iii) provide emergency medical services; (iv) expand accessibility; and (v) restore habitat for species important to visitors. For example, at Zion National Park, fees have been used to help repair trails and upgrade exhibits at the Zion Nature Center. At Joshua Tree National Park, entrance fees were used to plant over 1000 native plants, replace deteriorating picnic tables, and bring in school-aged children to

© Robert Manning and Elizabeth Perry 2024. *Conversations About Visiting and Managing the National Parks* (R.E. Manning and E.E Perry)
DOI: 10.1079/9781800626768.0065

learn about the park. At Dry Tortugas National Park, coral reef habitat was restored to improve fishing and snorkeling opportunities. Eighty percent of fees are retained by the parks that collect them, and the remaining fees are pooled and distributed to national parks that don't charge entrance or other fees.

Finally, compare the cost of visiting a national park for a week (a maximum of $35) with taking family/friends to a commercial theme park for a single day! From this perspective, the national parks are quite a bargain, as well as an investment in one of America's—and the world's—best ideas.

Reference

National Park Service (2024) Entrance Fees by Park. Available at: https://www.nps.gov/aboutus/entrance -fee-prices.htm (accessed 11 July 2024).

66 Entrance Passes

Post

On X, *markwarrenmusic* shared some advice with someone who was looking into how to plan for visiting multiple national parks:

> *National parks are what we do! (TBF we were rec majors in college.) Buy the year pass if you're going to more than 4 in a year ... Easiest coolest things to see ever!*

Response

As described in Conversation 65, the vast majority of the more than 400 national parks don't charge an entrance fee. But more than 100 do, and this may be a cause for concern among some park visitors, especially those who visit regularly. But the extensive "America the Beautiful-The National Parks and Federal Recreational Lands Access Pass" series offers a number of options that can substantially reduce these costs and even eliminate them in some cases. Most visitors weigh the cost of the annual pass against how many park trips they'll make that year when considering purchasing it, as *markwarrenmusic* states, but the pass is good beyond national parks too! All passes cover entrance fees at lands managed by the NPS and US Fish and Wildlife Service and standard day-use fees (sometimes called "amenity fees") at lands managed by the US Forest Service, the Bureau of Land Management, the Bureau of Reclamation, and the Army Corps of Engineers. This includes more than 2000 recreation areas managed by six federal agencies. Most fee revenues are used to improve and enhance visitor recreation services.

A recent change in policy is that all passes have one signature line for a single passholder. A pass covers the passholder and all occupants in a personal vehicle at sites that charge per vehicle, or the passholder and up to three additional adults (aged 16 and over) at sites that charge per person. Children aged 15 or under are admitted free. Motorcycles are treated the same as passenger vehicles, so each motorcycle is required to have a passholder and pass on board; this standardizes how motorcycles are treated for all pass types—one pass will allow in one motorcycle.

Entrance passes can be purchased in two ways: (i) in person at federal recreation sites that charge an entrance fee; and (ii) online. To find a location that issues interagency passes in person, search the list of all federal recreation sites where the passes are issued, including national parks, listed in the References at the end of this conversation. Many of the America the Beautiful-The National Parks and Federal Recreational Lands (Interagency) Passes are available to order from the online USGS Store (allow at least 3 weeks for order processing and delivery), also listed in the References. Note when making your purchase that Interagency Passes are non-refundable, non-transferable, cannot be extended and cannot be replaced if lost or stolen. Passholders must show a valid photo ID when using the passes. There are several types of passes as described below.

Annual pass

This pass is available to everyone and covers entrance fees and standard amenity day use fees as described above. The pass costs $80 for a calendar year.

Military annual pass

This free pass is available to current US military members and their dependents in

© Robert Manning and Elizabeth Perry 2024. *Conversations About Visiting and Managing the National Parks* (R.E. Manning and E.E Perry)
DOI: 10.1079/9781800626768.0066

the Army, Navy, Air Force, Marines, Coast Guard, and Space Force, as well as Reserve and National Guard members. Please check photo ID requirements before arriving. Online purchase of the pass at the online USGS Store requires a $10 processing fee. One of the following forms of documentation is required: (i) current members of the US Army, Air Force, Navy, Marines, Coast Guard, Space Force, and National Guard must have a valid Department of Defense common access card (DoD CAC); (ii) dependents of current US military members must have a valid Department of Defense (DD) form 1173 or Next Generation Uniformed Services ID (USID) card replacement; (iii) US Military Cadets must have a valid CAC card; or (iv) US Active Reservists (do not need to be deployed) must have a valid CAC card.

Military lifetime pass

This free pass is available to Gold Star Families with a valid Gold Star Family Voucher and US military veterans with a valid veteran ID. Gold Star Families are next of kin of a member of the US Armed Forces who lost their life in a "qualifying situation", such as a war, an international terrorist attack, or a military operation outside of the US while serving with the US Armed Forces, as explained in Department of Defense Instruction 1348.36. Gold Star Family members must self-certify by applying for a Military-Lifetime Pass or downloading and printing a special voucher to either present to the ranger, exchange for a Military Pass in person, or place on the vehicle dashboard at unstaffed sites. Gold Star Vouchers may be downloaded too.

Veterans are individuals who served in the US Armed Forces, including the National Guard and Reserves, and are able to present one of the following valid non-expired forms of identification when entering or using federal lands: (i) Department of Defense ID Card (DD Form 2, DD Form 2765, or Next Generation USID replacement); (ii) Veteran Health ID Card (VHIC); (iii) Veteran ID Card; or (iv) Veteran's designation on a state-issued US driver's license or ID card. When acquiring a pass in

person, the actual IDs listed above must be presented. As of September 2022, the Veterans Administration only provides a digital version of the Veteran ID Card noted in point iii above. When acquiring a pass online, photocopies or digital images are accepted. Form DD 214 is not accepted. If purchased from the USGS Store, your name will be printed on your pass.

Annual 4th grade pass

The Annual 4th Grade Pass is part of the NPS's Every Kid Outdoors Program. Fourth graders (and their families!), including home-schooled and free-choice learners 10 years of age, with a valid Every Kid Outdoors paper voucher can get a free pass. Follow this two-step process to get a pass: (i) get a paper voucher by visiting the Every Kid Outdoors website and following the instructions; and (ii) exchange the voucher for the Annual 4th Grade Pass at federal recreation sites that charge entrance or standard day use/amenity fees (find a list of these sites at the NPS pass pickup website United States Government (no date) in the References). Please note, digital versions of the paper voucher, such as on smartphones or tablets, are not accepted to exchange for an Annual 4th Grade Pass.

Senior pass

One of the advantages of getting older is the Senior Pass (sometimes—unofficially—called the "gezzer pass"), available to US citizens and permanent residents ages 62 and over. In addition to covering entrance fees, the Senior Pass may provide a 50% discount on some amenity fees charged for facilities and services such as camping, swimming, boat launch, and specialized interpretive services. The pass is available in two versions, an Annual Senior Pass ($20) and a Lifetime Senior Pass ($80); both are available in person at a federal recreation site and from the online USGS Store (nominal processing and shipping fees will be charged). Applicants must provide documentation of age and residency/citizenship.

Volunteer pass

This free annual pass is available to official volunteers in the parks with a minimum of 250 service hours (see Conversation 98 about the Volunteers-in-Parks (VIPS) program).

The National Parks and Federal recreational lands access pass

This interagency pass is available free for US citizens or permanent residents with permanent disabilities. Applicants must provide documentation of disability (does not have to be a 100% disability, but must severely limit one or more major life activities).

References

National Park Service (2022) America the Beautiful-The National Parks and Federal Recreational Lands Access Pass. Available at: https://www.nps.gov/subjects/accessibility/interagency-access-pass.htm (accessed 11 July 2024).

National Park Service (2024a) Entrance Passes. Available at: https://www.nps.gov/planyourvisit/passes.htm (accessed 11 July 2024).

National Park Service (2024b) Places to Get Interagency Passes. Available at: www.nps.gov/planyourvisit/pickup-pass-locations.htm (accessed 11 July 2024).

National Park Service (n.d.) Gold Star Family Voucher. Available at: https://www.nps.gov/customcf/goldstar/voucher.htm (accessed 11 July 2024).

United States Government (n.d.) Every Kid Outdoors. Available at: https://everykidoutdoors.gov/index.htm (accessed 11 July 2024).

USGS Store (n.d.a) Annual Pass. Available at: https://store.usgs.gov/pass (accessed 11 July 2024).

USGS Store (n.d.b) America the Beautiful National Parks & Federal Recreational Lands Passes. Available at: https://store.usgs.gov/recreational-passes (accessed 11 July 2024).

USGS Store (n.d.c) Military Pass. Available at: https://store.usgs.gov/MilitaryPass (accessed 11 July 2024).

67 Lodgings

Post

Steve L. spent several enjoyable days visiting Zion National Park, using the Zion Lodge for accommodations—the only hotel in the park. As noted in his review on Yelp, he enjoyed the advantage of staying in the park, close to many of the park's major attractions, rather than entering and exiting each day:

> *Zion Lodge is a rustic, historic lodge in the middle of Zion Canyon. The rooms are comfortable, but rustic; for example, the cabins don't have television, wifi, or coffee makers. Staying in Zion Lodge is all about being close to Zion's natural wonders. The Emerald Pools Trail, one of the highlights of the canyon, begins right across the river from the lodge, just a five minute walk.*

Response

Many of the larger parks of the National Park System, particularly those titled "national park", demand at least a few days to fully enjoy and appreciate them (see Conversation 1 for a description of the titles/names given to the units of the National Park System). That means you'll need lodging in or around these parks. Here's some information that can help you plan this aspect of your visit.

Lodgings in the parks

Most lodging facilities in the parks are managed by private concessioners (contracted by the NPS). Go to the official NPS website for the parks you're planning to visit and navigate to "Eating and Sleeping" and/or "Lodging". Here, there'll be a link to the company (sometimes more than one) that manages lodging facilities in the park; use these links to get descriptions, pricing, reservation policies, etc. In some of the most popular national parks, these facilities can be reserved a year or more in advance. Some national parks include grand historic hotels that were built many years ago to attract visitors to the parks. Examples include the El Tovar Hotel at Grand Canyon, Old Faithful Inn at Yellowstone, and Paradise Inn at Mount Rainier (see Conversations 68 and 69 about these grand national park lodges and more rustic lodgings in the backcountry of some national parks). These lodges are usually expensive and must be reserved well in advance. Because of the historic character of most of these properties, they may not meet contemporary standards of design and service, but they're often loved by those who use them.

Lodgings outside the parks

Of course, there are all types of lodgings outside many national parks, nearly all of them provided by private companies. Often, these facilities and related services are found in the park's "gateway towns", towns that have grown up on the borders of many national parks primarily to provide visitor facilities and services. Classic examples include Bar Harbor, Maine (Acadia National Park), Gatlinburg, Tennessee (Great Smoky Mountains National Park), Jackson, Wyoming (Grand Teton National Park), Estes Park, Colorado (Rocky Mountain National Park), and Moab, Utah (Arches National Park and Canyonlands National Park). Information on these facilities and services is readily available on the Internet and though demand is typically not as high as for lodgings in the parks, reservations should be made well in advance.

© Robert Manning and Elizabeth Perry 2024. *Conversations About Visiting and Managing the National Parks* (R.E. Manning and E.E Perry)
DOI: 10.1079/9781800626768.0067

Should you stay inside or outside the parks?

There are potentially important advantages to spending the night in the parks, as this can lead to a more immersive experience (e.g. you may see and/or hear nocturnal wildlife and stargazing can be great), and it may be more convenient and efficient because you're likely to find yourself substantially closer to attractions and trailheads and you won't have to wait in the lines that sometimes form at park entrance stations. The cost of hotel rooms in the parks can be higher than outside the parks, though this is not necessarily true for campsites, but weigh this against the potential conveniences of staying inside the parks. (See Conversation 39 for a description of camping in and around the national parks.)

68 Grand Lodges of the National Parks

Post

Michael S. recently had the pleasure of spending a few nights at the El Tovar Hotel on the South Rim of Grand Canyon National Park. Not surprisingly, his review comments on Yelp are highly positive:

History, luxury, and nature collide on the rim of the Grand Canyon at El Tovar. Since 1905, the El Tovar Hotel has been the superior lodging option at the South Rim's Grand Canyon Village. Relaxing on the back porch in rocking chairs sipping your drink of choice looking out at God's handiwork isn't too shabby a way to spend an afternoon.

Response

Sign us up! But later in the review, *Michael S.* notes that he paid several hundred dollars a night and had to make his reservation many months in advance. Maybe we'll stay in the campground after all. There's a long tradition of grand lodges operating in a number of national parks. In the early days of the national parks (the early 20th century primarily), grand lodges were often built to help draw visitors to these fledgling national parks. These lodges combined European influences of chalets and elegant country homes with the American character of log cabins and hunting lodges. This idiosyncratic and fanciful architectural style is often called "parkitecture", and is a careful blend of nature and culture, an attempt to sensitively incorporate humans into the surrounding wilderness. The massive scale of many of these hotels suggested the nation's vast western frontier, and they were constructed of native materials, usually timber and stone. These hotels have been renovated over the years to help bring them up to more modern standards. Today, they make especially attractive lodging opportunities, are located in prime park sites, and many are National Historic Landmarks. Room rates are often high because of demand and logistics; shop carefully for deals based on room type (e.g. rooms with shared baths and cabins) and season (any time other than summer). Here are some classic examples.

- *Old Faithful Inn*—Let's start at the beginning. The Old Faithful Inn, opened in 1904, was the first of the grand national park lodges, and is in Yellowstone, America's first national park. Sometimes referred to as "a giant log cabin", the massive scale of this timber-and-stone building is personified by the Great Hall, featuring lodgepole pine columns and beams that soar more than 75 ft. Public spaces are furnished with mission-style tables and chairs and oak writing desks with lamps that feature art-glass shades. The lodge is located directly adjacent to Old Faithful Geyser, a defining feature of the park.
- *The Ahwahnee*—The 1927 Ahwahnee may be the most elegant of the national park grand lodges. The six-story structure is sited on the edge of a meadow of Yosemite National Park, with views of several signature features, including Half Dome, Glacier Point, and Yosemite Falls. The building references a country estate and features a rough-cut granite exterior that blends the building into the rock formations of the surrounding cliffs, and floor-to-ceiling windows that maximize views. Indigenous crafters' basket-weave designs are featured extensively throughout the interior. The hotel includes many public rooms, but the cathedral-like Great Lounge and the 6630-ft^2 Dining Room are the most celebrated.
- *El Tovar*—Perched directly on the South Rim of the Grand Canyon, the El Tovar has welcomed visitors from all over the world starting in 1905. This architecturally

© Robert Manning and Elizabeth Perry 2024. *Conversations About Visiting and Managing the National Parks* (R.E. Manning and E.E Perry) DOI: 10.1079/9781800626768.0068

diverse lodge includes strong design elements of a Swiss chalet, a castle on the Rhine, and an American log cabin. The building is constructed primarily of stone and dark-stained wood and logs. The 89-ft-long Dining Room is a favorite of visitors. The hotel and companion building, the Hopi House, helped introduce the beauty of the Southwest and Indigenous arts to Americans in the East and others around the world.

- *Paradise Inn*—One of the many jewels of Mount Rainier National Park is the Paradise Inn, opened in 1917. Located in the park's aptly named Paradise Valley near the base of Mount Rainier, this location features what may be the most lavish display of wildflowers in the National Park System, along with in-your-face views of the glacier-clad namesake mountain. This is an especially large building featuring an exterior of native rock, walls covered in cedar shingles, and a steeply pitched roof designed to withstand the park's massive snowfalls. Popular elements of the hotel include the expansive Great Room with roaring fireplace and log framing, and the equally large Dining Room with 50-ft-high stone fireplace. Much of the furniture throughout the building is supersize and hand-made from local materials.

- *Bryce Canyon Lodge*—Sited just a short walk from the rim of magical Bryce Canyon stands its namesake lodge. Here, parkitecture is practiced at a smaller scale, one that offers a more intimate hotel experience. Opened in 1925, the lodge and a small number of associated cabins offer many of the features common to all the grand national park lodges—local building materials (primarily stone and wood), large fireplaces, a heavily shingled exterior laid in irregular courses, floor-to-ceiling windows, and a large dining area where guests gather after an active day in the park.

- *Many Glacier Hotel*—Simply called "Many" by its friends, this massive hotel, opened in 1915, sits proudly on the shores of Glacier National Park's Swiftcurrent Lake with views out over the lake and on to the park's signature glacier-covered mountains. Boats take visitors on tours and to nearby trailheads. Designed with strong Swiss-chalet elements, the hotel was constructed with timber and local stone. The exterior is stained and painted "national park brown", but is enlivened with a prominent gabled roof, long dormers, and wood shingle cladding. The towering Great Room is four stories, and guests can warm themselves around the large circular "campfire fireplace", while the Ptarmigan Dining Room features a huge stone fireplace with floor-to-ceiling windows.

- *LeConte Lodge*—All the grand lodges of the national parks are a pleasing blend of nature and culture, but Great Smoky Mountain National Park's LeConte Lodge tips strongly toward the former. Opened in the early 1930s, this is a small backcountry lodge complex composed of a common lounge and dining building and an associated group of small, primitive cabins. The cabins are hand-built, rough-hewn log structures with propane heat, kerosene lanterns, clean linens, warm Hudson Bay wool blankets, and a washbasin and soap for bathing. Hearty meals are served family style in the cozy lounge. Sited near the top of iconic Mount LeConte, the lodge is not accessible by road and requires a hike of 5 miles to reach it. Rough it in comfort!

Some visitors may consider these types of grand lodges to be inappropriate in the national parks (see Conversation 95 on the appropriateness of visitor facilities and services in the national parks). However, their historic role in park development, along with their popularity, suggests they are a permanent fixture of the landscape in some of the parks.

Insider tip: Lodges are open to the public, so enjoy them even if you're not staying there; tour their stately public spaces, take a break in their great rooms, and enjoy a meal in their fanciful dining rooms (but be sure to make a dinner reservation).

69 Backcountry Lodging

Post

The LeConte Lodge near the summit of Mount LeConte in Great Smoky Mountains National Park offers a unique and inviting experience for travelers, as *John K.* discussed on Tripadvisor:

> *LeConte Lodge was absolutely a fantastic experience and the most memorable trips we have done. We did Rainbow Falls Trail and underestimated hiking time up, but even with arriving late (past check in) the LeConte lodge team was fantastic.*

Response

Multi-day visits to the national parks are the most immersive way to experience them. Fortunately, there are lots of types of accommodations available for visitors to the national parks. (See Conversations 67–69 and 39 for more information on accommodations in the national parks, including lodgings and camping, respectively.) For example, some of the larger national parks have commercial accommodations that include contemporary motels, cabins, and historic lodges. These types of lodgings can usually be found outside the park as well, though this may not be as convenient. Camping is another option, but you must be prepared with an array of camping equipment or a camper/recreational vehicle of some type. Then there's backpacking, which may be the most immersive experience, but it's not for everyone; sleeping on the ground and eating freeze-dried food can discourage a lot of people. But there's another option in a few parks that's sometimes called "slackpacking". A few national parks include a variety of commercial lodgings in the backcountry of the park that offer comfort, convenience, and the companionship of like-minded people. These lodgings are characteristic of the extensive hut systems of Europe, Australia, and New Zealand. Here are some of the best options that span the geography of the National Park System.

High Sierra Camps loop (Yosemite National Park)

This remarkable multi-day route offers access to the strikingly beautiful wilderness of Yosemite National Park. Here, the park provides a series of five "camps"—clusters of large, semi-permanent tents and common areas—spaced an easy day's hiking apart; this adds up to about 50 miles of glorious hiking. Each tent has four to six dormitory-style beds with mattresses and pillows and a wood stove. Energetic young men and women prepare family-style dinners and breakfasts and serve them in large canvas-sided dining halls. All the camps have restrooms and some offer showers (though swimming in the park's lakes and streams is a refreshing—an understatement of the water temperature—alternative). The landscape of the High Sierra Camps Loop is classic John Muir country: mountains well above 10,000 ft, smooth granite domes, spacious meadows that support a rich stock of wildflowers, deep pine forests, and a ready supply of lovely streams and lakes. Of course, you can shorten this hike by using only one or more of the huts.

Grand Canyon Rim-to-Rim (Grand Canyon National Park)

Of all the fine hikes in the National Park System, this is one of the most iconic: a 20 mile or so cross section of the canyon's nearly two billion

DOI: 10.1079/9781800626768.0069

years of geological history, including crossing the Colorado River and hiking the canyon's most fabled trails. As the name suggests, the hike begins at various points along the rims of the canyon, descends to the Colorado River (the beating heart of the park), and climbs (slowly) back to the rim. Overnight lodging is at the bottom of Grand Canyon at Phantom Ranch, a rustic but colorful lodge with cabins, men's and women's dormitories, and a family-style restaurant. The hike is serviced by three trails: (i) South Kaibab (South Rim to Phantom Ranch); (ii) North Kaibab (North Rim to Phantom Ranch); and (iii) Bright Angel (South Rim to Phantom Ranch). Combine these in any way you see fit. The two classic routes are down the South Kaibab and up the Bright Angel (about 17 miles) and down the North Kaibab and up the Bright Angel (about 24 miles).

Garden Wall Trail (Glacier National Park)

The 12-mile Garden Wall Trail is an especially dramatic section of the much longer Highline Trail and is one of the most popular hikes in lovely Glacier National Park. Start the hike at Logan Pass as the trail is mostly downhill from there. Many hikers consider the Garden Wall Trail a long 1-day hike, but it can be a more leisurely and enjoyable 2-day slackpack using the historic Granite Park Chalet for your overnight. The Garden Wall features high alpine meadows, showy wildflowers (including the park's signature bear grass), and opportunities to see lots of wildlife, including mountain goats, bighorn sheep, marmots, pika, and even the occasional grizzly. At mile 7.6, you reach Granite Park Chalet, one of only two remaining backcountry huts constructed by the Great Northern Railroad in the early days of the park. The chalet is rustic, but comfortable and a bit of an adventure; it has 12 guest rooms, each with two to six bunks, and no electricity. A large kitchen is available for guests. In the morning, leave the Highline Trail and walk the remaining four miles to The Loop, the grand switchback on the Going-to-the-Sun Road. Options to return to your car at Logan Pass include leaving a second car at the large parking lot at The Loop or using the park's shuttle bus system.

Kapalaoa, Paliku, and Holua Wilderness Cabins (Haleakala National Park)

The vast crater of Haleakala National Park on the Hawaiian Island of Maui includes three cabins for hikers in the wilderness portion of the park; the cabins were built with help from the Civil Conservation Corps in 1937. Each cabin accommodates up to 14 people and includes beds, a wood stove, and a propane stove (all of the cabins are located above 6000 ft in elevation so the weather can be cold). Holua Cabin is located at the base of the crater wall in native scrublands that colonize the area's lava flows, Paliku Cabin is found at the base of a rainforest cliff, and Kapalaoa Cabin is at the east end of the wilderness in a grassy field. All cabins have pit toilets and water (which must be treated). The cabins are connected to crater-rim trailheads and require a hike of 4–9 miles. Hiking into the park's wild crater is a thrill, but can be challenging due to soft sand.

Mount LeConte (Great Smoky Mountains National Park)

Several trails lead to the summit of iconic Mount LeConte, a favorite of many Great Smokies' hikers. Alum Cave Trail is a good option because it features more open views and a number of natural attractions, including Alum Cave Bluffs, lots of rhododendrons, and distinctive Arch Rock. It's the shortest route to the summit (about 10 miles round-trip and 3000 ft of elevation gain and loss), and this makes for a long day on the trail. However, LeConte Lodge, located just below the summit, offers hikers the option of making this an easier and more memorable hike. The lodge and its accompanying cabins were built in the 1920s and require guests to "hike in" (there's no road access). Yes, some people might call LeConte a bit funky (rustic for sure), but think of it as romantic. There's no electricity nor phone service and bathing requires buckets and washbasins. But visitors enjoy hearty family-style meals and good comradery with like-minded hikers. Next morning, make a leisurely return hike to Alum Cave Trailhead.

Backcountry lodging in national parks is rare, but especially popular, and lodgings usually need to be reserved many months in advance and can even require participation in a lottery. They can also be expensive. Consult the park's official website for each option described above (there are more options in other national parks as well).

70 Commercial Services and Concessioners

Post

The major concessionaire at Crater Lake National Park recently changed, sparking this Reddit discussion:

MedSPAZ: Why can't the Park Service just run it themselves? Giving a National Park to a for profit corporation leaves a sour taste in my mouth.

Pine_Fuzz: Concessionaires in the Park Service have been around since their inception. I am not saying it's a good or bad thing. But this notion that people think that concessionaires are "running" the park is silly and shows folks don't know how public land management works.

Response

"Scenery is a hollow enjoyment to the tourist who sets out in the morning after an indigestible breakfast and a fitful night's sleep on an impossible bed". So spoke Stephen Mather, first Director of the NPS (cited in National Park Service, 2022). NPS employees have a great deal of expertise on topics that include natural and cultural resource management and visitor safety. But they tend not to be experienced in providing commercial visitor services such as hotels, restaurants, and stores, and so these types of facilities and services in the parks are generally managed (but not owned) by private companies that operate under various types of arrangements with the NPS. In the context of the national parks (as in Crater Lake National Park discussed in the post above), these companies are often called "concessioners" (or "concessionaires"), and they are administered under the auspices of the NPS Commercial Services Program.

Following Director Mather's lead, the NPS Commercial Services Program helps ensure that national park visitors have access to high-quality visitor facilities and services when in the parks. Agreements to provide these kinds of services fall into three general categories: (i) concessions; (ii) commercial use authorizations; and (iii) leases. Concessions usually apply to lodging, food, and retail services. Concession contracts specify the range of facilities and services the concessioner agrees to offer.

The rates the concessioner can charge for these services are approved by the NPS and must be comparable to those under similar conditions outside the park. Commercial use authorizations are granted to private businesses to permit small-scale commercial activities (e.g. guiding services). Leases can be issued for NPS land or certain structures that are not subject to authorization through a concession contract or commercial use authorization; leases are generally not of interest to park visitors.

Concessioners fill a vital role in helping the NPS carry out its mission. As *Pine_Fuzz* notes above, this is a supporting role. Private companies work with the agency to offer necessary and appropriate services to park visitors that parks do not provide directly. These arrangements build on the respective strengths of the public and private sectors to serve the diverse needs of park visitors. Moreover, this helps broaden the economic base of communities that surround the parks. The NPS Commercial Services Program administers nearly 500 concession contracts with gross revenues over $1 billion annually. NPS concessioners employ more than 25,000 people in a variety of jobs during peak seasons, providing services that include food and lodging, whitewater rafting adventures, motor coach tours, and many others.

Some concessioners are large companies that operate facilities and services nationally and internationally. For example, Xanterra Parks &

© Robert Manning and Elizabeth Perry 2024. *Conversations About Visiting and Managing the National Parks* (R.E. Manning and E.E Perry)
DOI: 10.1079/9781800626768.0070

Resorts, Inc. operates lodging and food services in several national parks including Yellowstone, Grand Canyon, Glacier, and Zion. But some concessioners are quite small; Jake's Horses, Inc., for example, is a local horse and mule guide and outfitter service in Yellowstone. Many national parks have no concessioners, while some of the large ones have a large number; Yellowstone National Park, for example, has 47 concessioners.

When visitors take advantage of facilities and services offered by concessioners, they should be aware that these facilities and services are offered by private companies, not the NPS. However, these companies are overseen by the NPS, and undergo periodic review, including concession visitor satisfaction surveys; be sure to ask for one if you'd like your opinions to count.

Reference

National Park Service (2022) Commercial Services Program. Available at: https://www.nps.gov/orgs/csp/index.htm (accessed 23 July 2024).

71 Guidebooks

Post

There are several good guidebooks to the national parks that can be very helpful to visitors. One of us (Bob) has written one on his favorite way of enjoying and appreciating the parks, by hiking them. *Kansas H.* reviewed the book on Amazon Books as follows:

> *I believe I have now purchased 3 of these and going for the 4th. Soft back, brilliant photos. Positive response from everyone gifted. Would recommend, especially if you are considering traveling to one of the National Parks.*

Response

Thanks, *Kansas H.*—you just made my day! (This book is briefly described at the conclusion of this conversation.) Given the importance and popularity of the national parks, it's not surprising that there are a number of guidebooks to them. Here are some of the most popular guidebooks to the National Park System, but keep in mind that there are even more guidebooks to individual national parks. There are also many books about the national parks—their history, management, photography, art, and other topics—and many of these are briefly described in Conversation 28. Note that some of the guidebooks described below are updated periodically, so be sure to consult the most recent editions as the National Park System evolves over time.

In Conversation 28, it was noted that there's been a long association between the national parks and the National Geographic Society, and this organization publishes several types of guidebooks to the national parks. The most comprehensive is *National Geographic Complete National Parks of the United States: 400+ Parks, Monuments, Battlefields,* *Historic Sites, Scenic Trails, Recreation Areas, and Seashores.* As the title suggests, this book covers the entire National Park System, and that's a big advantage. The book includes lovely photographs, maps, and trip advice, and is authoritative. Other National Geographic Society guidebooks include *National Geographic Secrets of the National Parks: the Experts' Guide to the Best Experiences Beyond the Tourist Trail,* and *National Geographic Atlas of the National Parks.* The former identifies and describes many places and features of the national parks that are less well known, but it includes only the units of the National Park System that are titled "National Parks" (see Conversation 1 on the titles/names of the national parks). The latter is an impressive introduction to many of the national parks that includes their natural and cultural history and a large collection of associated maps and graphics that are characteristic of an atlas.

Several guidebooks to the national parks are available from authoritative publishers of guidebooks to places around the world. These include *Moon USA National Parks: the Complete Guide to All 63 Parks, Fodor's the Complete Guide to the National Parks of the USA: All 63 Parks from Maine to American Samoa,* and *Lonely Planet National Parks of America.* These guides are useful, but they're limited to the current 63 national parks (though the books are periodically updated).

An independently published guidebook that enjoys good reviews is *Your Guidebook to the National Parks: the Complete Guide to All 63 National Parks.* As the title suggests, this book is limited to the current 63 national parks.

A Thinking Person's Guide to America's National Parks is a very different type of guidebook that addresses the history and management of the national parks, the diversity of issues and programs addressed in the National Park System, and where you can find good

© Robert Manning and Elizabeth Perry 2024. *Conversations About Visiting and Managing the National Parks* (R.E. Manning and E.E Perry)
DOI: 10.1079/9781800626768.0071

examples of these issues and programs. It addresses the full National Park System and is richly illustrated with color photographs.

Conversations 30–32 discuss new models of national parks, including national heritage areas, World Heritage Sites, and biosphere reserves. *America's National Heritage Areas: a Guide to the Nation's New Kind of National Park*, and *A Guide to America's World Heritage Sites: the Heritage of Humanity* describe the first two types of new models of national parks, including their visitor attractions.

If you're interested in hiking in the national parks, the award-winning *Walks of a Lifetime in America's National Parks* presents descriptions of each of the current 63 national parks and recommends the several hikes in each that best offer a sense of why these national parks are so important. The book is richly illustrated with color photographs. (And thanks for the kind book review, *Kansas H.*).

72 Specialized Services

Post

Kevin B. provided details of an experience with a guided tour of Independence National Historical Park on Tripadvisor:

> There's so much history here and it's amazing! ... Independence National Historical Park covers many historical attractions in [the] Old City and we were lucky enough to visit several of them. We booked a tour of Independence Hall (via recreation.gov) and it was a lovely tour. Our guide was knowledgeable and entertaining and it's so humbling to be standing where The Declaration of Independence and The Constitution were signed and adopted. It really gives you chills.

Response

Some national parks offer specialized services to visitors; examples include ranger-guided tours of caves at Carlsbad Caverns National Park and ranger-guided tours of Independence Hall at Independence National Historical Park. As *Kevin B.* notes above, rangers leading these tours can provide in-depth knowledge and a personalized experience. For these and other parks, this may be the only way to visit these sites. In addition, permits are often required for backpacking in the large backcountry and wilderness portions of most of the larger national parks. Permits are also required for some of the most popular hikes such as Half Dome in Yosemite National Park and Angels Landing in Zion National Park. Up-to-date information on reservations and permits for such specialized services is available on each park's official NPS website. The reservation/application process for many of these specialized services is managed by Recreation.gov (see Conversation 37).

© Robert Manning and Elizabeth Perry 2024. *Conversations About Visiting and Managing the National Parks* (R.E. Manning and E.E Perry)
DOI: 10.1079/9781800626768.0072

Part 3: Managing the National Parks

Introduction

73 Preservation Versus Use

Post

In 2016, the *National Parks Traveler* ran a story titled "National Park Service Ignoring Requirement To Establish Visitor Carrying Capacities" (Repanshek, 2016), which drew strong reactions from the readership. *John A.* pointed out the need to not just set capacities (the maximum number of visits that can be accommodated without unacceptable impacts), but to follow through with them, to help balance preservation and use:

> *The review ... looked primarily at whether parks have produced visitor carrying capacity plans. Plans are an important first step, but the MUCH more important thing is whether parks have implemented their visitor carrying capacity plans. That is where the rubber meets the road. A plan that is not implemented is worthless ... The NPS has long had a problem letting too many visitors into developed areas. Parks naturally want to accommodate the teeming hordes, even when it means decreasing the quality of the visitor experience or increasing resource impacts. It is hard to draw the line and exclude visitors, exclude their customers.*

Response

Yes, *John A.*, the issue you address is especially challenging: how to find the proper balance between use of the parks for recreation and preservation of park resources. Of course, part of the difficulty is that this may require limits on the amount and type of public use of the parks. National parks are established to protect these remarkable places *and* for the public to enjoy and appreciate them. Yellowstone National Park, established in 1872, is widely recognized as the first national park in America (and the world). The park was established to protect it from exploitative practices such as logging,

grazing, mining, and market hunting (see the Introduction to this book for more about the history of the national parks). But the enabling legislation stated that it was also to be "a public park or pleasuring ground of the benefit and enjoyment of the people" (National Archives, no date). Over the next several decades, Congress established more national parks, ultimately creating the National Park Service (NPS) to manage these areas. This new agency was required "to conserve the scenery and the natural and historic objects and the wildlife therein and to provide for the enjoyment of the same in such manner and by such means as will leave them unimpaired for the enjoyment of future generations" (United States Government, 2019, p. 1). (See Conversation 6 about the Organic Act establishing the NPS.)

This foundational twofold mission—preservation and use—has become more challenging in recent decades as recreational use of the national parks has rapidly grown to more than 300 million visits annually across the National Park System. Outdoor recreation in the national parks can result in damage to natural and cultural resources (e.g. trampling vegetation, compacting and eroding soils, polluting air and water, disrupting wildlife, disturbing historical and cultural artifacts; see Conversation 85 for more about this) and the quality of the visitor experience (crowding, traffic congestion, construction and maintenance of visitor facilities and services, conflicting recreation activities; see Conversation 86 about this). How much and what kinds of recreation can be accommodated in the parks without endangering park resources and the quality of the visitor experience? As *John A.* notes, this issue is often called "carrying capacity".

Carrying capacity has a rich history in the natural resource professions. For example, in wildlife and range management, carrying capacity refers to the number of animals of any one species that can be maintained in a given

DOI: 10.1079/9781800626768.0073

habitat. But in its most generic form, carrying capacity is a fundamental concept in natural resources management, referring to the ultimate limits to growth in the use of environmental resources. It's even been applied to the human carrying capacity of the Earth. The basic concept of carrying capacity has evolved into the more contemporary notion of sustainability, which was famously defined by the World Commission on Environment and Development as development that meets "the needs of the present without compromising the ability of future generations to meet their own needs" (Brundtland, 1987, p. 16). Application of sustainability to national parks requires consideration of the types and levels of use these areas can accommodate while leaving them "unimpaired for the enjoyment of future generations" (United States Government, 2019, p. 1) as demanded by the legislation establishing the NPS.

Perhaps the first concern over the issue of preservation vs use in the national parks was recorded in the mid-1930s when a NPS report asked "How large a crowd can be turned loose in a wilderness without destroying its essential qualities?" (Sumner, 1936, p. 58). Later, it became clear that this issue has two important components, the natural environment and the social environment; not only are the natural resources of an area affected by recreation, but also the quality of the recreation experience.

Research on this issue has documented the fact that rising visitor use can have increasing impacts on both the natural and the social environments of parks as illustrated in Fig. 73.1. Here, X_1 amount of visitor use may cause Y_1 amount of environmental and/or social impact, while X_2 amount of visitor use may cause Y_2 amount of impact. But which of these points—Y_1 or Y_2, or some other point along the vertical axis—represents the maximum acceptable amount of impact and, therefore, the maximum acceptable level of use? This issue is sometimes called the "limits of acceptable change" and is a foundational concept in national park management.

Experience suggests that the answer to the limits of acceptable change question can only be determined through formulation of management objectives and associated indicators and standards of quality (sometimes, the term "desired conditions" is used for management objectives, and "thresholds of quality" is used for standards of quality). This approach to addressing the issue of preservation vs use/carrying capacity focuses on defining the types of park and outdoor recreation conditions to be provided as the key to determining the maximum levels of impact that are acceptable. Management objectives/desired conditions are broad, narrative statements defining the type of park and outdoor recreation opportunities to be provided and maintained, including the condition of

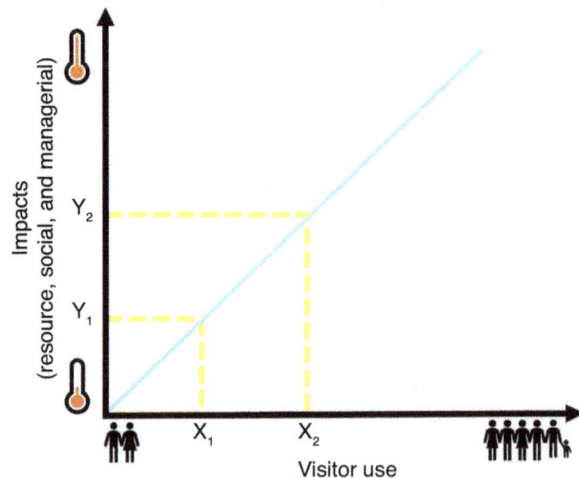

Fig. 73.1. Limits of acceptable change. Adapted from Manning *et al.* (2022).

natural and cultural resources and the type of recreation experience. Indicators of quality are more specific, measurable variables reflecting the essence or meaning of management objectives/desired conditions; they are quantifiable proxies or empirical measures of management objectives/desired conditions. Indicators of quality may include elements of the resource and social environments. Standards/thresholds of quality define the minimum acceptable condition of indicator variables.

An example may help illuminate these ideas and terms. The Wilderness Act of 1964 states that areas included in the National Wilderness Preservation System (many of which are in the national parks) are to be managed to provide "opportunities for solitude" (Wilderness Connect, no date), and this is an appropriate management objective/desired condition. (See Conversation 21 for a discussion of wilderness.) Moreover, research on wilderness use suggests that the number of other visitors encountered along trails and at campsites is important in defining solitude for wilderness visitors. Thus, the number of trail and camp encounters are potentially good indicators of wilderness quality. Research also suggests that many wilderness visitors

have normative standards about how many trail and camp encounters can be experienced before opportunities for solitude decline to an unacceptable degree. For example, a number of studies suggest that many wilderness visitors prefer to see no more than five other groups per day along trails, and to camp out of sight and sound of other groups. Thus, a maximum of five encounters per day along trails and no other groups encountered in camps may be good standards/thresholds of quality for a wilderness area. This approach can be used to address a variety of experiential impacts of recreation, as well environmental impacts such as trampling of vegetation, soil erosion, and disturbance of wildlife (see Conversations 85 and 86 for more about the environmental and social impacts of outdoor recreation).

The NPS and other federal land management agencies have adopted this approach to determining the carrying capacity/sustainability of park and recreation areas, and the approach is outlined in the *Visitor Use Management Framework* (Interagency Visitor Use Management Council, 2016) and illustrated in Fig. 73.2. The framework is defined by three primary steps: (i) formulate management objectives/desired conditions and associated

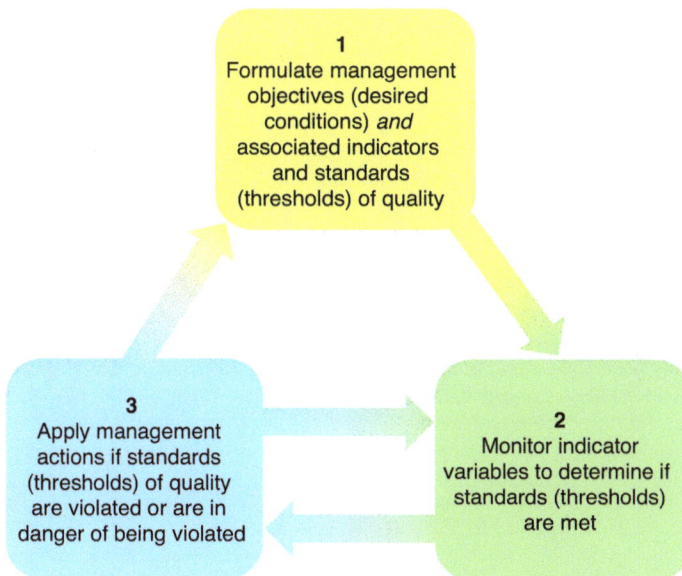

Fig. 73.2. Three-step visitor use management. Adapted from Manning *et al.* (2022).

indicators and standards/thresholds of quality; (ii) monitor indicator variables to determine if standards/thresholds are met; and (iii) apply management actions if standards/thresholds are violated or are in danger of being violated. (See Conversation 89 on the types of management actions that can be applied.) This quantitative approach to addressing the inherent trade-offs between preservation and use of national parks and related areas is being widely adopted throughout the US and internationally. Going beyond the plan and into the "action" portion of the work is now where the rubber is meeting the road (Repanshek, 2016; Sumner, 1936).

References

Brundtland, G. (1987) Report of the World Commission on Environment and Development. United Nations General Assembly document A/42/427. United Nations, New York. Available at: http://www.un-docu ments.net/ocf-ov.htm (accessed 11 July 2024).

Interagency Visitor Use Management Council (2016) *Visitor Use Management Framework: A Guide to Providing Sustainable Outdoor Recreation*. US National Park Service, Denver, Colorado.

Leung, Y., Spenceley, A., Hvenegaard, G. and Buckely, R. (2018) *Tourism and Visitor Management in Protected Areas: Guidelines of Sustainability*, Best Practice Protected Area Guidelines Series No. 27. International Union for Conservation of Nature (IUCN), Gland, Switzerland.

Manning, R. (2007) *Parks and Carrying Capacity: Commons Without Tragedy*. Island Press, Washington, DC.

Manning, R.E., Budruk, M., Goonan, K., Hallo, J., Laven, D., Lawson, S., McCown, R., Minteer, B., Newman, P., Perry, E., Pettengill, P., Reigner, N., Valliere, W., van Riper, C. and Xiao, X. (2022) *Studies in Outdoor Recreation: Search and Research for Satisfaction*, 4th edn. Oregon State University Press, Corvallis, Oregon.

National Archives (n.d.) Act Establishing Yellowstone National Park (1872). Enrolled Acts and Resolutions of Congress, 1789–1996; General Records of the United States Government; Record Group 11. Available at: https://www.archives.gov/milestone-documents/act-establishing-yellowstone-national -park (accessed 18 July 2024).

Repanshek, K. (2016) National Park Service ignoring requirement to establish visitor carrying capacities. *National Parks Traveler*, July 14. Available at: https://www.nationalparkstraveler.org/2016/07/peer -national-park-service-ignoring-requirement-establish-visitor-carrying-capacities (accessed 24 July 2024).

Sumner, E.L. (1936) *Special report on a wildlife study in the High Sierra in Sequoia and Yosemite National Parks and adjacent territory*. U.S. National Park Service Records, National Archives, Washington DC. Available at: https://www.npshistory.com/publications/yose/high-sierra-wildlife.pdf (accessed July 2024).

United States Government (2019) National Park Service Organic Act. An Act to establish a National Park Service, and for other purposes. Public Law (United States) 64–235, H.R. 15522, 39 Statute 535, enacted August 25, 1916. Available at: https://www.govinfo.gov/content/pkg/COMPS-1725/pdf/CO MPS-1725.pdf (accessed 18 July 2024).

Wilderness Connect (n.d.) The Wilderness Act. An Act to establish a National Wilderness Preservation System for the permanent good of the whole people, and for other purposes. Public Law 88-577 (16 U.S.C. 1131-1136). 88th Congress, Second Session, September 3, 1964. Available at: https://wilder ness.net/learn-about-wilderness/key-laws/wilderness-act/ (accessed 16 July 2024).

74 Common Property Resources

Post

rjtwatts shared a succinct overview of the "tragedy of the commons" concept in the national parks on X:

> *Over Exploiting the Resource? Theory of Tragedy of the Commons predicts that in the case of National Parks – which are held in common and open to all – the values that visitors seek will be steadily eroded, and overuse will lead inevitably to exhaustion and destruction.*

Response

Precisely, *rjtwatts*. A famous paper on the inherent tension between the use and preservation of the environment was published several decades ago in the prestigious scholarly journal, *Science*. Hauntingly titled, "The Tragedy of the Commons", the paper identified and discussed a set of environmental problems that have no technical solutions, but must be resolved through collective social action. Written by Garrett Hardin, the paper argued that the ultimate prescription for managing what Hardin called "common property resources" (or simply, the "commons") such as national parks was "mutual coercion, mutually agreed upon"; without such collective action, environmental (and related social) tragedy is inevitable (Hardin, 1968).

Hardin began his paper with an illustration using perhaps the oldest and simplest example of an environmental commons, a shared pasture:

> Picture a pasture open to all. It is expected that each herdsman will try to keep as many cattle as possible on [this] commons ... What is the utility of adding one more animal? ... Since the herdsman receives all the proceeds of the sale of the additional animal, the positive utility [to the herdsman] is nearly +1 ... Since, however,

the effects of overgrazing are shared by all the herdsmen, the negative utility for any particular ... herdsman is only a fraction of -1. Adding together the ... partial utilities, the rational herdsman concludes that the only sensible course for him to pursue is to add another animal to [the] herd. And another; and another ... Therein is the tragedy. Each man is locked into a system that [causes] him to increase his herd without limit – in a world that is limited ... Freedom in a commons brings ruin to all.

(Hardin, 1968, p. 1244)

Hardin went on to explore other examples of environmental commons, ultimately addressing human population growth. One of his examples of the tragedy of the commons—one that resonates more urgently each year—is national parks:

> The National Parks present another instance of the working out of the tragedy of the commons. At present, they are open to all without limit. The parks themselves are limited in extent—there is only one Yosemite Valley—whereas population seems to grow without limit. The values that visitors seek in the parks are steadily eroded. Plainly, we must soon cease to treat the parks as commons or they will be of no value to anyone.

(Hardin, 1968, p. 1245)

In the post above, *rjtwatts* picked up on this, centering a national park's population—visitors—exhausting its environmental resources and social appeal.

The concept of the tragedy to the commons has become one of the most compelling and powerful concepts in the environmental literature. Hardin and others have noted that the issue of managing common property resources has a long history. In fact, nascent interest in the "commons" was expressed by Aristotle, who wrote "For that which is common to the greatest number has the least care bestowed upon it. Everyone thinks chiefly of his own, hardly at

© Robert Manning and Elizabeth Perry 2024. *Conversations About Visiting and Managing the National Parks* (R.E. Manning and E.E Perry)
DOI: 10.1079/9781800626768.0074

all of the common interest; and only when he is himself concerned as an individual" (Aristotle cited in McGlynn, 2015, p. 1).

As noted above, Hardin's solution to avoid the tragedy of the commons is "mutual coercion, mutually agreed upon", and this is what's being done in an increasing number of national parks. For example, limits on the number of visits to some national parks (or locations within parks) are being established to control the environmental and social impacts of park visitation. (See Conversations 85 and 86 about the environmental and social impacts of outdoor recreation, and Conversation 89 about the ways park visitation can and is being managed.) While such coercions may be distasteful because they limit individual freedom, they're ultimately needed to protect the parks and the greater welfare of society. Hardin rationalized this when he wrote that "Freedom is the recognition of necessity" (which he credits to the philosopher Hegel). We rely on the NPS to act in the best interests of society through management of the national parks, and this sometimes requires limits on the amount or type of visitor use.

Conversation 73 describes how the national parks and related areas are addressing the issue of use vs preservation, and Conversations 89 and 91 describe the management practices that can be used to implement resulting decisions (Hardin, 1968).

References

Hardin, G. (1968) The tragedy of the commons. *Science* 162, 1243–1248. Available at: http://dx.doi.org/1 0.1126/science.162.3859.1243 (accessed 17 October 2024).

Manning, R. (2007) *Parks and Carrying Capacity: Commons without Tragedy*. Island Press, Washington, DC.

Manning, R.E., Budruk, M., Goonan, K., Hallo, J., Laven, D., Lawson, S., McCown, R., Minteer, B., Newman, P., Perry, E., Pettengill, P., Reigner, N., Valliere, W., van Riper, C. and Xiao, X. (2022) *Studies in Outdoor Recreation: Search and Research for Satisfaction*, 4th edn. Oregon State University Press, Corvallis, Oregon.

McGlynn, C. (2015) Aristotle's economic defence of private property. *The Student Economic Review* Vol. XXIX. Trinity College Dublin. Available at: https://www.tcd.ie/Economics/assets/pdf/SER/2015/Mc Glynn,%20Aristotles%20Economic%20Defense%20of%20Private%20Prpoerty.pdf (accessed 24 July 2024).

Natural and Cultural Resources

75 Science

Post

LadyG60 shared her recent experience in Pinnacles National Park on Tripadvisor, where the science of conservation biology and the park's habitat have brought the California condor back from the brink of extinction:

> *The condors are magnificent, what a success story. I had wrongly thought I'd seen them previously but they were buzzards; once actually in the Pinnacles, at elevation, we were fortunate to spot two or three condors in flight and/or resting on the rock face.*

Response

The success of the campaign to help the American condor is truly remarkable, *LadyG60*, and is a success story of science in the national parks. The more than 85 million acres of diverse natural and historical landscapes in the National Park System offer unusual opportunities to conduct research and expand our knowledge (see Conversations 9 and 10 for more information about the natural and cultural diversity of the national parks). This research can tell us much more about these places, including the natural and cultural history of the nation, the effects of our growing population on the environment, the people who visit the parks (and those who don't), and how these visits might best be managed to offer high-quality experiences and protect park resources. The resulting knowledge can offer important guidance on how to manage the national parks (and perhaps the greater world) in an informed way.

The National Park System includes many of the remaining relatively undisturbed natural ecosystems in the country, and these parks represent vital reservoirs of knowledge. Celebrated conservationist Aldo Leopold wrote that such areas represent "a base datum of normality" compared to the places in which we live, and went on to caution us that "to keep every cog and wheel is the first precaution of intelligent tinkering" (Leopold, 2020, p. 190). Our grand experiment of living in the natural world must be informed by understanding our potential impacts on the environment. The national parks represent many of the essential cogs and wheels that Leopold references, and we should take advantage of the parks as research laboratories. The National Park Service (NPS) includes a staff of scientists to help do this (though the agency is thinly staffed in this regard), and works with faculty and students at many universities as well. Some parks include Research Learning Centers that are composed of scientists, educators, and volunteers who gather information and help apply it to park management.

The Schoodic Education and Research Center at Maine's Acadia National Park is a good example of science in action in the national parks. Here, a group of scientists, park staff, university faculty and graduate students, citizen scientists, and schoolchildren conduct a program of field-based science, coursework, conferences, and public lectures that focus on research in the park, its findings, and its management implications. For example, the park conducts an annual BioBlitz, a 2-day event that inventories all species of a given group of plants and/or animals within the park, expanding our knowledge and monitoring the park's ecological health.

Pinnacles National Park in California is another good example of natural science in the parks, and the subject of *LadyG60*'s admiration. The park offers good habitat for the critically endangered California condor. Once extinct in the wild, there were only 22 condors in captivity when they were reintroduced in the park. NPS staff monitor the birds, which have now increased to about 400 individuals that can be found at Pinnacles and other national parks,

© Robert Manning and Elizabeth Perry 2024. *Conversations About Visiting and Managing the National Parks* (R.E. Manning and E.E Perry)
DOI: 10.1079/9781800626768.0075

including Grand Canyon. With a wingspan of nearly 10 ft, these are magnificent animals that are a marker of improved environmental conditions and that are a highlight for park visitors.

The social sciences and humanities have also contributed to our knowledge of American history and prehistory and have helped inform national park management. For example, substantive programs of archeology have helped reveal the rich prehistory of the Southwest and other locations. Archeological and ethnographic research at Mesa Verde National Park, for example, is expanding our understanding of prehistoric and historic occupations of this region, linking findings to the regional histories of the greater Southwest, and contributing to more informed management and interpretation of a host of national parks and public lands. Another example is the ways in which NPS historians and collaborators have helped collect, store, and interpret many of the artifacts, papers, and other materials associated with the Civil War, and findings have helped inform management and interpretation of the many Civil-War-related national parks, including Gettysburg National Military Park. This iconic park includes a library of books, manuscripts, and other materials that help the park tell the story of this tragic war, including its causes and consequences, and that help park staff interpret the war to visitors. A third example is the way in which NPS staff, academics, and students study the American Civil Rights Movement; findings help inform management and interpretation of the many national parks that help tell this continuing story.

A program of natural and social science is also conducted in the national parks that's designed to learn more about national park visitors, including how the parks can provide for high-quality park experiences and how to minimize the potential impacts of visitor use. For example, a program of natural science has studied the environmental impacts outdoor recreation—trampling of groundcover vegetation, soil compaction, disturbance of wildlife, water pollution, diminished natural quiet and natural darkness—and offers insights into how these impacts can be minimized (see Conversation 85 for more about this). Similarly, a program of social science has identified efficient ways to measure the number of visits to the national parks, and conducted visitor surveys that define the characteristics of visitors (and by default the characteristics of those who don't visit the parks), the economic impact of visitation, and offers insights into a number of issues that affect the quality of the visitor experience and how to manage these issues (see Conversations 3, 25, and 86–91 for more about this).

References

Hammitt, W.E., Cole, D.N. and Monz, C.A. (2015) *Wildland Recreation: Ecology and Management*, 3rd edn. Wiley Blackwell, Hoboken, New Jersey.

Leopold, A. (2020) *A Sand County Almanac*. Oxford University Press, New York.

Manning, R., Anderson, A. and Pettengill, P. (2017) *Managing Outdoor Recreation: Case Studies in the National Parks*, 2nd edn. CAB International, Boston, Massachusetts.

Manning, R.E., Budruk, M., Goonan, K., Hallo, J. and Laven, D., Lawson, S., McCown, R., Minteer, B., Newman, P., Perry, E., Pettengill, P., Reigner, N., Valliere, W., van Riper, C. and Xiao, X. (2022) *Studies in Outdoor Recreation: Search and Research for Satisfaction*, 4th edn. Oregon State University Press, Corvallis, Oregon.

Soukup, M. (2016) Reservoirs of knowledge. In: Manning, R., Diamant, R., Mitchell, N. and Harmon, D. (eds) *A Thinking Person's Guide to America's National Parks*. Braziller Publishers, New York, pp. 93–104.

76 Climate Change

Post

Alcatraz Island is facing climate change pressures, including sea level rise, that compound the difficulties of preserving the prison and other structures. A new effort, detailed in a *New York Times* article (Knight, 2024), aims to capture the entire island in 3-D, allowing for remote exploration and a catalog of current conditions as climate change continues to impact the national park. Not all are in agreement about the need for this, as *Russ J.* shared in a reader comment on the story:

> *Fans of penitentiary facilities are of course entitled to treat this site as important and worth preserving. But trying to present Alcatraz as a meaningful indicator of climate change smacks of opportunism and dishonesty. If people refuse to see the evidence of climate change that is readily apparent everywhere, I doubt looking at a rusty old prison is going to change their minds.*

Response

Russ J., we agree that there are numerous examples evidencing climate change in the national parks and beyond; and that for some, Alcatraz Island may not be the prime example. However, we also know that climate change is affecting all national parks (again, and beyond) and that we need more invested climate stewards. Consider that the climate change story at Alcatraz may inspire some who are interested in the history of the island to dig a little deeper into climate impacts, make connections between their curiosities and climate, and, hopefully, engage in actions toward a responsive future. This could be "fans of penitentiary facilities", but also those interested in the Indians of All Tribes occupation, the flora and fauna of the island, and its representation throughout time and cultures in the San Francisco Bay. Let's explore the subject of climate change and the national parks a bit more.

Human-caused climate change has been called an "existential threat" to humanity; it endangers the integrity of the natural and cultural world, our ways of life, and perhaps our very existence. The contemporary climate crisis is primarily driven by excessive greenhouse gas emissions that collect in the atmosphere, trapping the sun's heat, warming the planet, and leading to a cascading series of impacts. The principal source of greenhouse gasses is burning of fossil fuels including coal, oil, and natural gas, along with massive global deforestation which reduces the degree to which forests capture and trap/sequester greenhouse gasses.

The National Park System is on the front lines of this crisis. Many national parks are located in extreme and vulnerable environments such as high elevations, Arctic regions, the arid south-western US, large wetlands, and extensive forests and coastlines; these are locations where the effects of climate change tend to appear early and with more severity. Examples of these effects include glacial melt, reduction of snow cover, drought, declining river flows, increasing wildfires, severe storms, extensive tree mortality, shifting biomes, sea level rise, ocean warming and acidification, coral bleaching, loss of biodiversity, invasive species, and loss of archeological and historical sites and associated artifacts.

In response to these threats, the NPS has developed its Climate Change Response Strategy (updated in 2023). This plan includes an integrated strategy to apply across the National Park System. First, the strategy begins with understanding the science behind climate change as a way to make informed decisions about national park management. For example, what are global trends and projections about climate change, how are park resources affected, and how might management actions be effective? Second, this is followed by adapting to climate change. For

DOI: 10.1079/9781800626768.0076

example, as stream water temperatures have risen in response to climate change, native trout in Glacier National Park are being relocated to cooler sections of these streams. Other examples include prescribed fire in selected forests (see Conversation 77), propagation and planting of warm-water resistant corals, and expanding coastal wetlands to absorb storm water surges and sea level rise. There are a host of adaptation strategies for cultural resources as well, including stabilizing shorelines to protect historic structures, moving historic buildings to higher ground, and documenting historic and archeological sites before they are ultimately inundated by sea level rise. Third, the NPS is working to mitigate the foundational causes of climate change. For example, the agency is adopting a variety of climate-friendly practices in the parks, including reducing greenhouse gas emissions in park operations, building and retrofitting visitor centers and other facilities to meet carbon reduction objectives (see Conversation 50 on visitor centers), shifting from fossil fuels to renewable energy sources, and developing public transit options in parks to reduce reliance on automobiles. Fourth, the NPS is making climate change an important component of its public education and interpretive programs. As noted in Conversation 13, the national parks are increasingly known as "America's classroom", and many of the parks' educational and interpretive programs are addressing the increasingly important issue of climate change, including

how the lessons learned in the parks might be applied in the communities in which park visitors live. The NPS publication, "Climate Change in National Parks" is a useful guide (see National Park Service (2023a) in the References at the end of the conversation).

Recent research has also explored the effects of climate change on recreational use of national parks and related areas. The changing climate has altered recreation conditions in varying seasons, primarily manifested in winter and summer recreation and tourism activities. For example, warming temperatures in the winter season have reduced the length of snow-sports seasons and depth of snowpack, and increased the volatility of natural snow conditions, and this is undercutting the quality of winter recreation experiences. Under future climate change projections, the length of the snow season is expected to substantially decline. Research also suggests that climate change is likely to negatively affect summer outdoor recreation conditions in regionally specific ways, such as increasing average daily summer temperature, increasing the number of days over 90°F, increasing the number of rainy days per week, and increasing the number of biting insects across the Northeast. In addition, the changing climate (e.g. warming temperatures and more and stronger hurricanes) is expected to result in limited accessibility to recreation resources that are damaged and/or temporarily closed for restoration.

References

Gonzalez, P. (2020) Human-caused climate change in United States national parks and solutions for the future. *Parks Stewardship Forum* 32(2), 188–210.

Knight, H. (2024) One way to preserve Alcatraz? Capture everything in 3-D. *New York Times,* February 28 2024. Available at: https://www.nytimes.com/2024/02/28/us/alcatraz-island-3d-map.html (accessed 23 July 2024).

National Park Service (2023a) Climate Change in National Parks. Available at: https://www.nps.gov/s ubjects/climatechange/upload/2023-03-03-UPDATE-CC-Unigrid-compliant.pdf (accessed 12 July 2024).

National Park Service (2023b) Climate Change and Your National Parks. Available at: https://www.nps.go v/subjects/climatechange/index.htm (accessed 12 July 2024).

77 Wildfire

Post

The NPS posted this photo (taken by *M. Quinn*) of smoke at Grand Canyon National Park on Wikimedia Commons, explaining that the origin of the smoke is a controlled burn to simulate the natural effects of fire in the park's ecosystem. The smoke can limit the physical activities of visitors and certainly decreases the stunning beauty of the Canyon. But these effects are temporary and controlled burns maintain the naturalness of the park and help to prevent conflagrations that can occur without periodic small fires.

Grand Canyon National Park, Wikimedia Commons/Grand Canyon NPS.

Response

In 1988, wildfires memorably burned in Yellowstone National Park, affecting about a third of this 2.2 million acre world-famous national park. These fires began an intensive period of research on wildfires and a lively debate on public policy regarding wildfires, particularly in national parks.

Most people are now well aware of the fact that wildfires in forests and other natural environments have increased in frequency and intensity. This is largely due to the multiple and cascading effects of climate change and the historic policy of extinguishing all wildfires as soon as possible. Climate change has resulted in hotter and drier weather in many parts of the world, and this makes forests and other natural environments more susceptible to wildfires. This change in weather has also allowed some forest insects to extend their range, damaging or killing many trees and making them more likely to catch fire. Moreover, public policy toward wildfires has historically focused on putting them out as quickly as possible, and this has led to unnatural accumulation of dead wood on the forest floor that contributes to the size and intensity of many contemporary wildfires. Unnatural prevention of wildfires has also affected the composition of trees and other species. For example, some trees, such as giant sequoias (and the lodgepole pines that burned in Yellowstone), are serotinous, meaning cones can remain on the tree for years, long after the seed is mature, and these seeds are only released when the cones open triggered by the heat from fire.

Fire has also been purposely used for many millennia by Indigenous peoples. Sometimes called "cultural burning", fire was integral to many Indigenous peoples' ways of life. Across North America and the Pacific islands, these peoples used fire to clear areas for crops and travel, to manage the land for specific species of both plants and animals, to hunt game, and for many other important uses. Managed fire was also a tool that promoted ecological diversity and reduced the risk of catastrophic wildfires.

Of course, wildfires in the national parks can have detrimental effects. The danger they can present to visitors can lead to park closures when and where warranted, and fires can kill some species of wildlife. Moreover, smoke can obscure views in the parks, can have detrimental health implications for some park visitors (and NPS staff), and leave behind charred forests and otherwise altered or damaged landscapes (as the above photo by *M. Quinn* documents).

Nevertheless, fire is a natural and important influence in some forests and other environments; indeed, many fires are caused by lightning. Because of this, wildfire policy has changed over the past few decades to allow some wildfires to burn under certain conditions, as long as these fires don't threaten public safety or public and private property. This policy is applied particularly in the wilderness portions of large national parks (see Conversation 21 about wilderness). Under certain conditions, the NPS even sets fires to simulate the natural role of fire; this is often called "prescribed fire".

Visitors to national parks should understand and appreciate the natural role of fire in some ecosystems and why the NPS may let some wildfires burn when human health and property aren't threatened. If a wildfire occurs in a national park you're visiting, be sure to follow directions given by park officials, and support new wildfire policies that are being adopted in the national parks.

78 Natural Darkness

Post

Joshua Tree National Park is renowned for its dark skies and stargazing, as *Ren Z.* noted on Google Reviews:

This is a truly beautiful place to visit. Exceeded my expectations. I was there for a nighttime photography shoot but I wish that I had been able to do some exploring beforehand. The peacefulness of the desert at night is almost surreal.

Response

National parks have been established to protect a variety of natural and cultural resources. Prominent examples include landscape features (e.g. mountains, lakes, and rivers), wildlife, vegetation, cultural artifacts, and historic sites and buildings. But the definition of what constitutes a "resource" has evolved substantially over the more than 150 years of national parks in America.

One of the newly recognized resources in national parks is "natural darkness": darkness undiminished by human-caused light. Many visitors like *Ren Z.* enjoy looking up into the night sky in national parks. Of course, natural darkness has been present in the national parks from their inception, but it's only recently been added to the agenda of park managers and scientists and is just now entering more widely into the public conscience. As the world becomes more widely bathed in the glare of human-caused light, natural darkness is rapidly disappearing and national parks are some of the last refuges of this increasingly scarce and valuable resource.

Emergence of natural darkness as an important national park resource is a function of a growing consciousness of its value and a crisis over its rapid disappearance. For millennia, our ancestors looked to the night sky in their enduring efforts to understand the physical and metaphysical worlds, and this suggests that night skies are an important cultural resource. Moreover, human culture is conventionally organized around the rhythms of the sun, moon, and stars, observations of the night sky are embodied in the religions and mythology of cultures around the globe and over time, and the celestial world has been the inspiration for art, literature, and other forms of cultural expression.

But natural darkness is being lost as the population and related development grow. Even the dark skies at Joshua Tree National Park, the subject of *Ren Z.*'s photography, are at risk from nearby light sources and more people—carrying their own lights—visiting the parks for a nighttime experience. Human-caused light is pervasive in a world where commerce and other human activity occur around the clock. An increasing number of national park visitors can't see the Milky Way from their home communities and relish the opportunity to experience natural darkness and to see and experience a pristine night sky in the national parks.

Contemporary science has extended the importance of natural darkness by demonstrating its vital role in the biological world; many of the world's species, estimated as half or more of all animals, are nocturnal and rely on the absence of light for breeding and feeding patterns, seasonal migrations, and other necessary behaviors. A classic example is the marine turtle. Turtle hatchlings emerge at night from their nests on ocean beaches and instinctively crawl toward the lighted horizon. Traditionally, this has been the sea as it reflects the light of celestial bodies. But now the land is often lighted from nearby development, and this attracts many turtle hatchlings that ultimately die from predation, exhaustion, or desiccation. Hundreds

DOI: 10.1079/9781800626768.0078

of thousands of turtle hatchlings die each year in Florida alone.

Recent research on the experiential component of natural darkness is evident in a program of study at Acadia National Park. A large majority of park visitors reported that the quality of the night sky at Acadia is important to them and that the park should be managed to protect the quality of the night sky. For example, many respondents reported seeing features of the night sky (e.g. moon, stars, constellations), and that this substantially added to the quality of their visit. Likewise, many visitors reported that they didn't see many sources of human-caused light in the park (e.g. car headlights, lighted buildings) and that this also substantially added to the quality of their experience. Minimum standards for night sky conditions (i.e. the absence of most human-caused light) were also identified in this program of study. Acadia and many other national parks are now being managed to help protect natural darkness, including working with surrounding towns to adopt state-of-the-art outdoor lighting practices, certification by the International Dark-Sky Association as an International Dark Sky Park, and periodic "star parties" in the national parks to celebrate the night sky as an important park resource.

Natural darkness is sometimes referred to as an "ecosystem service" of the national parks; see Conversation 26 for more about this.

References

Manning, R., Newman, P., Barber, J., Monz, C., Hallo, J. *et al.* (2018) *Natural Quiet and Natural Darkness: the "New" Resources of the National Parks*. University Press of New England, Lebanon, New Hampshire.

79 Natural Quiet

Post

Daryan S. mentioned the absence of human-caused sound in a Google Review of Redwood National and State Parks:

> *So beautiful and quiet! Really interesting to see trees so big! Well maintained roads and lots of places to stop!*

Response

National parks have been established to protect a variety of natural and cultural resources. Prominent examples include landscape features (e.g. mountains, lakes, rivers), wildlife, vegetation, cultural artifacts, and historic sites and buildings. But the definition of what constitutes a "resource" has expanded substantially over the more than 150 years of national parks in America. (The concept of the "ecosystem services" provided by national parks is another way to think about the values of national parks such as natural quiet; see Conversation 26 for more about this.)

One of the newly recognized resources in national parks is "natural quiet": the sounds of nature uninterrupted by human-caused noise. This was one of the things that *Daryan S.* especially appreciated at Redwood National and State Parks. Of course, natural quiet has been present in the national parks from their inception, but it's only recently been added to the agenda of park managers and scientists, and is just now entering more widely into the public consciousness. As the world becomes a noisier place, natural quiet is disappearing, and national parks are some of the last refuges for this increasingly scarce and valuable resource. A day in the redwood forest, especially along its lesser-visited paths, can remind visitors of the experience of "quiet".

Many of the sounds of nature are iconic manifestations of national parks—wolves howling, elk bugling, thundering waterfalls, and the cathedral-like quiet of ancient rainforests. These and other "soundscapes" are vital components of the integrity and authenticity of national parks. Unfortunately, excessive human-caused noise has become a pervasive problem throughout society, and this noise is increasingly migrating and drifting into many national parks. Transportation is a prime source of noise in many parks—cars and other vehicles on park roads and aircraft overhead. Park visitors can also generate substantial noise through talking on cellphones and boisterous behavior.

Noise can have important biological and ecological impacts. An increasing number of studies have found that acoustical cues play important roles in animal behavior, including predator–prey interactions, reproductive cycles, and territoriality. Masking of these cues by human-caused noise can threaten wildlife.

Noise can also substantially detract from the quality of visitors' experiences in national parks; it's an unwanted distraction and can mask the sounds of nature that can contribute to the quality of visiting the parks. Studies spanning many years have documented that escaping noisy cities and enjoying the sounds of nature are important motivations for visiting national parks and related areas. In fact, a national survey found that 72% of Americans reported that opportunities to experience the sounds of nature are a very important reason for preserving national parks. Another survey found that 91% of park visitors considered enjoyment of the sounds of nature as a very important reason for visiting these areas. Research has also documented that human-caused noise such as airplanes and automobiles can increase perceived crowding in national parks and related areas. Moreover, a number of studies have documented conflicts between motorized and non-motorized recreation, and the noise associated with motorized recreation is one of the causes of this conflict. A series of focus group sessions with visitors and other stakeholders at Yosemite National Park found a number of noise-related issues that participants reported as detracting from the quality of their park experiences, including noise from tour buses, automobiles, generators, aircraft over-flights, machinery, construction, and radios.

A program of noise-related research conducted at Muir Woods National Monument identified a number of factors that visitors felt increased the quality of their experiences at the park, including the sound of water flowing in Redwood Creek, birds calling, and wind blowing in the trees. Variables that decreased the quality of visitors' experiences included visitor-caused noise such as talking loudly and boisterous behavior. This program of research also identified minimum standards for visitor-caused noise (i.e. the maximum amount of noise acceptable to visitors) and found that these noise thresholds were sometimes violated in the park.

Many national parks and related outdoor recreation areas are now being managed to minimize human-caused noise. For example, aircraft overflights in some national parks are being regulated, quiet electric and natural gas-powered public transit systems are being established in some national parks as an alternative to noisy cars, and visitors are asked to limit the noise they generate in national parks to minimize crowding and conflict (Manning *et al.*, 2018).

Reference

Manning, R., Newman, P., Barber, J., Monz, C., Hallo, J. *et al.* (2018) *Natural Quiet and Natural Darkness: The "New" Resources of the National Parks*. University Press of New England, Lebanon, New Hampshire.

80 Human Health and Well-Being

Post

In celebration of National Park Week, *Katie B.*, working with Outdoor Explorers for All, posted the following on LinkedIn about park programming, veterans and their families, and well-being connections:

> *The strong connection between our program and the National Park Service extends far beyond the funding provided by NPS ... We work closely together to create unforgettable adventures for military families, like tidepooling at Olympic National Park, exploring caves at Timpanogos Cave National Monument, and beachcombing at Fire Island National Seashore. It's like planning the best family vacation ever, every single day! ... To witness the love, respect, and genuine commitment that National Park Rangers (so many of them being #Veterans themselves!) have for their work and the military families we serve at Blue Star Families is truly heartwarming. By working alongside those who share our belief in the transformative power of fresh air and the #outdoors, we are able to positively impact the mental health and overall well-being of those who serve our country and their families.*

Response

Those sound like remarkably meaningful experiences for veterans and their families, *Katie B.*! We can certainly understand how exploring the national parks can have such positive health and well-being impacts. There's a growing body of literature on the role that national parks and related areas play in improving human health and well-being. While participants in outdoor recreation have intuitively recognized the connections between parks and human health for a very long time, only recently have social-ecological studies advanced our understanding of the interconnectedness. In particular, research has begun to recognize and document the role of parks and outdoor recreation in facilitating psychological well-being amid growing concerns over societal mental health issues. Veteran-focused programs are a good example of that recognition and action toward improved mental and physical health via outdoor recreation.

The physical health benefits from visiting and taking part in recreational activities in national parks and related areas have been noted through empirical studies for several decades. Increasing evidence from these studies suggests that exercising outdoors, such as in national parks and protected areas, has greater positive effects on physical health than indoor exercise.

Psychological well-being is more difficult to define, but is increasingly recognized as an important component of overall human health. Research within the context of national parks and related areas has led to important policies and programs that strive to facilitate psychological well-being. For example, several countries now have "Healthy Parks, Healthy People" programs, and park and outdoor recreation managers are beginning to work with physicians and insurance providers to facilitate park prescription or "ParkRX" programs.

The recent COVID-19 pandemic, declared by the World Health Organization in March 2020, inevitably created a global focus around health and well-being. Despite some park closures and restrictions implemented during at least the initial pandemic declaration in an attempt to limit virus transmission, park visits and outdoor recreation flourished. Human health studies documented the negative influences of the pandemic on both physical and psychological well-being; meanwhile park and outdoor recreation-specific research noted that the simultaneous increase in outdoor recreation participation was driven by motivations to relieve stress and to support mental health, while pursuing physical health through exercise

DOI: 10.1079/9781800626768.0080

outside. Related research suggests that the pandemic resulted in greater participation in outdoor recreation, and predicts that these new participants are likely to continue this activity long after the pandemic has ended.

Despite the documented positive influences national parks and outdoor recreation can have on human health and well-being, historic inequities remain with regard to public access to these places and activities. The pandemic further highlighted the need to create equitable, safe access to national parks and related areas for all groups in society. NPS initiatives to establish more national parks in and around urban areas, along with efforts to make national parks more relevant and appealing to traditionally underserved populations, are helping to address these issues (see Conversations 19 and 93 for more about this).

Outdoor recreation in national parks and related areas has increasingly been correlated with human health and well-being. (Some observers suggest that human health and well-being is an "ecosystem service" provided by national parks; see Conversation 26 for more about this.) As a result, a variety of public health organizations such as the American Public Health Association and the American Academy of Pediatrics, now promote outdoor recreation as a vital component of human well-being, based on a growing body of empirical research.

Reference

Manning, R.E., Budruk, M., Goonan, K., Hallo, J. and Laven, D., Lawson, S., McCown, R., Minteer, B., Newman, P., Perry, E., Pettengill, P., Reigner, N., Valliere, W., van Riper, C. and Xiao, X. (2022) *Studies in Outdoor Recreation: Search and Research for Satisfaction*, 4th edn. Oregon State University Press, Corvallis, Oregon.

81 Dynamic Nature

Post

Controlling nature isn't an option when it comes to the magnificent eruptions of Kilauea at Hawaii Volcanoes National Park—only managing the human response to it. This image from Flickr shows lava from an active eruption entering the sea.

Hawaii Volcanoes National Park, National Park Service.

Response

Perhaps nothing conjures the image of "dynamic nature" as much as extreme events, especially ones with fire or lava. How we reconcile these natural, dynamic events with national park management has changed over the course of history of parks and park science. When Congress famously established Yellowstone National Park in 1872 (see the Introduction to this book for a history of the national parks), the act explicitly called for "the preservation, from injury or spoilation, of all timber, mineral deposits, natural curiosities, or wonders" included in the park (National Archives, no date). This basic mandate was ratified in the 1916 Organic Act

that created the NPS to manage the growing number of national parks, and the early leaders of the agency presumed that their mission was to ensure that little or nothing changed within park boundaries. This was a reasonable assumption given the state of natural science and associated thinking at the time.

But that assumption began to change by the late 1930s, when the new science of ecology emerged, emphasizing the often complex interactions among species and their relationships with the broader natural environment. Consequently, nature could be—and often was—dynamic rather than perpetually stable. Therefore, shouldn't the national parks be managed in ways that allowed—even enabled and celebrated—such change?

By the 1960s, the foundational dynamic character of nature—and its potentially profound effect on park management policy—was becoming undeniable. For example, findings from an NPS-commissioned study of groves of giant sequoias in Yosemite National Park suggested an entirely new paradigm for park management. The study found that the cones of these magnificent trees were serotinous, meaning they opened to disperse seeds only with the heat of fire. Moreover, the bark of the trees had adapted in ways that protected the trees from periodic and naturally occurring ground fires—it was a foot or more thick and non-resinous. Finally, eliminating naturally-occurring ground fires encouraged growth of competing tree species that were not naturally resistant to fire, and this inhibited growth of sequoia seedlings. By "protecting" the groves from fire for decades, the NPS was unknowingly endangering their reproduction.

In an analogous way, an emerging knowledge of and appreciation for predator–prey relationships—another example of the dynamic character of natural processes—reset national park management. Until that time, the NPS

© Robert Manning and Elizabeth Perry 2024. *Conversations About Visiting and Managing the National Parks* (R.E. Manning and E.E Perry)
DOI: 10.1079/9781800626768.0081

favored selected species in Yellowstone such as elk (majestic animals that visitors enjoyed seeing) and eliminated others such as wolves (that visitors didn't favor because they killed elk and were the subject of unfortunate mythology). But this led to explosive growth in elk populations, many of which prematurely died because they overgrazed the park's browse (e.g. young willows and aspens) they depended on.

Experiences in other national parks have magnified the importance of natural processes and contributed to the growing emphasis on maintaining the role of such processes in the national parks. An obvious example is the foundational role of volcanoes and other geological processes in many national parks, such as in the image sparking this conversation. For example, Hawaii Volcanoes National Park was established to protect the volcanic landscapes created by periodic natural eruptions of Kilauea and Mauna Loa Volcanoes (and others), and the park is managed in ways that don't attempt to interfere (e.g. visitors are kept away from periodic eruptions, lava flows, and other hazards, rather than somehow trying to control these volcanic processes). Similarly, the NPS attempted to control periodic wildfires in most national parks, only to find that such fires are often a natural occurrence. Moreover, extinguishing such fires can lead to more unnatural conflagrations caused by the extreme buildup of dead and down trees that fuel such larger fires (see Conversation 77 for more about wildfire in the national parks). All of this history and science have led to a greater appreciation of the dynamic character of much of the natural environment and to a new and more ecologically informed program of national park management.

However, more recent human-caused climate change has presented still another new challenge to park management (see Conversation 76 on climate change in the national parks). For example, as the climate continues to warm and dry in the American Southwest, there's concern that saguaro cactuses may not be viable in Saguaro National Park, and the same fate may apply to Joshua trees in their namesake national park. Should the NPS consider replanting these species to cooler, wetter climates to "save" them? What effect might this have on the indigenous plants and animals in these new areas?

The science of ecology is informing and revolutionizing NPS management policy. But sometimes the more we know highlights how little we know. Moreover, science can help inform policy, including national park management, but informed public policy often has vital societal and philosophical components as well. What do we want our national parks to be, and how can science help inform the answer to this foundational question? It seems undeniable that the deliberations of society—the workings of an informed environmental philosophy—should and will play an important role in formulating national park management policy; and this policy may be just as dynamic as the natural environment itself.

References

National Archives (n.d.) Act Establishing Yellowstone National Park (1872). Enrolled Acts and Resolutions of Congress, 1789–1996; General Records of the United States Government; Record Group 11. Available at: https://www.archives.gov/milestone-documents/act-establishing-yellowstone-national -park (accessed 23 July 2024).

Tweed, W. (2016) Dynamic nature. In: Manning, R., Diamant, R., Mitchell, N. and Harmon, D. (eds) *A Thinking Person's Guide to America's National Parks*. Braziller Publishers, New York, pp. 81–92.

82 Evolution of Parks and Wilderness

Post

Theoretical discussions abound about the evolution of parks and wilderness, but these considerations aren't just for scientists and academics. William Cronon, a historian, has written extensively on our collective evolution of thought on parks and wilderness, including in a timeless edited book of essays from diverse perspectives, *Uncommon Ground: Rethinking the Human Place in Nature* (Cronon, 1996a). Reviewing this book on Amazon in a post titled "Theorizing the Environment: Not Just for Scientists", *Lara C.* notes:

> *This book is indeed about "rethinking" the environment outside of the usual realms of political advocacy. The editor, William Cronon, is an historian, and this book is the result of a multi-disciplinary conference of scholars working in surprising niches of environmental studies. What makes this anthology so important is that many of the essays in it emphasize that our views of the environment, nature, and wilderness are "narratives" that are entangled with religion, culture, politics, and race—not just science. Cronon's introduction explores the concept of "wilderness" through time to the modern preservationist notion of a pristine, human-free zone, and the quandary that idea presents: wilderness preservation requires that all humans be removed from it …*

Response

Yes, *Lara C.* (and Dr. Cronon)—there is a strong entanglement between cultures and the concept of nature. Parks and wilderness continue to evolve in the traditional ecological context. Landscapes are shaped and reshaped by geological processes, and plants and animals evolve in response to the vagaries of genetic mutation and competitive advantage. Of course, some of these processes are now modified by climate change as noted in Conversation 76. But just as importantly, human thinking about parks and wilderness is evolving as well, and this has potentially important implications for use and management of these places.

Several conversations in this book reflect the increasing number of visits to the national parks and the associated environmental and experiential impacts (e.g. see Conversations 85–88). This concern started relatively early in American history and fueled the conservation, wilderness, and environmental movements of the 20th and 21st centuries. For example, 20th-century luminary conservationist Aldo Leopold famously wrote that "All conservation of wildness is self-defeating, for to cherish we must see and fondle, and when enough have seen and fondled, there is no wilderness left to cherish" (Leopold, 2020, p. 101). A few decades later, in his classic treatment of the history of American thought about wilderness, Roderick Nash wrote that, ironically, "the very increase in appreciation of wilderness threatened to prove its undoing. Having made extraordinary gains in the public's estimation in the last century, wilderness could well be loved to death in the next" (Nash, 2001, p. 316). Characteristically, environmentalist Ed Abbey put all this more bluntly, railing against the devastating consequences of "industrial tourism" to the nation's parks and wilderness (Abbey, 1990).

But this narrative of the damaging consequences of humans on nature reached a fork in the path more recently when historian William Cronon published a paper titled "The trouble with wilderness" (Cronon, 1996b). (Themes of this work are present throughout *Uncommon Ground*, the book reviewed in *Lara C.*'s post above.) In the parlance of the academic community, Cronon "deconstructed" the concept of wilderness, arguing that it was less natural and more cultural than traditionally

© Robert Manning and Elizabeth Perry 2024. *Conversations About Visiting and Managing the National Parks* (R.E. Manning and E.E Perry)
DOI: 10.1079/9781800626768.0082

thought. In particular, the natural environment conventionally honored in wilderness had been substantially altered through the long presence and actions of Indigenous peoples, and that such alterations have been more recently exacerbated by climate change, human-caused extinctions, large-scale land conversions, rapid urbanization, and the emergence of the Anthropocene (the "age of humans") more broadly. Consequently, he suggested that we recognize the world as a blend of the natural and cultural, and begin paying more attention and care to the "cultural landscapes" where most of us live, work, and play. In his words, "We need to embrace the full continuum of a natural landscape that is also cultural, in which the city, the suburb, the pastoral, and the wild each has its proper place, which we permit ourselves to celebrate without needlessly denigrating the others" (Cronon, 1996b, p. 24). (See Conversation 11 for more about cultural landscapes.)

This evolution of thought doesn't suggest that we abandon the American wilderness tradition as represented by the establishment of national parks beginning in 1872 and the establishment of the National Wilderness Preservation System in 1964. Rather, it means that we should examine the traditional concept of wilderness more closely by acknowledging its historical and cultural components, and extend our concern to the cultural landscapes closer to home as well. In these ways, we accept that all landscapes are some blend of the natural and cultural, and honor and protect the elements that we find so pleasing and useful in all of these cultural landscapes.

In reality, the National Park System sets a good example for these historical, cultural, and philosophical lessons: it's comprised of more than 400 national parks that range from Statue of Liberty National Monument to Gateway National Recreation Area, to Cape Cod National Seashore, to Yellowstone National Park, to Gates of Arctic National Park and Preserve. Moreover, the relatively new "models" of parks represented by national heritage areas, World Heritage Sites, and biosphere reserves (see Conversations 30–32 and 83 for more about this) present other useful and effective examples of the creative blending of nature and culture.

References

Abbey, E. (1990) *Desert Solitaire: A Season in the Wilderness*. Simon & Schuster, New York.

Cronon, W. (1996a) *Uncommon Ground: Rethinking the Human Place in Nature*. W.W. Norton & Co, New York.

Cronon, W. (1996b) The trouble with wilderness: Or, getting back to the wrong nature. *Environmental History* 1(1), 7–28. Available at: http://www.jstor.org/stable/3985059

Leopold, A. (2020) *A Sand County Almanac*. Oxford University Press, New York.

Minteer, B.A. (2015) *After Preservation: Saving American Nature in the Age of Humans*. University of Chicago Press, Chicago, Illinois.

Manning, R.E., Budruk, M., Goonan, K., Hallo, J. and Laven, D., Lawson, S., McCown, R., Minteer, B., Newman, P., Perry, E., Pettengill, P., Reigner, N., Valliere, W., van Riper, C. and Xiao, X. (2022) *Studies in Outdoor Recreation: Search and Research for Satisfaction*, 4th edn. Oregon State University Press, Corvallis, Oregon.

Minteer, B.A. and Manning, R.E. (2003) *Reconstructing Conservation: Finding Common Ground*. Island Press, Washington, DC.

Nash, R. (2001) *Wilderness and the American Mind*, 4th edn. Yale University Press, New Haven, Connecticut.

83 New Models of Parks

Post

The concept of national parks has grown and evolved into new models, including "cultural landscapes" that span broad geographic regions. The John H. Chafee Blackstone River Valley National Heritage Corridor in Massachusetts and Rhode Island is a good example, taking a regional approach to narrating the story of industrial growth, pollution, and contemporary environmental and economic revitalization. The boundaries of this new kind of park were recently expanded, and the park was highlighted as part of the national "America the Beautiful" initiative. A Google Review by *Katya M.* describes the expanse and diversity of this park:

This is a connected series of interesting and unique places. Bicycle path, walking and hiking trails, historical buildings and much more. Each time I go to a different place that is connected I am [learning] more about the history and industrial history of the area. Quite worth spending some time and checking it out. Some inspired person developed 101 Things You've Got To Do aka the Blackstone Bucket List which has given me ideas I had never considered.

Response

The connected and regional nature of the John H. Chafee Blackstone River Valley National Heritage Corridor (let's call it "Blackstone River Valley" for short) exemplifies one of America's new models of parks, and it's heartening that you've found so much to explore there, *Katya M.* Conversation 82 addressed evolving thoughts about parks and wilderness from historical and philosophical perspectives. But this evolution can be found on the ground as well as in the mind; new models of parks, wilderness, and related areas, along with advancing management regimes, have followed directly on the heels of their forward-thinking foundational philosophy. For example, concern about growing use of national parks and wilderness—as reflected in both environmental and experiential impacts—has drawn serious attention from academics and park managers alike, and this has brought advances in science and park practice.

Conceptual frameworks such as preservation vs use, carrying capacity, common property resources, limits of acceptable change, and the modern notion of sustainability have guided management of many conventional parks and wilderness areas toward more restrictive management regimes. These include: (i) use limits (see Conversation 91); (ii) public transit systems in parks to reduce environmental impacts, crowding, and congestion (see Conversation 92); and (iii) development and application of the national Leave No Trace program and its spinoffs that have advanced an agenda designed to limit recreation-related impacts to parks and associated areas (see Conversation 60). Limits on public use of oversubscribed sites are increasingly common in the national parks; for example, the opportunity to hike to the summit of Half Dome in Yosemite National Park, one of the most iconic hikes in all the national parks, is strictly limited to those fortunate enough to have (literally) won the lottery for this privilege (see Conversation 91).

But parks themselves are also changing in very different ways to keep up with their evolving philosophical underpinnings. For example, many Americans are beginning to come to terms with their unfortunate historic relationship with Indigenous peoples. As a result, several national parks are now co-managed with local tribes, park staff (some of them Indigenous) are using their highly developed interpretative talents to tell stories that celebrate the Indigenous presence

DOI: 10.1079/9781800626768.0083

on the land from prehistory to the present, and Indigenous peoples have been granted subsistence use rights in several Alaskan national parks.

New kinds of parks have also emerged, including national heritage areas (NHAs), World Heritage Sites, and biosphere reserves (see Conversations 30–32 for more about these). Blackstone River Valley that *Katya M.* describes in her posting at the beginning of this conversation is a good example of these new models of parks. This park is a large geographic region of 465,000 acres spread over two states and that includes 48 miles of its namesake river. This NHA weaves the story of the land and people throughout much prehistoric and historic time, and is managed by diverse partner organizations. The NHA includes the much smaller national park, Blackstone River Valley National Historical Park.

New models of national parks and related areas are evolving in response to the critique that many parks should be considered "cultural landscapes", where both natural and cultural resources are celebrated and protected and where people live, work, and play. The word "heritage" has come into the vocabulary of those who study and manage parks and references both park "resources" (the objective natural and cultural histories of places) as well as the more subjective meanings and values that have been assigned to them. This is reflected in the new models of US national parks established beginning in the 1960s, designated in lived-in places such as Cape Cod (Cape Cod National Seashore), New York City (Gateway National Recreation Area), San Francisco (Golden Gate National Recreation Area), Chicago (Indiana Dunes National Park), and Cleveland (Cuyahoga Valley National Park), all urban and urban-proximate regions. This new model of national parks continues to be advanced in the NPS's Urban Agenda (see Conversation 19).

NHAs have expanded into a network of more than 60 areas scattered around the nation, large areas that celebrate their distinctive natural and cultural heritage. Moreover, these NHAs are planned and managed by local citizens' groups (with technical and financial support from the NPS) and are primarily private lands. This new kind of national park follows models developed in Europe and elsewhere, often in locations with high population densities, and are based on partnerships among government at all levels, non-profit organizations, private enterprise, and interested citizens. Some are established adjacent to or surrounding national parks, supporting a more ecologically and historically informed approach to large landscape-scale conservation where conventional national parks serve as a protected core and NHAs offer buffers to urbanization and incompatible development. (See Conversation 32 for more about landscape-scale conservation.)

Conservation of a sample of the large geophysical region of the Great Basin geographic province that comprises much of the American West takes this landscape-scale form. Great Basin National Park is the core area of nearly 80,000 acres of this basin and range landscape that's owned and closely managed by the NPS, and this is complemented by the massive, more than ten-million-acre Great Basin National Heritage Area that links the park with surrounding national forests, tribal lands, and numerous small communities in the states of Nevada and Utah.

Adrian Phillips, former Chair of the World Commission on Protected Areas of the International Union for Conservation of Nature (IUCN), prepared a table (adapted here as Fig. 83.1) to illustrate the evolution of parks "as they were" and "as they are becoming", and the dynamic is provocative, even stunning. A more recent report by IUCN, *Tourism and Visitor Management in Protected Areas: Guidelines for Sustainability* (Leung *et al.*, 2018), also advances alternative models of parks that adopt many of the qualities outlined in Fig. 83.1, some of which embrace tourism as a form of economic development and as a means to offset the potential costs of parks to local people (e.g. foregone economic opportunities, congestion, and rising prices borne by locals).

These new models of parks are responding to underlying shifts in thinking about parks and related areas and offer a number of important benefits that can help managers meet the increasingly complex sets of challenges now facing parks and protected areas worldwide. For example, community-based approaches like NHAs offer opportunities to link actors across institutional as well as geographic scales through diverse social networks. The power and

Reserved for conservation Established mainly to protect wildlife & scenery Managed mainly for visitors & tourists Valued as wilderness About protection	**Objectives**	Run with concurrent social & economic objectives Established also for scientific, economic, & cultural values Managed with consideration about locals Valued for the cultural importance of "wilderness" About restoration & rehabilitation too
Run by central government	**Governance**	Run by diverse partnerships
Planned & managed against people Managed without regard to locals' opinions	**Locals**	Run with, for, & sometimes by locals Managed to meet the needs of locals
Developed separately Managed as "islands"	**Contexts**	Planned as part of regional to international systems Developed as "networks"
Viewed primarily as a national asset Viewed only as a national concern	**Perceptions**	Viewed also as a community asset Viewed also as an international concern
Funded by taxpayers	**Finances**	Funded by diverse sources
Managed reactively with short timescale Managed in a technocratic way Managed by scientists & natural resource experts Expert-led	**Management**	Managed adaptively with a long-term perspective Managed with political considerations Managed by multi-skilled individuals Draws on local & traditional knowledge

As protected areas were...   **As protected areas are becoming...**

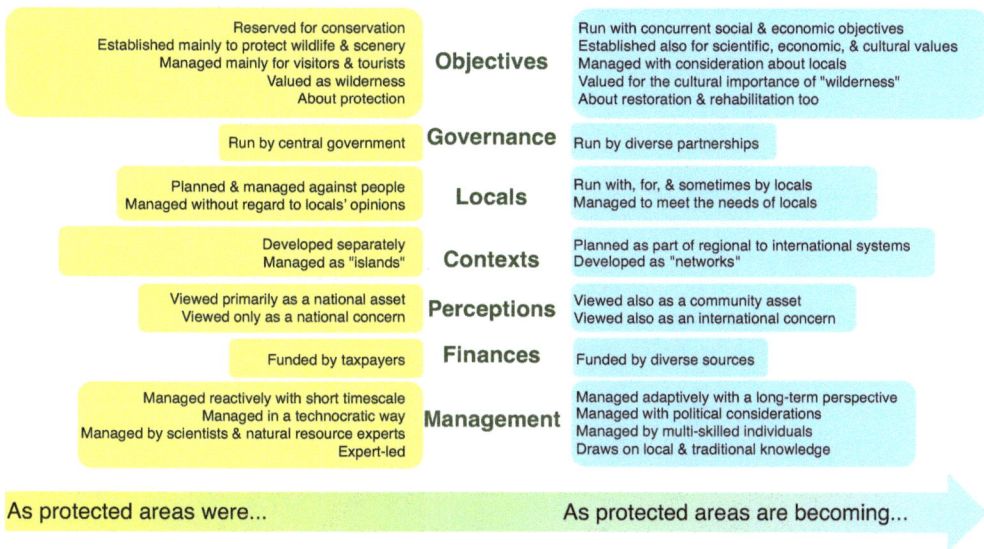

Fig. 83.1. The dynamic evolution of parks. Adapted from Phillips (2003).

potential of such networks lies in their ability to encourage and facilitate collective action that would otherwise exceed the capacity of any specific actor to undertake independently. This role is especially important when outdoor recreation interests intersect with ecological restoration and community development needs.

Blackstone River Valley, the subject of *Katya M.*'s post and one of the growing number of NHAs, offers insight into this issue. At the time of designation of the NHA in 1986, the US Environmental Protection Agency characterized the Blackstone River as one of the most toxic rivers in the nation. The river, which runs through Worcester, Massachusetts, on its way to Providence, Rhode Island, traverses a number of municipal boundaries and two state borders. Over 1.2 million people made their home in the Blackstone River Valley at the time of designation, and high levels of toxic contaminants rendered the river unusable from an outdoor recreation perspective, so much so that the town of Providence buried a section of the river under a blanket of concrete. Not long after its designation, the management team, composed of a wide spectrum of stakeholders, crafted and mobilized a long-term river restoration effort to create new opportunities for outdoor recreation

and community development in the area, and the success of this cooperative effort has been remarkable.

Another benefit offered by these new models of parks is the opportunity to engage broad segments of society in the management of natural and cultural resources. As suggested in Fig. 83.1, new models of parks and protected areas have adopted collaborative forms of governance that have the potential to include historically underrepresented and perpetually disenfranchised voices in the decision making and management of park resources, which in turn, can help ensure that parks remain relevant to the publics they're intended to serve. Conversation 93 discusses racial and ethnic diversity in the context of national parks and outdoor recreation more broadly, and it's difficult to overstate the importance of associated issues (e.g. chronic underrepresentation of minority racial and ethnic groups in national parks). Parks need the capacity to anticipate and respond to changing environmental and social conditions while also serving as platforms for civic discourse. New park models that rely on shared forms of governance provide opportunities for such dialogue.

The concept and practice of park management has evolved substantially over the last 150 years and this evolution continues. Societies everywhere face substantial socio-ecological changes: (i) climate change and all its associated and cascading impacts are altering many cherished outdoor recreation landscapes; (ii) traditionally underrepresented groups in society are growing in presence and power; and (iii) environmental thought is advancing and diversifying. (See Conversations 76, 93, and 82 for more about these issues.) This means that national parks and related areas will have to be highly adaptive and prepared to respond to a range of issues, including the capacity to "reach out" as well as "protect within".

Jon Jarvis, recent Director of the NPS, was fond of saying that "America invented the idea of national parks, the idea went around the world, and it came back different" (Manning, 2022, p. 2). As suggested in Conversation 82, parks and wilderness can be considered social constructs, ideas created by society and heavily influenced by knowledge and culture. It seems appropriate that the social constructions of parks and wilderness vary across geography and culture, and with the flow of time as well, and that this should be reflected in the range of parks, wilderness, and other models of parks and outdoor recreation areas (and their management regimes) we find scattered across the global landscape. It also suggests that these models will (and probably should) be diverse and continue their evolution.

References

Laven, D., Manning, R., Ventriss, C. and Mitchell, N. (2010) Evaluating national heritage areas: Theory, methods, and application. *Environmental Management* 46, 195–212.

Leung, Y., Spenceley, A., Hvenegaard, G. and Buckely, R. (2018) *Tourism and Visitor Management in Protected Areas: Guidelines for Sustainability*, Best Practice Protected Area Guidelines Series No. 27. International Union for Conservation of Nature (IUCN), Gland, Switzerland.

Manning, R. (2022) *America's National Heritage Areas: A Guide to the Nation's New Kind of National Park*. Globe Pequot Press, Guilford, Connecticut.

Manning, R. (2024) *A Guide to U.S. World Heritage Sites: The Heritage of Humanity*. Globe Pequot Press, Guilford, Connecticut.

National Park Service (2019). Available at: https://www.nps.gov/subjects/urban/index.htm (accessed 15 July 2024).

Phillips, A. (2003) Turning ideas on their head: The new paradigm for protected areas. *The George Wright Forum* 20(2), 8–32.

Stanfield McCown, R., Laven, D., Manning, R. and Mitchell, N. (2012) Engaging new and diverse audiences in the national parks. *The George Wright Forum* 29(2), 272–284.

84 Historic Preservation

Post

Responding to a Facebook post by the NPS Historic Preservation Training Center (HPTC) on their Aspiring Preservationist Programs, *Amy L.* noted:

> *I did an Americorps Vista project on new paints for lead paint encapsulation right out of college at Fort Vancouver [National Historic Site] – made a huge impression on my career and experience at our parks. Recommend 100 percent.*

Response

Historic preservation is a fascinating field with many in-depth considerations. It sounds like you found this fascination to be a lasting one, *Amy L!* As we discuss the national parks' cultural history and resources (see Conversation 10), we recognize that there is a science and training to adequately caring for the human histories in these parks. This is vital to the preservation of the historic resources as objects, but also as pathways providing opportunity for connection between our past and present.

To do so, the NPS follows a set of standards for historic preservation. Other organizations also follow the NPS's lead in these standards and best practices. Consistency and high quality of these efforts are important when restoring historic buildings, replicating historic fencing or travel paths, or caring for museum artifacts, for example.

Related, the NPS also maintains the National Register of Historic Places, which is the US's official list of important historic sites (see Conversation 24 from more about this). Listing here can assist in raising awareness and coordination on preservation of these places. The NPS not only lists these places on a register, but can also lend their technical preservation expertise

and services to help restore or stabilize historic buildings. If a private entity has a building listed on the National Register and would like to rehabilitate it, the NPS can assist with administering tax incentive programs for this work.

The NPS HPTC is a well-known leader in the science of historic preservation and restoration. They complete such projects within the National Park System and provide employees, interns, and students working with them the training needed for such tasks. Training in the HPTC consists of both knowledge about preservation philosophy and experience in specialized skill sets (e.g. masonry, wood crafting, millwork, metal work, carpentry). Advanced learning in these trades is crucially needed within the NPS and across historic preservation, especially with the challenges of climate change and urbanization further affecting the viability of many structures. The HPTC's Traditional Trades Advancement Program is a 6-month commitment for young adults and veterans to learn these skills and get a competitive edge in the workforce (see Conversation 97). The Historic Stewards and Build Up Technical Internship programs are other opportunities for skills enhancement.

People with interest in careers related to historic preservation, risk management, construction, planning and design, and maintenance have all found benefit in the hands-on learning at HPTC and problem solving about how to apply these techniques in individualized contexts within the national parks. For example, rehabilitating a historic building at a Timucuan Ecological and Historic Preserve on the Atlantic Coast of Florida and another at Sleeping Bear Dunes National Lakeshore on the shore of Lake Michigan in Michigan may have some similarities in dealing with coastal structures but undoubtedly differences in approach based on the location and age of the buildings. The NPS historic preservation program works to

© Robert Manning and Elizabeth Perry 2024. *Conversations About Visiting and Managing the National Parks* (R.E. Manning and E.E Perry)
DOI: 10.1079/9781800626768.0084

preserve the diverse range of history present in the parks, from the restoration of the prison facility on Alcatraz Island to the care of Civil War structures at Fort Sumter and Fort Moultrie to the complicated presentation of buildings and reactors associated with the Manhattan Project National Historical Park. If you are interested in the science and skill of maintaining such resources, as *Amy L.* was, check out the opportunities available with the HPTC, discover more on the "History" section of your favorite national park's website, or chat up a ranger while there.

References

Conservation Legacy (2024) NPS Historic Preservation & Training Center. Available at: https://stewardsle gacy.org/hptc (accessed 14 July 2024).
National Park Service (2022) Historic Preservation Training Center. Available at: https://www.nps.gov/org s/1098/index.htm (accessed 15 July 2024).

Outdoor Recreation

85 Environmental Impacts of Outdoor Recreation

Post

Outdoor recreation can impact the environment, including sensitive substrates such as cryptobiotic soils (communities of organisms living on the soil surface in arid ecosystems such as alpine mountain tops). After *Spaceman_the_SkierCO* reposted a story on Reddit by the *Denver Gazette* titled "Stepping (or camping) on this "living soil" can cause 1,000 years of damage and early snowmelt" (McKee, 2024), many shared about learning not to disrupt these living and slow-growing biotic crusts on alpine soils. A few, such as those below, had rhymes to keep folks impact aware:

> *River_Pigeon: Don't bust the crust*
>
> *Machaco: Tiptoe through the crypto*

Response

Absolutely, *River_Pigeon* and *Machaco*—stay off those fragile soils! Outdoor recreation activities such as hiking and camping are popular and welcome ways to enjoy and appreciate national parks. But they can impact vital park resources such as soil, vegetation, water, wildlife, and historical/archeological sites. Given the rise in popularity of outdoor recreation, these impacts must be understood, managed, and minimized. A substantial scientific and professional literature—often called "recreation ecology"—has developed to document and understand these impacts, guide visitor behavior, and direct park management.

Research demonstrates that impacts to soil generally begin when the organic layer on the soil surface (leaves, composting vegetation) is scuffed away by passing hikers, bikers, and stock (e.g. horses) and by concentrated use at sites like trails and campsites. This reduces the fertility of the soil and makes it more vulnerable to compaction, thereby inhibiting plant growth and altering soil organisms. This, in turn, reduces water infiltration leading to soil erosion. These impacts can occur rapidly even under relatively low levels of use. This is especially true for the cryptobiotic soils mentioned in the Reddit thread above.

Impacts to vegetation can occur at all structural levels. For example, when groundcover vegetation is trampled, it can be threatened by direct breakage and bruising. Soil compaction and resulting reduction of water infiltration (as noted above) can also lead to reduced plant vigor and reproduction. Shrubs and saplings can also be damaged when visitors leave developed trails and campsites, create social trails, and search for firewood. Also mature trees can be damaged when they are scavenged for firewood and used to hang hot lanterns. All of these impacts can occur quickly, alter natural forest composition, and lead to invasion of exotic species.

Research suggests that recreation-related impacts to streams and lakes may be relatively uncommon, but that it can be serious when it does occur. A primary concern, of course, is that visitors sometimes swim in this water and/or use it as a source of drinking water, and this has the potential to lead to disease. An increase in suspended matter and water turbidity (generally caused by soil erosion) is a more common problem, and this can reduce water clarity, diminish oxygen levels, and affect plant and animal composition and productivity.

Recreation-related impacts to wildlife are dependent on several contexts, including time of year, breeding season, animal age, type of habitat, and experience of wildlife with humans. These impacts can be direct (e.g. disturbance by recreationists) or indirect (e.g. impacts to vegetation). The primary impact is harassment of wildlife, intentional or unintentional, which can lead to physiological and psychological stress. This problem is greatly enhanced during winter when stress is already high. Other impacts include habituation/taming of wild animals and feeding wildlife. All of these potential impacts can lead to reductions in wildlife populations and/or changes in species composition.

Historical and cultural sites can also be damaged by visitors, though less is known about this. Recreation visitors may cause such damage inadvertently, such as camping in or on such sites. But the more common problem is visitors removing historical/archeological artifacts. Graffiti and vandalism are also common problems.

Of course, all of these potential impacts should be minimized by park visitors. The national Leave No Trace program has been designed to help do this, and is discussed in Conversation 60. Moreover, recreation-related impacts must be addressed by park managers, and alternative management strategies and practices are described in Conversation 89. Perhaps, in the spirit of the rhymes for cryptobiotic soil impacts noted at the beginning of this conversation, a more general one for environmental impacts could be "Love the parks, tread with care, minimize your impacts there!"

References

Hammitt, W.E., Cole, D.N. and Monz, C.A. (2015) *Wildland Recreation: Ecology and Management*. Wiley Blackwell, New York.

McKee, S. (2024, April 15) Stepping on this 'living soil' can cause 1,000 years of damage and early snowmelt. *Denver Gazette*. Available at: https://denvergazette.com/outtherecolorado/adventures/stepping-on-this-living-soil-can-cause-1-000-years-of-damage-and-early-snowmelt/article_24cb450e-fb49-11ee-bccf-0375e9f3a1ca.html (accessed 23 July 2024).

86 Social Impacts of Outdoor Recreation

Post

A video caught two people knocking over a rock formation at Lake Mead National Recreation Area, a unit of the National Park System. When the National Park Service (NPS) released the video in an attempt to catch the culprits, it sparked substantial and passionate discussion on social media. The video was shared across Facebook, with *Jim C.* adding a comment to it:

> *As a person who enjoys going around the country and seeing unique places in the national parks, this really makes me sad. Help share this to hopefully catch the 2 on this video.*

Response

We agree, *Jim C.*, this video saddens us too. Intentionally destructive behavior has no place in the outdoors, especially in the protected landscapes of national parks. Conversation 85 described a variety of environmental impacts of outdoor recreation, including damage to soils, vegetation, water, wildlife, and historical/archeological sites. Moreover, these impacts can be exacerbated by rising numbers of visits and inappropriate visitor behavior. *Jim C.*'s post highlights an extreme case of inappropriate—indeed, criminal—visitor behavior. A companion concern addresses the social impacts of outdoor recreation, sometimes called experiential impacts. Of course these two types of impacts—environmental and social—can be closely related in that environmental degradation of national parks caused by outdoor recreation can diminish the quality of the recreation experience. For example, destruction of groundcover vegetation and resulting soil erosion can have important aesthetic consequences, and this can diminish the quality of the recreation experience. Impacts to water quality, wildlife, and historical and archeological sites can affect the quality of the recreation experience as well; diminished opportunities to see wildlife in their natural habitat, for example, can lead to disappointment. It's this diminished experience that *Jim C.*'s post addresses, as this natural formation at Lake Mead National Recreation Area now no longer stands for others to enjoy.

Crowding and conflict are the two other primary sources of social/experiential impacts of outdoor recreation. Crowding is especially vulnerable to the rising number of visits to the national parks, particularly in the larger national parks and the wilderness portions of these parks that are often associated with opportunities for solitude. While the number of visitors encountered in the parks can be important in defining crowding, visitor behavior can be important as well; examples include large groups, boisterous behavior, environmentally insensitive behavior (e.g. walking off designated trails), and inherently conflicting activities (e.g. motorized and non-motorized activities). Crowding is discussed in Conversation 87, and ways to avoid crowding in the national parks is discussed in Conversation 55.

Conflict differs from crowding in that it generally addresses the interaction and behavior of visitors rather than their sheer number. For example, there may not be too many visitors on a trail, but hikers seeking peace and quiet may be disturbed by bikers who ride too fast. (To be fair, bikers may be disturbed by hikers who travel slowly and fail to keep to the right.) Conflict may also be tied to social values. For example, some canoeists may object to motorboaters because these groups can have very different worldviews about what types of recreation activities are appropriate in a national park. Conflict is discussed in more detail in Conversation 88.

Like the environmental impacts caused by outdoor recreation, the social/experiential

© Robert Manning and Elizabeth Perry 2024. *Conversations About Visiting and Managing the National Parks* (R.E. Manning and E.E Perry)
DOI: 10.1079/9781800626768.0086

impacts of outdoor recreation should be mini-mized by park visitors. The national Leave No Trace program has been designed to help do this, and is outlined in Conversation 60. Moreover, recreation-related impacts must be addressed by park managers, and alternative management strategies and tactics/practices are described in Conversation 89.

87 Crowding

Post

Nearly countless posts across social media, stories in the news, and personal accounts on blogs and videos discuss one aspect of national parks: the crowds. On Reddit, one thread centers not only on the issue of crowding but also discusses some realistic answers. It was started by *Stock_Code_8632*'s question:

> As a nature lover, there is nothing as fascinating as American national parks. I have never been but that's one of my top goals to visit a few of them, however, I like the nature because it's peaceful and quiet. From my research it seems like these national parks are completely mobbed by hordes of people therefore making it pointless to go. Seems to kind of defeat the purpose of going to connect with nature when there are crowds of humans everywhere. Maybe these articles are exaggerated and you can find peace in these parks or go off season? Or the crowds are always there?

Other responses suggested some of the nuances associated with crowding in the national parks, topics like varying use levels among parks, locations within parks, and times of the year. Other responses addressed the importance of accommodating as many visitors to the national parks as possible.

> *travelinmatt76:* Avoid weekends and major holidays, go on off season days.

> *manhattanabe:* Each park has different levels of access. The parts you can drive to can be very crowded. The parts that are a 2 day hike will be empty. There is something for everyone.

> *thattogoguy:* I'd also say to look at attendance rates for each park annually; Some parks will have well over 1–2 million visitors a year, some even higher. Some parks don't even have 10,000. There's also lesser visited parks that are more remote, like North Cascades in Washington, which you can easily drive to, it just takes time, and there aren't as many immediate amenities for people. Those parks open up over time. North Cascades is a great place for people looking to really rough it for a bit.

> *calcade:* Park ranger here. Just want to remind you that national parks are far more than nature and solitude. We have that, too, but our parks welcome everyone. We preserve nature, culture and history as well. Sometimes that means there are many people around, but that is because so many folks want to enjoy the park. I think that's a great thing, albeit challenging in some ways.

Response

Where to start with crowding? Well, *Stock_Code_8632* does a good job of getting the conversation rolling. Crowding in the national parks is an important issue that has grown in intensity over the years. As noted in Conversation 3, there are now more than 300 million annual visits to the national parks, and that's caused many parks to feel more crowded (though this has been offset, at least to some degree, by the establishment of more national parks). But given the fact that many people associate the national parks with opportunities for solitude—particularly the natural parks like Yellowstone, Yosemite, and Great Smoky Mountains—this is a problem. The problem of crowding is especially vital in the wilderness portions of many national parks, as these areas are required by the Wilderness Act of 1964 to provide "opportunities for solitude" (see Conversation 21 on wilderness).

As described in Conversations 73 and 74, there's been a longstanding concern over the "carrying capacity" of national parks and related areas; how much and kinds of uses can be accommodated in the national parks without too much impact to natural and cultural resources. Carrying capacity has an equally important social or experiential dimension as well: how many visits can be accommodated

© Robert Manning and Elizabeth Perry 2024. *Conversations About Visiting and Managing the National Parks* (R.E. Manning and E.E Perry)
DOI: 10.1079/9781800626768.0087

without unacceptable degradation of the quality of the visitor experience. Also crowding is often considered an important component of "social carrying capacity". But many studies have found relatively little statistical relationship between the number of visits to national parks, visitor reports of perceived crowding, and measures of overall satisfaction by visitors. Why is this and what are the implications of this research?

Research has found that some visitors "cope" with crowding through "displacement"; that is, if they find some parks (or places within parks) to be too crowded, they visit other less heavily used parks, visit less heavily used portions of parks, or visit during less heavily used times (as suggested by some of the posts above). Or some visitors may stop visiting the parks entirely, though this may be rare. Another line of research has found that judgements of crowding are related to some characteristics of visitors. It's obvious, for example, that visitors who seek out the national parks to find solitude are more sensitive to crowding; this is in contrast to visitors who are motivated more strongly to enjoy the beauty and environmental significance of national parks and to "see the sights". Another line of research has found that crowding can also be related to the characteristics of other visitors who are encountered in the national parks. For example, when some visitors are behaving in ways that bother others, this can cause visitors to feel more crowded. Classic examples of behaviors that can cause feelings of crowding include large groups, boisterous behavior, environmentally insensitive behavior (e.g. walking off designated trails), and inherently conflicting activities (hikers, bikers, and horseback riders on the same trails; paddling canoeists and motorboats on the same lakes; hunters and non-hunters in the same areas; see Conversation 88 on conflict among recreationists). A final line of research addresses the effects of "situational" variables on crowding. For example, feelings of crowding can be more pronounced in the wilderness portion of parks than in more developed areas, and can even be affected by the environmental quality of an

area (e.g. an area that's been degraded by visitors through soil compaction and erosion and littering can feel more crowded than the same area that is less impacted). We see echoes of all of these in the responses to *Stock_Code_8632*.

There are potentially important implications of this body of research for both park managers and visitors. First, some visitors feel crowded in the national parks, at least in some places and times, and this should be addressed by park managers when and where possible. Conversation 89 discusses the range of actions that can be taken by managers to control the environmental and social impacts of increasing levels of visitor use. Of course, limits can be placed on the number of visits allowed, and this is happening in many parks. But limiting visitor use denies access to the parks and this infringes on the mandate of the NPS to "provide for the enjoyment" of the parks as specified in the agency's Organic Act of 1916, and it may undercut public support for the national parks. Other options include minimizing crowding through educational programs aimed at reducing visitor behaviors that exacerbate crowding, separating conflicting uses, maintaining the environmental quality of the parks, and accommodating large numbers of visitors through facilities and services such as public transit systems that reduce competition for limited parking spaces (see Conversation 92).

Visitors can also minimize perceived crowding through visiting less heavily used parks and/or time periods, following park rules and regulations, minimizing their environmental and social impacts (e.g. adopting Leave No Trace practices as discussed in Conversation 60), adjusting their expectations with more realistic assessments of current and future use levels, avoiding areas with inherently conflicting uses, and understanding that the portions of the national parks that have been reserved for relatively low use levels (the wilderness portions of the parks, for example) may require permits and that this may require a special application process. See Conversation 55 for more ways visitors can avoid unacceptable crowding in the national parks.

Reference

Manning, R.E., Budruk, M., Goonan, K., Hallo, J. and Laven, D., Lawson, S., McCown, R., Minteer, B., Newman, P., Perry, E., Pettengill, P., Reigner, N., Valliere, W., van Riper, C. and Xiao, X. (2022) *Studies in Outdoor Recreation: Search and Research for Satisfaction*, 4th edn. Oregon State University Press, Corvallis, Oregon.

88 Conflict Among Recreation Activities

Post

Conflict can occur within or between activity groups in any national park. On the George Washington Memorial Parkway in Washington, DC, drivers on the road for their commute or for leisure encounter other drivers as well as multiple pedestrian and multi-use trail crossings and well-used pull-outs and parking lots for specific scenic and historic sites along the parkway. *Mike R.* spoke to the beauty and danger in this mix of activities from a driver's perspective on Yelp:

> *I have a love/hate relationship with this road. First off it's one of the prettiest in the DC area. Looking out at the Potomac, the views are difficult to put into words. Please don't get distracted by it, but hope you'll stop at one of the viewing spots ... On the other side of the spectrum, non drivers amok here. There are a fair amount of accidents due to careless folks.*

Response

Conversations 87 and 55 address crowding in national parks and related areas, including how to avoid it and its management implications. A separate but related issue concerns potential conflict among recreation visitors/groups. Crowding and conflict may be related issues (e.g. crowding may increase the potential for conflict and vice versa), but they can also be distinguished. Crowding is generally a function of problems associated with increased demand and competition for park access, while conflict addresses problems associated with the interaction of park visitors. It sounds like *Mike R.* is directly speaking to conflict among the different ways people are moving through and enjoying their time along the George Washington Memorial Parkway. This is a bit of an update

to the many classic examples of the potential for conflict among different types of park visitors: (i) hikers and bikers; (ii) canoeists and motorboaters; (iii) skiers and snowboarders; (iv) hikers/bikers and equestrians; (v) canoeists and anglers; (vi) hunters and non-hunters; and (vii) cross-country skiers and snowmobilers.

Research on conflict in national parks and related areas suggests that it generally falls into one of two types. The first is conflict that is derived from "goal interference" or "interpersonal conflict"; this type of conflict is associated with motivations and related behavioral issues (see Conversation 90 on motivations for recreation). For example, hikers seeking a quiet and peaceful walk in nature may experience conflict with bikers who wish to travel faster as part of an adventurous outing. The reverse may be true as well: bikers may object to the presence of hikers who may block the trail because of their slow pace of travel, or failure to keep to the right of the trail. Judging from *Mike R.*'s post and knowledge of the uses along the George Washington Memorial Parkway, the interpersonal conflicts stem from the intersection of vehicles on the roadways with walkers, runners, bikers, etc. on the pathways at frequent and often confusing junctures—especially for non-locals who are sightseeing in the area as DC tourists. Add into this that many use both the parkway and the pathways (notably the Mount Vernon Trail) for vehicle or bike-based commuting rather than strictly in their free time and it's no wonder that people with different goals may experience some level of "goal interference"-related conflict in this national park.

The second type of conflict is based on "social values" and may stem from alternative worldviews about the foundational meaning of national parks and appropriate recreation activities. In this type of conflict, visitors may not even interact for conflict to exist. For example, some national park visitors may object

© Robert Manning and Elizabeth Perry 2024. *Conversations About Visiting and Managing the National Parks* (R.E. Manning and E.E Perry)
DOI: 10.1079/9781800626768.0088

to biking, hunting, or motorized recreation on philosophical grounds.

Conflict among recreation visitors can be managed in three ways. First, conflicting activities can be separated or "zoned" to minimize personal interaction. For example, biking in national parks is often allowed only on roads, not trails; in this way, interaction and conflict between bikers and hikers is minimized. Second, rules and regulations can be applied to minimize conflict; for example, bikers can be required to slow down in the presence of hikers (correspondingly, hikers can be encouraged to walk on the right side of the trail), motorboaters can be required to slow down and minimize their wake in the presence of canoeists, and hikers can be required to stop and step off the trail to allow equestrians to safely pass. Third, educational programs can be undertaken to improve mutual understanding among potentially conflicting recreation participants. In the case of visitors to national parks, it's likely that all visitors are drawn to these areas because of their mutual interest in the natural and cultural history of these areas, and this shared interest might be used as the basis for finding empathy among visitors, and this might in turn lead to more compatible activities, practices, and behaviors.

Research and management experience have made it clear that there is often some level of conflict among recreation groups, and that this often needs to be managed. Visitors can play an important role in this process by thinking carefully about how their activities might affect other visitors and adapting their behavior accordingly. Alternatively, if conflicts prove to be unavoidable, then managers should separate these activities (spatially or temporally) to keep one type of activity from inappropriately driving the other away. In some cases, this may mean that some activities are not allowed in national parks or related areas.

Reference

Manning, R.E., Budruk, M., Goonan, K., Hallo, J. and Laven, D., Lawson, S., McCown, R., Minteer, B., Newman, P., Perry, E., Pettengill, P., Reigner, N., Valliere, W., van Riper, C. and Xiao, X. (2022) *Studies in Outdoor Recreation: Search and Research for Satisfaction*, 4th edn. Oregon State University Press, Corvallis, Oregon.

89 Managing Outdoor Recreation

Post

Management strategies and practices assist in protecting the quality of park resources and visitor experience. Muir Woods National Monument, a bit north of San Francisco, California, has implemented some such management to control outdoor recreation and its impacts. *SwimMamaBear* on Tripadvisor spoke to a few of these in a review:

> *Take the shuttle and don't stress over the drive or worry about parking reservation … We were glad we were unable to reserve parking because the [$3/ person] shuttle was so easy and convenient for our group of four … I think the signs encouraging respect for the habitat and need for quiet could be emphasized by park personnel as tickets are purchased and with entry. The signs alone did not deliver the message as many seemed to think it was not a serious reminder. The sound meter at the cafe/ gift shop is a good reminder but not highly visible. It would be great to have another meter located along the trail if it could be done without compromise to environment … Seeing trails soon to be re-routed made me feel personnel are vigilant in observing growth patterns and taking steps to protect and conserve this forest habitat with as little disruption as possible while still allowing the public to visit.*

Response

SwimMamaBear offers an insightful perspective on the range of management practices that can be applied in the context of national parks, and she illustrates this discussion in the context of Muir Woods National Monument. Here, park staff are managing outdoor recreation in several ways, including providing a shuttle bus system to access the park (at a lower price than parking nearby) to alleviate parking pressure and vehicle pollution near the park entrance, encouraging quiet recreation through signage and sound meters, and adjusting trails to minimize environmental impacts while still accommodating public use. These are all crucial measures in this park's management, and represent approaches used across the National Park System.

As discussed in Conversation 3, visitor use of the national parks has increased substantially over the last few decades and now exceeds 300 million visits annually. This requires more attention to managing outdoor recreation in the parks to maximize its benefits and minimize potential environmental and social impacts (see Conversations 85 and 86 for a discussion of these issues). It can be useful to think systematically and creatively about management options and their potential effectiveness, and this can be advanced by identifying the management options available and the contexts in which they can be applied, and then arraying these management options and contexts in an organized format.

One way to think about management options is to categorize them into strategies and tactics/practices. There are four basic strategies for managing visitor use to limit its environmental and social impacts: (i) limit use (to reduce the amount of use and associated impacts); (ii) increase the supply opportunities (to spread out use and reduce the severity of impacts); (iii) reduce the impact of use (by modifying the type and/or character of use); and (iv) "harden" park resources and/or the visitor experience (to make both more resistant to use and its potential impacts).

There are six basic categories of management tactics/practices that can be used to advance these four strategies: (i) information/ education; (ii) rationing/allocation of use; (iii) rules/regulations; (iv) law enforcement; (v) zoning; and (vi) facility development/site design/ maintenance. Moreover, these four management strategies and six tactics/practices can be applied in a variety of park and outdoor recreation

© Robert Manning and Elizabeth Perry 2024. *Conversations About Visiting and Managing the National Parks* (R.E. Manning and E.E Perry) DOI: 10.1079/9781800626768.0089

Address problem(s) through combining management strategies and practices	Problems: Impacts to...															
	Resource (environment)								Social (experiential)			Managerial (facilities and services)				
Management strategy: Limit use (Other strategies: increase supply, reduce impact of use, and harden park resources and/or the visitor experience)	Soil	Vegetation	Water	Wildlife	Air	Natural quiet	Natural darkness	Historical/cultural	Crowding	Conflict	Depreciative behavior	Attraction sites	Trails	Campgrounds/campsites	Roads/parking	Interpretive facilities/programs
Information/education	1	7	13	19	25	31	37	43	49	55	61	67	73	79	85	91
Rationing/allocation	2	8	14	20	26	32	38	44	50	56	62	68	74	80	86	92
Rules/regulations	3	9	15	21	27	33	39	45	51	57	63	69	75	81	87	93
Law enforcement	4	10	16	22	28	34	40	46	52	58	64	70	76	82	88	94
Zoning	5	11	17	23	29	35	41	47	53	59	65	71	77	83	89	95
Facility development/ site design/maintenance	6	12	18	24	30	36	42	48	54	60	66	72	78	84	90	96

(Management Practices — left-side vertical label)

Fig. 89.1. Management matrix for management strategy "Limit use" indicating how to address problems of protecting both the quality of park resources and the visitor experience through combining management strategies and practices. Adapted from Manning *et al*. (2022).

contexts, including attraction sites, trails, campgrounds/campsites, roads and parking lots, and at interpretive facilities and programs. When all of these options—strategies, tactics/practices, and contexts—are arrayed in a series of matrices as illustrated in Fig. 89.1, the wide variety of management options becomes apparent. This is magnified by the fact that the figure is for the management strategy of "limiting use" only (as indicated by the phrase "Limit use" in the middle of the left-hand column); three more matrices address the three additional strategies of increasing the supply opportunities, reducing the impact of use, and "hardening" park resources and/or the visitor experience. (All four of these matrices and related materials can be found in the book, *Managing Outdoor Recreation: Case Studies in the National Parks* (Manning *et al*., 2017), listed in the References at the end of this conversation.) Each of the four matrices includes 96 cells or management alternatives, and the four matrices together include 384 cells or management alternatives. This matrix

approach encourages park managers and visitors to think comprehensively and creatively about all the possible management alternatives, and not simply those that are commonly applied or administratively easy. In matrix-speak, this allows for "thinking outside the box" by "thinking within the cells".

There are several corollaries to using these four management matrices. First, most of the impacts and problems associated with outdoor recreation can be addressed by more than one management strategy and/or practice. Crowding, for example, can be addressed by the strategy of limiting use (e.g. using the practice of raising fees or the practice of conducting a lottery for use permits), increasing the supply of recreation opportunities (e.g. using the practice of informing visitors about substitute recreation opportunities or the practice of developing additional facilities such as trails), and reducing the impact of use (e.g. using the practice of education about the national Leave No Trace (LNT) principles (see Conversation 60) or a regulation against cellphones to limit visitor-caused noise that can contribute to perceived crowding). In the post above on Muir Woods, we see strategies of limiting use (encouraging shuttle use from a more remote parking area to limit entrance area crowding and air-quality concerns) and reducing impacts of use (creating interpretive signage and trail design to support natural quiet and functioning forest systems).

Second, recreation management strategies and practices can address multiple problems. For example, the strategy of reducing the impact of use and the associated practice of information/education can be used to address impacts to a number of park resources, including soils, vegetation, water, wildlife, and air. The LNT program has been designed specifically for this purpose. Information/education can also be used to reduce crowding by dispersing use to other sites/parks, minimizing conflict by suggesting appropriate visitor behavior, limiting depreciative behaviors by explaining why littering and graffiti are inappropriate, and "hardening" the visitor experience by helping to shape realistic expectations of visitors about park conditions.

Third, each of the six categories of management practices can be employed to advance more than one of the four management strategies, and this effectively expands management options exponentially. For example, the management practice of information/education can be used to reduce use at a problem site or park (by informing visitors of the problems being experienced at the site or park and/or by informing them of the advantages of alternative sites or parks, for instance), or to reduce the impact of use (by educating visitors about LNT behaviors). It's important to design and apply management practices in ways that will advance the strategies that are chosen to solve management problems. It's also important to take advantage of the ways in which one management practice might be used to advance more than one management strategy.

Fourth, outdoor recreation management strategies can be advanced by more than one management practice. For example, the management strategy of limiting use can be used by informing visitors of alternative outdoor recreation opportunities, rationing use through a permit system, and implementing a rule that limits group size. The management strategy of reducing the impact of use can be advanced by educating visitors about LNT practices, rationing use through a permit system, implementing a rule against the use of campfires above tree line, and developing tent pads to harden fragile soils and vegetation.

Classifying outdoor recreation management options by the criteria noted above (or any other useful classification system) allows for a more systematic and comprehensive assessment of management options that can address high levels of visitor use in the national parks and their potential environmental and social impacts. This can make for a good management tool. But it can also be useful to visitors and others interested in the national parks. The NPS is a government agency and is open to public input on potential management actions; park plans are updated periodically and this is an especially good time to make management suggestions based on thoughtful consideration of the full range of potential management actions and personal observations derived from visiting the parks.

References

Manning, R., Anderson, A. and Pettengill, P. (2017) *Managing Outdoor Recreation: Case Studies in the National Parks*, 2nd edn. CAB International, Boston, Massachusetts.

Manning, R.E., Budruk, M., Goonan, K., Hallo, J. and Laven, D., Lawson, S., McCown, R., Minteer, B., Newman, P., Perry, E., Pettengill, P., Reigner, N., Valliere, W., van Riper, C. and Xiao, X. (2022) *Studies in Outdoor Recreation: Search and Research for Satisfaction*, 4th edn. Oregon State University Press, Corvallis, Oregon.

90 Motivations and Benefits in Outdoor Recreation

Post

In a thread on X, *59nationalparks* posed the following question:

> *Q10 #ParkChat This year ParkRx Day is a fee-free day in US National Parks so everyone can get out and enjoy the health benefits of the great outdoors. It's part of #NationalParkWeek. How do you think Park visits help to improve your health?*

Many responded with their personal health benefits (and beyond) from engaging in outdoor recreation, including *joovy*:

> *Mental health, clarity, & perspective plus quality family time. There's something about being out in the vastness of a park or learning about its history. Sometimes we all need to take a step away and listen to the world around us. #parkchat #nationalparkweek*

Response

Indeed, park visits can improve our lives and our well-being, *59nationalparks* and *joovy*; what a wonderful question-and-answer thread. A number of studies over the past few decades have documented the underlying motivations for visiting parks and participating in outdoor recreation, along with the multiple benefits that can be gained. For example, an early study of visitors to parks and outdoor recreation areas noted that many anglers returning from a day of fishing reported being highly satisfied with their activity even though they hadn't caught any fish. Similar studies of hunters found the same thing: many hunters were very satisfied with their experience even though they bagged no game. Why is that? Further research found that outdoor recreation participants choose activities to fulfill a range of motivations such as spending time in nature, getting away from the routine of work, and sharing experiences with friends and family. While it would be nice if anglers caught fish and hunters bagged game, at least occasionally, participants are often driven by a range of other more fundamental motives and can be highly satisfied with their experiences when these other motivations are realized.

These seemingly simple findings suggest a very different perspective on outdoor recreation—a revelation, really—one that focuses more directly on motivations rather than activities. In this sense, activities are a means to an end, and not necessarily an end in themselves. Related research has documented a wide range of motivations for visiting national parks and related areas and participating in a variety of outdoor recreation activities. These motivations include meeting challenges, getting exercise, taking risks, escaping crowds, enjoying scenery, finding peace and calm, developing skills, learning new things, and a host of others. This research is consistent with psychological theory which suggests that most human behavior is goal oriented or aimed at meeting some need.

Follow-up research has found that when participants in outdoor recreation fulfill at least some of their motivations, they receive a variety of benefits, and that these benefits can accrue to individuals, society at large, the economy, and the environment. For example, personal benefits from meeting a challenge might include personal growth and development, social benefits derived from an enjoyable family camping trip might lead to greater family solidarity, economic benefits from escaping the demands of everyday life might include enhanced work productivity, and environmental benefits from a wilderness hike might include greater support for environmental protection. The response above from

© Robert Manning and Elizabeth Perry 2024. *Conversations About Visiting and Managing the National Parks* (R.E. Manning and E.E Perry)
DOI: 10.1079/9781800626768.0090

joovy references many of these types of benefits. This program of research is related to the more recent development of the concept of ecosystem services described in Conversation 26; for example, being active in the out-of-doors can lead to greater human health and well-being.

This line of research is inherently interesting, but it also has potentially important implications. For example, it suggests the importance of parks and outdoor recreation to individuals and society at large. It also suggests that people should probably think carefully about their motivations for visiting national parks and related areas, and choose thoughtfully among outdoor recreation opportunities and activities that might best fulfill these motivations. A corollary is that there might be multiple activities that fulfill the same motivations, and that these activities can be substituted for one another when desired or necessary. Finally, this perspective on outdoor recreation can help park managers design opportunities for outdoor recreation that are more likely to meet the motivations of park visitors and that are more likely to lead to a variety of potential personal and societal benefits.

Reference

Manning, R.E., Budruk, M., Goonan, K., Hallo, J. and Laven, D., Lawson, S., McCown, R., Minteer, B., Newman, P., Perry, E., Pettengill, P., Reigner, N., Valliere, W., van Riper, C. and Xiao, X. (2022) *Studies in Outdoor Recreation: Search and Research for Satisfaction*, 4th edn. Oregon State University Press, Corvallis, Oregon.

91 Rationing and Allocating Visit Use

Post

This iconic photo of Yosemite Valley in Yosemite National Park was posted on Wikimedia Commons by *Thomas W.* and highlights the stunning beauty of the park as well as the types of outdoor recreation opportunities it offers:

Half Dome with Eastern Yosemite Valley, Thomas Wolf, www.foto-tw.de/ Wikimedia Commons.

Response

Thomas W.'s photo is a classic view of Yosemite Valley, one of the principal features of Yosemite National Park. Nearly sheer granite walls rise thousands of feet from the valley floor and the distinctive Half Dome is prominent on the upper right side of the photo. The photo illustrates how glaciers have carved many national park landscapes, eroding great valleys and rounding and polishing vast granite surfaces as the glaciers of the last ice age of some 10,000 years ago advanced and retreated (often many times). Half Dome may be the quintessential example in the national parks of glacial action, where these rivers of ice have dramatically cleaved this massive rounded granite dome.

The summit of Half Dome has beckoned adventurous hikers for decades and is well known as one of the most iconic hikes in all the national parks. In fact, the hike became so popular that the NPS has limited the number of hikers because of safety considerations (too many hikers on the top of the dome make it too time-consuming to evacuate the area when thunder and lightning storms approach). The hike now requires a permit that is issued through a lottery system.

An increasing number of popular attractions in the national parks—campsites, hotel rooms, hikes, ranger programs, even park entrance—are now limited and require advance arrangements. This raises the challenging issue of how to best allocate scarce recreation opportunities in the national parks. These opportunities must be allocated efficiently (i.e. employ a method that's relatively easy to use for both the public and the NPS), but must be equitable too, given the public and democratic character of the parks.

There are five basic allocation alternatives: (i) reservations; (ii) lotteries; (iii) queuing/first come, first served; (iv) pricing; and (v) merit. All are used in the National Park System and each has potential advantages and disadvantages. For example, reservation systems tend to favor visitors who are willing and able to plan ahead, but can be difficult and costly to administer. Lotteries are often viewed as eminently fair, but can also be difficult and costly to administer, and offer no advantage to visitors who are more deeply committed to the opportunity. First-come, first-served systems favor visitors who have more leisure time or who live relatively close to a park, but are relatively easy to administer. Pricing is a commonly used practice in American society to allocate scarce resources, but may discriminate against potential visitors with low incomes, and this may be considered undemocratic. Merit systems, where visitors must demonstrate their "worthiness" (e.g. their knowledge of Leave No Trace practices or technical abilities to safely

DOI: 10.1079/9781800626768.0091

climb mountains), are used sparingly, but may have the important side benefits of lowering the environmental and social impacts of use and contributing to public safety.

As demand for the national parks continues to increase, opportunities to visit them and find desired facilities and services will become more challenging. This will often require advance planning, making reservations, participating in lotteries, etc. Visitors should become familiar with the national parks they're interested in by examining their official NPS websites to determine what opportunities, facilities, and services are offered and how to access them. These arrangements must often be made at the national website, Recreation.gov (see Conversation 37). Become familiar with this website as you plan your visits and make your arrangements well in advance.

Reference

Manning, R.E., Budruk, M., Goonan, K., Hallo, J. and Laven, D., Lawson, S., McCown, R., Minteer, B., Newman, P., Perry, E., Pettengill, P., Reigner, N., Valliere, W., van Riper, C. and Xiao, X. (2022) *Studies in Outdoor Recreation: Search and Research for Satisfaction*, 4th edn. Oregon State University Press, Corvallis, Oregon.

92 Sustainable Transportation

Post

Diamond Brand shared an article by *Outside Magazine* on LinkedIn on car-free national park experiences, with the caption:

National parks are experiencing record numbers of visitors, and unfortunately for the environment, record numbers of vehicles. But that's not to say you need a car to climb El Capitan, hike Angel's Landing, or survive the hairpin turns on Glacier's Going-to-the-Sun Road. You don't. In fact, Yosemite, Zion, and Glacier are just a few of our country's national parks offering public transportation to mitigate the effects of mass tourism. #campingideas #nocarcamping #sustainablecamping #sustainability #nationalparks

Response

Yes, an increasing number of national parks are providing public transportation within park boundaries and this is an exciting development. Transportation and national parks have been inextricably linked from the very beginning of the national parks as visitors must access them from their home communities. Millions of visitors travel to, from, and within national parks each year. Moreover, many national parks include extensive networks of transportation corridors—roads, trails, bike paths, waterways, public transit—that link a vast array of attraction sites—viewpoints, historical and cultural sites, visitors centers, campgrounds, gateway communities. The inherent complexities of this intersection between transportation and national parks demand explicit management and research attention.

But transportation is more than a means of access to national parks—it can be a form of recreation itself, offering many visitors their primary opportunities to experience and enjoy the parks. For example, the iconic roads of many national parks—Going-to-the-Sun Road in Glacier National Park, Tioga Road in Yosemite National Park, Trail Ridge Road in Rocky Mountain National Park, and the Park Loop Road in Acadia National Park—were designed for visitors to experience the parks in their cars and are important manifestations of the historic and contemporary linkages between transportation and outdoor recreation. In fact, entire parks, such as Blue Ridge Parkway, have been designed specifically for this purpose. All of these roads were a response to demand for "driving for pleasure", an historically popular outdoor activity in national parks and related areas (see Conversation 40 on scenic drives in the national parks).

Transportation can be even more than this; it's also an important tool for managing national parks. The transportation networks and linkages in parks help determine where parks visitors travel (and where they don't) and can be used by park managers to help deliver the "right" number of visitors to the "right" places at the "right" times as a way of protecting park resources and the quality of the visitor experience.

A body of research has begun to explore the relationships between transportation and national parks. Some studies have addressed the environmental impacts of transportation such as wildlife disturbance. For example, a large, multidisciplinary study was conducted at Denali National Park and Preserve to help assess the potential impacts to wildlife of alternative numbers of buses that travel the Denali Park Road. The study included tracking grizzly bears and Dahl sheep (by means of radio collars) and monitoring their movements near the Denali Park Road under alternative levels of vehicle traffic. Study findings were used to help guide development of the Denali Park Road Vehicle Management Plan.

Several studies have addressed standards for crowding and conflicting recreation uses on

© Robert Manning and Elizabeth Perry 2024. *Conversations About Visiting and Managing the National Parks* (R.E. Manning and E.E Perry)
DOI: 10.1079/9781800626768.0092

multiple types of transportation corridors in the National Park System. For example, a survey of visitors driving on Acadia National Park's scenic Loop Road were shown photographs of alternative numbers of vehicles along a representative portion of the road, and respondents were asked to rate the acceptability of each photo. Resulting data suggest the maximum number of vehicles that can use the road without violating crowding-related standards of quality. The study included a similar analysis of the maximum acceptable number of hikers and bicycles on the park's carriage roads and the maximum number of riders on the park's Island Explorer shuttle buses.

As *Diamond Brand*'s post above discusses, an increasing number of national parks have established public transit systems to help limit environmental and experiential impacts of automobiles and use such transit systems as a park management tool. For example, a study at Rocky Mountain National Park determined standards for both environmental and experiential conditions at selected recreation sites in the popular Bear Lake Corridor portion of the park. A computer-based simulation model of the shuttle bus system that serves this area was then developed to help design routing and scheduling of the shuttle bus system to deliver the "right" number of visitors to the "right" sites at the "right" times in an effort to maintain high-quality environmental and experiential conditions. (See Conversation 62 about taking the bus in national parks that offer this option as a way to limit the environmental and social impacts of cars in the parks.)

Reference

Manning, R., Lawson, S., Newman, P., Hallo, J. and Monz, C. (2014) *Sustainable Transportation in the National Parks: From Acadia to Zion*. University Press of New England, Lebanon, New Hampshire.

93 Underrepresented Groups/Discrimination

Post

Sha recently visited Yosemite National Park and posted the following comments on Yelp about what he felt were several instances of racial discrimination by NPS and concession employees:

Terribly racist time at Yosemite! Blatant white supremacy and racism LIVE at Yosemite.

Response

Sha raises an increasingly vital issue in the national parks. Minority racial and ethnic groups have been substantially underrepresented in the national parks for decades. Research suggests this has happened for three reasons: (i) historic societal discrimination against these groups that has resulted in educational and economic disadvantages that diminish knowledge of the national parks and the economic means to visit them; (ii) the traditional focus of the parks (and parks research) is on the dominant white American cultural heritage as opposed to that of underrepresented groups; and (iii) the perceived interpersonal and institutional mistreatment of minority racial/ethnic groups as manifested in *Sha*'s experience at Yosemite.

The candid and painful observations of *Sha* at Yosemite, along with the research that's been conducted on this topic, are suggestive of several approaches that are beginning to successfully address this problem. For example, more national parks have been established in or near urban areas, making them more accessible and at less cost to large populations of minority racial and ethnic groups, and public transportation options are available to enhance access to potential visitors who don't own automobiles. Gateway National Recreation Area (New York City and northern New Jersey), Golden Gate National Recreation Area (San Francisco Bay area), and Cuyahoga Valley National Park (outside Cleveland and Akron) are good examples. Also more national parks have been established to celebrate the history of minority racial and ethnic groups; for example, many national parks address the American Civil Rights Movement.

Existing national parks are also being reinterpreted to develop and tell stories that recognize and honor the important roles that Black, Hispanic, Indigenous, and other minorities have played in the national parks. Yosemite is a good example of this. Award-winning NPS ranger Shelton Johnson has developed and presented a series of interpretive programs that celebrate the vital role of the Army's Buffalo Soldiers, an all-Black unit of the Cavalry, in protecting the park before the NPS was established. Little Bighorn Battlefield National Monument is another example in which a national park has been reinterpreted to offer a more balanced and inclusive story of American history. This site was originally named Custer Battlefield National Monument and focused primarily on the US Army's 7th Cavalry, but more recently the name of the site has been changed to Little Bighorn Battlefield National Monument, and a memorial to the Lakota and Cheyenne warriors who fought there has been constructed.

The NPS more broadly is reexamining its programs, policies, and staff interactions to be more proactive in promoting racial and ethnic harmony. For example, more rangers of color are being recruited to the agency, entrance fee policies should be designed to ensure they don't discriminate against selected groups, and the size of campsites might be expanded

DOI: 10.1079/9781800626768.0093

to accommodate the extended families that are often characteristic of Hispanic visitors. These are just a few of potentially many options that can help address underrepresentation of minority racial and ethnic groups in the national parks and the racially-related problems they may experience on their visits.

The NPS is keenly aware of the issues raised by *Sha* and is working to address them, and park visitation by racial and ethnic minorities is increasing. But these issues are deeply ingrained in American society and it will take some time before they're fully resolved in the national parks.

Reference

Manning, R.E., Budruk, M., Goonan, K., Hallo, J. and Laven, D., Lawson, S., McCown, R., Minteer, B., Newman, P., Perry, E., Pettengill, P., Reigner, N., Valliere, W., van Riper, C. and Xiao, X. (2022) *Studies in Outdoor Recreation: Search and Research for Satisfaction*, 4th edn. Oregon State University Press, Corvallis, Oregon.

94 International Visitors

Post

On X during the COVID-19 pandemic, *JohnDWalke* pondered his previous trips to national parks and how many international visitors he encountered:

> *During my last visit to national parks, pre-COVID – Bryce Canyon, Zion, Grand Canyon – it was striking how many international visitors there were, and how much in awe they appeared to be of America's special places & the national parks system. Can't wait to travel again.*

Response

Now that the pandemic is reasonably managed, *JohnDWalke*, we hope you and those from other countries are visiting the national parks again too. International visitors are welcome in US national parks, just as Americans can visit most national parks and related areas around the world. Many Americans travel internationally and visits to iconic places such as Ecuador's Galapagos Islands, Egypt's pyramids, Australia's Great Barrier Reef, Asia's Himalayas, and Africa's great wildlife parks are often important parts of their itineraries. In a like manner, many international visitors make a point of visiting some of the most iconic US national parks, including Yellowstone, Yosemite, Grand Canyon, Statue of Liberty, and many more. It's no wonder *JohnDWalke* notes the "awe" that these special places in the US evoke. In fact, it's estimated that more than a third of all international visitors to the US include a stop in at least one national park (though this accounts for a very small percentage of all US national park visitors, about 5%).

But what about the fees charged to international visitors? The current policy is that international visitors to US national parks pay the same entrance fees as US visitors, and international visitors can purchase annual passes to the national parks at the same cost charged to Americans (see Conversations 65 and 66 for more about national park entrance fees and passes). Is this appropriate?

Many countries charge higher entrance fees to non-residents, sometimes substantially higher, often called "dual" or "differential" pricing formats. For example, foreign tourists to the Galapagos Islands pay a fee of $200, while Ecuadorians pay a small fraction of that amount. Entry to Sagarmatha National Park in Nepal—the gateway to Mount Everest and treks in the Himalayas—costs $30 for foreigners, $15 for SAARC (South Asian Association for Regional Cooperation) nationals, and $1 for Nepalis. A recent study suggests that the NPS institute this type of "tiered" pricing system, arguing that this could raise substantial revenues for the NPS—perhaps as much as several hundred million dollars—and that this would help maintain the national parks. But given the relatively small percentage of all visitors to the US national parks represented by foreign tourists, the amount of additional money raised would be a small percentage of the NPS annual budget.

Should international visitors be charged higher entrance fees to US national parks? The primary arguments in favor of this note that foreign visitors don't pay US taxes like residents do (tax revenue is the primary source of funding for the NPS), increasing fees for foreign visitors would raise additional revenue to manage and protect the national parks, and modest increases in entrance fees for foreign visitors would be a small proportion of the total trip costs for such visitors. Primary arguments against this policy include: (i) potentially escalating "price wars" among nations; (ii) the foundational democratic character of US national parks welcoming all visitors; (iii) a national pride in sharing our national parks

© Robert Manning and Elizabeth Perry 2024. *Conversations About Visiting and Managing the National Parks* (R.E. Manning and E.E Perry)
DOI: 10.1079/9781800626768.0094

with the citizens of the world; and (iv) the administrative challenges of determining the nationality of national park visitors. So, should international visitors be charged higher entrance fees to US national parks? What do you think?

References

Repanshek, K. (2024) Traveler's view: Should international national park visitors be charged more. *National Parks Traveler, 5 January*. Available at: https://www.nationalparkstraveler.org/2024/01/travelers-view-should-international-national-park-visitors-be-charged-more (accessed 16 July 2024).

Watkins, T. (2023) How overseas visitors can help steward our national parks. *PERC*. Available at: https://www.perc.org/2023/12/21/how-international-visitors-can-help-steward-our-national-parks/ (accessed 16 July 2024).

95 Park-Dependent Recreation

Post

Torrey J. recently used Yelp to post the following review of Badger Pass Ski Area in Yosemite National Park:

> *Badger Pass Ski Area truly rules! While this ski area is on the smaller side, there really is something for everyone here.*

Response

Thanks for this posting, *Torrey J.*—we think some readers might be surprised that there's an alpine (downhill) ski area in this iconic national park. Given the scenery it offers skiers, it's no wonder you reviewed your experience very positively. But this raises the question of what types of recreation activities are appropriate in national parks (and what aren't). Let's talk about this ...

In Part 1 of this book, Conversation 12 discussed the central role of recreation in the national parks, noting that the National Park System is sometimes called "America's Playground". In Part 2, several conversations described the major types of recreation activities that are especially popular in the national parks. But does this mean that all types of outdoor recreation are appropriate in the National Park System? How about golf? Tennis?

Some observers have approached this issue by suggesting that only certain types of recreation should be offered in the national parks, describing these activities as "park dependent". These are recreation activities that focus on the underlying purpose of the parks and that often require the size and naturalness that are featured in many national parks; other forms of recreation that don't require these qualities should be accommodated elsewhere.

Joe Sax, a Professor at the University of Michigan, wrote a small but powerful book several decades ago that raised and discussed this issue. The book, *Mountains Without Handrails: Reflections on the National Parks* (Sax, 1980), introduced the concept of "reflective recreation", activities that encourage visitors to focus on the underlying purpose of the national parks—preservation of natural and cultural environments that help tell the story of America. He used words and phrases such as "self-directed", "engaged activities", "unmediated experiences", and "engagement with nature" to explain his thinking, concluding that recreation in the national parks had a moral component to it in which we focus on the natural and cultural resources the parks were established to protect. His thinking was an outgrowth of the writings of iconic American landscape architect Frederick Law Olmstead, who was instrumental in management of Yosemite Valley before it was established as a national park, and who described national parks as places "to stir the contemplative faculty" (Sax, 1980). Sax and Olmstead both implicitly suggest the "re-creation" roots of the contemporary word "recreation".

The NPS has sometimes struggled with this issue, and the history with Yosemite National Park is a good case study. For example, the NPS allowed construction of a golf course in the park in 1918, and it still offers this activity. Yes, this is a lovely place to play golf, but in hindsight many people would argue that this iconic national park isn't an appropriate place for a golf course and there are lots of opportunities to play golf in attractive locations outside the park. There's only one Yosemite National Park and it should be reserved for activities that are more park oriented and "dependent", such as hiking and camping. This thinking is based on the fact that activities such as hiking and camping are focused more directly on experiencing and appreciating the park's distinctive natural and cultural history.

© Robert Manning and Elizabeth Perry 2024. *Conversations About Visiting and Managing the National Parks* (R.E. Manning and E.E Perry)
DOI: 10.1079/9781800626768.0095

The same might be said about Badger Pass Ski Area that was constructed in the heart of Yosemite National Park in 1935. This alpine ski area still offers fine opportunities for skiing (as *Torrey J.* describes in his post) , but there are many ski areas in the Sierra Nevada Mountains. Yosemite probably shouldn't devote part of this rare and magnificent national park to a recreation activity that can readily be found outside the park and isn't focused on the natural and cultural resources for which the park was established.

A third example is more contentious: the lovely and historic Ahwahnee hotel in Yosemite Valley. This is one of the grand lodges constructed in several early national parks to attract visitors (see Conversation 68 for more about this). Some people would argue that the hotel is an historic resource that should be protected, and that has a lot of validity. Nevertheless, the hotel offers a degree of luxury that's not affordable to most park visitors and that emphasizes facilities and services that are an attraction in and of themselves and have little or no connection to the park. As noted in Conversation 70, most of the hotels and associated commercial facilities and services in the national parks are operated by private companies (called concessioners), and the company that recently managed the Ahwahnee hotel advertised it as follows:

> It's not just another American convention hotel ... It's a great American castle ... All your worldly needs are provided for ... when you go the barber or the hairdresser or the gift shops ... This isn't no-man's land. Or primitive wilderness. This is civilization.
>
> (Sax, 1976)

This seems inappropriate.

Other examples of this type of issue are more obvious. For example, from about 1890 until World War II, grizzly bears at Yellowstone National Park gathered each evening at the park's garbage dump to feed, and this became an especially popular visitor attraction. The NPS even constructed bleachers (stands) for visitors to watch the artificial gathering of park wildlife. Of course, this was ultimately discontinued (and the park's garbage trucked out of the park) because it was not consistent with the park's wilderness character and for the detrimental effects it had on the park's bear population. Similarly, the "Yosemite Firefall" was conducted each evening at Yosemite from 1872 to 1968. Each evening, a bonfire was constructed at Glacier Point, high above Yosemite Valley, and the large bed of glowing embers was pushed over the cliff to create a "glowing waterfall" for the entertainment of visitors in the Valley. This spectacle ended when it became clear that it was an inappropriate attraction for a national park.

The issue of what recreation activities (and associated facilities and services) are appropriate (or not) in the national parks can be challenging and can shift over time as ecological and cultural knowledge and sensibilities evolve. But Professor Sax offers us a filter that can be useful in thinking about this: to what degree do these activities focus on the underlying purpose of national parks and the natural and cultural resources they were established to protect? Indeed, what recreation activities and associated facilities and services are most "park dependent" and have the highest claim in our National Park System? The title of Sax's book, *Mountains without Handrails*, is a metaphor: what recreation activities invite us to enjoy and appreciate the parks on their own terms, with as little mediation (i.e. facilities and services) as possible? Though he didn't suggest this, he might have agreed that "recreation" isn't even the best term to describe our activities in the national parks as it may be too suggestive of pure "entertainment".

References

Miles, J. (2020) Essay: Revisiting mountains without handrails. *National Parks Traveler*, May 31. Available at: https://www.nationalparkstraveler.org/2020/05/essay-revisiting-mountains-without-handrails (accessed 16 July 2024).

Sax, J. (1980) *Mountains Without Handrails: Reflections on the National Parks*. University of Michigan Press, Ann Arbor, Michigan.

Sax, J.L. (1976) America's national parks: Their principles, purposes, and prospects. *Natural History*. Available at: https://www.naturalhistorymag.com/picks-from-the-past/271452/america-s-national-parks-their-principles-purposes-and-prospects (accessed 23 July 2024).

What You Can Do to Help the National Parks

96 Be a National Park Steward

Post

Citizen scientists lend their insights and enthusiasm to helping the National Park Service (NPS) expand datasets that their staff alone couldn't maintain. A YouTube video by *hike734* highlights such an experience:

> *A really great program in Glacier National Park for wannabe biologists such as myself is the Citizen Science Program which is part of the Crown of the Continent Research Learning Center. This program is partially funded by my sponsor, the Glacier National Park Fund and is a great way for folks to get involved with some real science.*

Response

The national parks were established to protect vital natural and cultural resources and to offer outstanding recreation opportunities, but they need our help. We're fortunate to have a National Park System that includes more than 400 areas (e.g. national parks, national monuments, national historic sites) totaling more than 85 million acres, but the NPS is a small agency of only about 20,000 employees (about the same size staff as Disney World!) and receives annual funding of less than 1/15th of 1% of the federal budget. This has led to an accumulating list of deferred maintenance in the parks that's in the billions of dollars. The parks face a host of issues, including loss of biodiversity, habitat fragmentation, intensive development on park borders, invasive species, crumbling infrastructure, limited staff, impacts to park resources and the quality of the visitor experience caused by increasing visitation, estrangement of many young people from nature, and underrepresentation of selected racial and ethnic groups as visitors.

Perhaps the two most pressing issues are climate change and social change. As we continue to burn vast quantities of fossil fuels, the resulting warmer and less stable climate fundamentally threatens the integrity of our National Park System. Greenhouse gasses lead to a cascade of environmental consequences, including melting glaciers and ice packs, rising sea levels, more frequent weather extremes, more intense wildfires, and species extinctions. Climate models suggest that: (i) glaciers in Glacier National Park will disappear within the next few decades; (ii) namesake plants in Joshua Tree National Park and Saguaro National Park may soon be unsustainable; (iii) freshwater wetlands in Everglades National Park may be contaminated by massive saltwater intrusion; (iv) coral reefs at Virgin Islands National Park and others may die from bleaching; and (v) wildfires in many national parks will increase in frequency and intensity.

We're also undergoing substantial social change. Our population continues to rise, but just as importantly, it's becoming substantially more diverse, and the National Park System must adapt accordingly. Existing parks must be reinterpreted to tell more inclusive stories; for example, the role of the African American Buffalo Soldiers in protecting the national parks in their formative years should be told throughout the National Park System. Also new parks must be added that tell the stories of more culturally diverse people, including African Americans, Hispanics, Indigenous peoples, youth, the LGBTIQA + community, and others. Society has also become more polarized and divisive, and national parks can help bring us back together; there's a long history of support for the national parks among the American people and across the aisles of Congress that can help combat growing partisanship and incivility. This is a function of the fundamental democratic character of the national park idea.

© Robert Manning and Elizabeth Perry 2024. *Conversations About Visiting and Managing the National Parks* (R.E. Manning and E.E Perry)
DOI: 10.1079/9781800626768.0096

This is a big agenda and the national parks and the NPS need our help to facilitate this work. As the YouTube video and description above relate, *hike734* answered that call by volunteering to help conduct a program of citizen science in the national parks. Fortunately, there are a number of partner groups that help support the national parks, including friends groups, volunteers, concessioners, universities, and generous donors (we like to call these people and entities "parkners" and "parknerships"). But ultimately, it's up to all of us who love the national parks to support them. Rachel Carson, author of *Silent Spring*, an exposé of the environmental impacts of DDT (dichlorodiphenyltrichloroethane) and other pesticides, wrote that "no carefree love of the planet is now possible" (cited in Manning *et al.*, 2016, p. 275), and this message should resonate with all of us who love the national parks: if we love them, then we must help care for them.

There's a long and storied history of individual championship of national parks: (i) Theodore Roosevelt using his presidential powers to create so many national parks; (ii) the Rockefeller family's gifts of land and money to form and expand a number of national parks; (iii) more ordinary people such as John Muir (who once modestly described himself as "an unknown nobody"; cited in Manning, 2024) and his campaign to create Yosemite National Park; (iv) Enos Mills and his support for Rocky Mountain National Park; and (v) Marjorie Stoneman Douglas whose book, *The Everglades: River of Grass* (1947), was instrumental in establishing Everglades National Park.

All of us can be national park heroes by:

- volunteering to maintain trails or staff visitor centers;
- welcoming visitors from underrepresented racial and ethnic groups;
- participating in programs of citizen science by monitoring ecologically and culturally sensitive sites;
- joining friends groups and philanthropic organizations such as the National Park Foundation, National Parks Conservation Association, and local equivalents;
- living our lives in ways that decrease the need for more and more natural resources; and
- considering the welfare of the national parks when voting in local, state and national elections.

More ways to support national parks are often posted on national park websites at "Get Involved". Think about how you can best support the national parks and exercise your responsibility as a national park steward.

References

Manning, R. (2024) On Earth Day, Americans need to step up and protect their national parks. *San Francisco Chronicle*. Available at: https://www.sfchronicle.com/opinion/openforum/article/earth-day-national-parks-19409050.php (accessed 24 July 2024).

Manning, R., Diamant, R., Mitchell, N. and Harmon, D. (2016) A national park system for the 21st century. In: Manning, R., Diamant, R., Mitchell, N. and Harmon, D. (eds) *A Thinking Person's Guide to America's National Parks*. Braziller Publishers, New York, pp. 261–278.

Stoneman Douglas, M. (1947) *The Everglades: River of Grass*. Pineapple Press, Sarasota, Florida.

97 Be a Friend of the National Parks

Post

"Friends groups" sometimes step in for more-than-the-usual support, such as *Emma G.* wrote about on X during a recent federal government shutdown:

In Tucson, it's the community who stepped up to take care of Saguaro National Park during the shutdown. I talked to the Executive Director of Friends of Saguaro National Park yesterday about what the nonprofit does to keep the park clean.

Response

Conversation 96 discusses becoming a volunteer with the National Park Service, including the ways in which it can make such important contributions to the national parks, as well as the many personal benefits it offers. The NPS is thinly funded and staffed, and it needs all the help it can get. There are other ways to contribute to the national parks as well, including joining in the work of one of the more than 200 non-profit, philanthropic organizations that partner with the national parks nationwide. In the official parlance of the NPS, many of these non-profit organizations are known as "cooperating associations" and have developed formal agreements with the parks they partner with. More informally, these organizations are known as "friends groups"; consider joining these organizations and becoming a "friend" of the national parks in the process. *Emma G.*'s posting above references the good work of the Friends of Saguaro National Park that assisted with vital park functions (e.g. educating visitors, cleaning restrooms) when NPS staff were unable to work during the 2019 federal government shutdown.

The work that friends do for the parks is nearly as diverse as the National Park System itself. For example, you can: (i) volunteer at visitor centers to help visitors plan their activities; (ii) conduct trail maintenance; (iii) help reconstruct historic buildings; (iv) assist with fieldwork of park scientists; (v) help organize park archives; (vi) work in a park bookstore; (vii) help administer the NPS Junior Ranger Program; (viii) restore park habitat; and (ix) support educational and interpretive programming. In all these ways, and more, you can help protect park resources and enhance visitor understanding, knowledge, and appreciation of national parks. Of course, if time doesn't allow, you can donate to these organizations to further their mission and objectives.

The National Park Foundation (NPF) is the largest of the NPS friends groups. It was established by Congress in 1967 as the official charity of America's national parks and non-profit partner to the NPS. NPF raises private funds to help protect the National Park System through critical conservation and preservation efforts. The organization also runs a host of programs that connect people with their natural and cultural heritage, and engage the next generation of park stewards. Find out more and become a part of the national park community at the NPF link, National Park Foundation (2024), in the References at the end of this conversation.

Two examples of friends groups that are associated more specifically with a particular national park are Friends of Acadia and Golden Gate National Parks Conservancy. Acadia National Park, established in 1919, protects 47,000 acres in Maine that includes rugged coastline, granite mountains, unique cultural resources, scarce communities of plant and animal life, brilliant night skies, and a host of outdoor recreation opportunities. The close proximity of the park to large population centers means that it's heavily visited and needs careful management attention. Friends of Acadia (friendsofacadia.org) helps support and expand the programs of the NPS such as

© Robert Manning and Elizabeth Perry 2024. *Conversations About Visiting and Managing the National Parks* (R.E. Manning and E.E Perry)
DOI: 10.1079/9781800626768.0097

the Ridge Runners, a group of park employees and volunteers who help educate visitors about Leave No Trace practices (see Conversation 60).

Golden Gate National Recreation Area is a more recent park, established in 1972. Located in the San Francisco Bay area, this sprawling park protects a great variety of natural and cultural resources, including iconic Muir Woods, Alcatraz Island, Crissy Field, the Marin Headlands, Stinson Beach, Lands End, and the historic Presidio. The park offers outstanding outdoor recreation opportunities to the residents of this large metropolitan region, and is now one of the most heavily visited units of the National Park System. Golden Gate National Parks Conservancy (parksconservancy.org) helps protect this vital national park through a suite of programs that are administered by professional staff and a host of volunteers. Consider joining this progressive and effective friends group.

Gifts can also be made directly to the NPS. Donations can be directed to the general needs of the National Park System or a specific park, in support of a specific program or project. Donations are tax deductible under section 170(c)(1) of the Internal Revenue Code. Checks should be made out to the NPS and should include a covering letter specifying whether the gift is intended to support the overall work of the NPS or a specific program area. Checks can be sent to: National Park Service Accounting Operations Center, c/o RDMT Deposits, 13461 Sunrise Valley Drive, Herndon, VA 20171. The NPS is often asked how to bequeath all or part of an estate to the agency. The following language may be included in a will: "to the National Park Service, an agency of the United States of America, Washington, D.C. 20240, for the support of its programs and activities."

Thanks for being a friend of the national parks!

References

Find Your Park (n.d.) Friends Groups. Available at: https://findyourpark.com/get-involved/friends-groups (accessed July 2024).
National Park Foundation (2024). Available at: www.nationalparks.org (accessed 16 July 2024).

98 Volunteering

Post

Volunteers with the Juan Bautista de Anza National Historic Trail can serve as a Trails and Rails docent, interacting with the public on scenic train rides along the California coast (part of the historic trail's route). Prospective volunteers complete a training day before serving, as *Steve* enthused about on X:

> *Tomorrow, my wife and I are going for training to be NPS volunteer docents on the rails and I couldn't be more excited.*

Response

There are lots of reasons to volunteer: (i) it's a way to contribute to the causes you believe are important; (ii) you learn a lot about what you're interested in; (iii) it can reduce stress and makes you healthier; (iv) it promotes personal growth and self-esteem; (v) it can help strengthen your community; (vi) it encourages civic responsibility; and (vii) it's a way to give back to your community. Maybe most important of all, it can make a difference! If you enjoy visiting the national parks and think they're important, consider volunteering in the national parks. As the NPS is severely underfunded and thinly staffed, the agency needs volunteers to help manage and protect the parks. There are lots of good opportunities to volunteer in the national parks.

There's a long history of voluntarism in the national parks going all the way back to the establishment of Yellowstone National Park in 1872 and creation of the NPS in 1916. Private citizens have played important roles in managing and protecting the parks and in helping people enjoy their visits to the parks. This heritage of volunteers was formalized in 1969 with Congressional passage of the Volunteers

in Parks Act. Now, hundreds of thousands of Volunteers-in-Parks (VIPS) serve in nearly every aspect of park operations and management. You can volunteer for a day or up to a year or more, and can work close to home or at a distant park you haven't yet visited. In the case of those looking to be a Trails and Rails docent on the Juan Bautista de Anza National Historic Trail like *Steve*, volunteers commit to at least two day trips per year, riding the train and engaging passengers in discussion, adding to their park experience. Examples of other volunteer activities include:

- maintain trails and historic buildings;
- assist park staff on research projects;
- serve as the official "host" of a campground;
- swear in Junior Rangers;
- staff visitor centers, helping people plan their visits and answering questions;
- help conduct guided walks and campfire talks; and
- staff park libraries, archives, and museum collections.

Get started by reading the NPS website on volunteering, National Park Service (2024a), listed in the References at the end of the conversation; be sure to watch the short video on the website. The volunteering news website, National Park Service (2024b), is also useful and includes lots of examples of volunteer positions and projects. There's even a *Volunteers-in-Parks Reference Manual* that's useful to NPS employees, partners, and volunteers.

To find a volunteer opportunity, follow these steps:

1. Visit Volunteer.gov (2024) and see current volunteer opportunities for the NPS and other agencies. You can search by park, state, or activity.
2. Visit the volunteer webpage for a specific national park by logging onto the official

DOI: 10.1079/9781800626768.0098

NPS website of the park you're interested in and then clicking on the "Get Involved" option.
3. Explore the NPS special Volunteer Programs website, National Park Service (2023b), to find volunteer activities focused on special programs, interest groups, and activities. Examples include Girl Scouts and Boy Scouts, citizen science, National Parks BioBlitz, Community Volunteer Ambassador Program, International Volunteers-in-Parks, and the Artist-in-Residence Program.
4. Participate in a volunteer event, see National Park Service (2023a) for the Volunteer Events Calendar. These are held regularly at many parks; examples include the Birthday of Martin Luther King, Jr., National Volunteer Week, Earth Day, National Trails Day, 9/11 Remembrance and Service, and National Public Lands Day.

If you decide to volunteer, follow these steps:

1. Apply to a current volunteer opportunity at the website: Volunteer.gov.
2. Receive confirmation of your volunteer position provided by your supervisor.
3. Complete the required volunteer paperwork (provided by your supervisor).
4. Complete the "onboarding" process that will be explained by your supervisor.
5. Report your contributions (e.g. hours worked, activities, accomplishments) to your supervisor.

In addition to the satisfaction of contributing to the work of managing and protecting the national parks, volunteers with a minimum of 250 service hours are eligible for an annual Volunteer Pass to the National Park System (see Conversation 66 for more on entrance passes). There's also an award program for volunteers that applies to individuals, youth, groups, volunteer programs, and lifetime achievement.

References

National Park Service (2023a) Volunteer with Us – Volunteer Events Calendar. Available at: https://www.nps.gov/subjects/volunteer/vip-events.htm (accessed 16 July 2024).
National Park Service (2023b) Volunteer with Us – Volunteer Programs. Available at: https://www.nps.gov/subjects/volunteer/programs.htm (accessed 16 July 2024).
National Park Service (2024a) Volunteer with Us. Available at: https://www.nps.gov/getinvolved/volunteer.htm (accessed 16 July 2024).
National Park Service (2024b) Volunteer with Us – News & Stories. Available at: https://www.nps.gov/subjects/volunteer/news.htm (accessed 16 July 2024).
Volunteer.gov (2024) Federal Volunteer Opportunities. Available at: https://www.volunteer.gov (accessed 16 July 2024).

99 Work for the NPS

Post

Matthew promoted an open position in the NPS on LinkedIn, sharing:

The Outdoors can be your Office. Do you enjoy being outside? Does helping people motivate you? Are you interested in a rewarding job on a dynamic team? Consider working for the National Park Service in Chiricahua National Monument as a Park Ranger focused on Preventative Search and Rescue (PSAR). This full-time, entry-level position is open for the next four days or the first 50 candidates. Details on the position and application process are available on USAJobs.

Response

There's been a long legacy of appreciation of the national parks leading to efforts to help protect them. We suggest ways to do this in Conversations 97 and 98 by working with "friends groups" associated with the national parks and volunteering in the national parks. But you can take this to a whole new level by working for the NPS! The agency has a workforce of about 20,000 employees (that may sound like a lot, but it's not nearly enough to manage the more than 400 national parks, the more than 85 million acres of land that they include, and the more than 300 million annual visits they accommodate; moreover, many employees are only seasonal).

The largest number and most iconic type of NPS employees are national park "rangers", and they have a well-deserved reputation for their efforts in managing the parks' natural and cultural resources and assisting park visitors. *Matthew* emphasizes the appeal of such positions in the opening line of his above posting: "The Outdoors can be your Office". Rangers are generally divided into two types: (i) interpreters (see Conversation 52); and (ii) law enforcement rangers. But the NPS also includes many other types of employees, including mechanics, engineers, office staff, historians, natural resource specialists, museum curators, scientists, firefighters, search and rescue personnel, and many others. Given the size and diversity of the National Park System, employees work in a great variety of locations, including remote natural areas, urban parks, regional offices scattered around the country, and the national office in Washington, DC.

All open permanent and seasonal positions with the NPS are listed on the website, USAJobs. This site also includes internship and volunteer opportunities; completing one of these can help qualify you for seasonal and permanent positions. Seasonal positions for the summer are usually posted between October and February, and seasonal positions for parks that are visited primarily during the winter (e.g. Everglades National Park) are usually posted in July and August. Some of the more popular national parks often receive hundreds of applications for only a handful of positions, so consider some of the less well-known and smaller national parks. Some positions, like the one advertised in the above posting by *Matthew*, are limited to those who apply quickly. Qualified veterans can be given higher priority. The NPS is also committed to increasing the cultural diversity of its staff and draws from all segments of society.

Another path to employment in the NPS is through an increasing number of college and university programs in parks, outdoor recreation, forestry, wildlife management, and related departments. These are usually 4-year degree programs for students with defined interests in professional careers with the NPS and related agencies and organizations.

© Robert Manning and Elizabeth Perry 2024. *Conversations About Visiting and Managing the National Parks* (R.E. Manning and E.E Perry)
DOI: 10.1079/9781800626768.0099

For more information, including profiles of NPS employees and associated videos, see the NPS websites noted below (National Park Service, 2023, 2024; USAJobs, 2024).

References

National Park Service (2023) Applying for a Job with the National Park Service. Available at: https://www.nps.gov/aboutus/how-to-apply.htm (accessed 17 July 2024).

National Park Service (2024) Become a Law Enforcement Ranger. Available at: https://www.nps.gov/aboutus/become-a-law-enforcement-ranger.htm (accessed 17 July 2024).

USAJobs (2024) National Park Service Open Positions. Available at: https://www.usajobs.gov/Search?a=IN10 (accessed 17 July 2024).

100 National Park Heroes and Heroines

Post

A recent string of comments on Reddit was initiated by *themanwithahorse*, who posted the following:

> *Big thanks to President Teddy Roosevelt for establishing the first national parks!*

Response

Thanks for your post, *themanwithahorse*—it's very generous and appropriate for us to express our thanks to the people who were instrumental in establishing and protecting our national parks, and TR should be high on this list (though we clarify a few things about this below). The National Park System tells many of the stories of the nation's natural and cultural history and features many heroes and heroines in the process. These heroes and heroines can be thought of in three basic categories: (i) the people who have been instrumental in establishing and managing the parks; (ii) the heroic figures in American history that are honored in the national parks; and (iii) ordinary citizens like most of us who care about the parks and do what we can for them.

Let's begin with those who have played foundational roles in the national parks. Certainly, John Muir would be on most people's list, as he's often called the father of the national park idea. Muir was a prodigious hiker in the Sierra Nevada Mountains of California in the late 19th and early 20th centuries, and vigorously campaigned for establishing Yosemite National Park. His powerful writing and speaking were instrumental in the crusade for this national park and others, and he remains an inspirational figure in the national parks and conservation more broadly. (It must be noted,

however, that recent scholarship has found some disappointingly bigoted writing by Muir about the Indigenous peoples who occupied the Sierra Nevada Mountains, home of his beloved Yosemite.) President Theodore Roosevelt was a contemporary of Muir and is generally considered the "conservation president", helping to establish five national parks (though they were early national parks, they weren't the first parks as *themanwithahorse* suggests) and signing the landmark Antiquities Act which led to establishment of many national monuments and national parks (see Conversation 5 on the Antiquities Act).

Stephen Mather, Horace Albright, and George Melendez Wright were early and iconic leaders of the NPS. Mather was a wealthy industrialist who lobbied for establishment of the NPS and was appointed its first director, aggressively advancing the national park idea and making the national parks more accessible. Horace Albright was Mather's assistant and eventually director of the NPS, successfully carrying on expansion of the National Park System. Wright was a wildlife biologist and named by Albright as the first chief of the newly established NPS Wildlife Division and was a strong advocate for integrating science into national park management.

The national parks have benefited substantially from wealthy families and individuals through donations of land and money. Perhaps the best example is the Rockefeller family, who contributed land and funds that helped establish several national parks, including Acadia, Great Smoky Mountains, Grand Teton, and Virgin Islands.

But many national parks benefited from the passion and work of more ordinary citizens from all walks of life. Enos Mills came from a family of homesteaders and had only a rudimentary education, but his support of Rocky Mountain National Park was instrumental in its

© Robert Manning and Elizabeth Perry 2024. *Conversations About Visiting and Managing the National Parks* (R.E. Manning and E.E Perry)
DOI: 10.1079/9781800626768.0100

establishment. Marjorie Stoneman Douglas was a journalist whose book, *The Everglades: River of Grass* (1947), advanced the movement to establish Everglades National Park, the first to be created for primarily ecological reasons. Virginia McClurg and Lucy Peabody were among the "Mothers of Mesa Verde National Park", helping to found the Colorado Cliff Dwellers Association that worked to establish this early cultural national park. Captain Charles Young was only the third African American to graduate from West Point and helped lead the Army's iconic Buffalo Soldiers that protected the early national parks before the NPS was established. Mardy Murie worked alongside her more famous wildlife biologist husband, Olaus Murie, to guide establishment and management of national parks for their wildlife values.

A second category of national park heroes and heroines include the large number of Americans, some luminaries and others less well known, who are celebrated in the National Park System. Examples include:

- George Washington (George Washington Birthplace National Monument, Independence National Historical Park, Washington Monument, and others);
- Abraham Lincoln (Abraham Lincoln Birthplace National Historical Park, Lincoln Memorial, Gettysburg National Military Park);
- Harriet Tubman, known as the "conductor" of the Underground Railroad (Harriet Tubman National Historical Park);
- Captain Meriwether Lewis and Second Lieutenant William Clark who led the Lewis and Clark Expedition (Lewis and Clark National Historical Park);
- César E. Chávez who promoted agricultural laborers' rights and worker justice (César E. Chávez National Monument);
- civil rights activist Martin Luther King, Jr. (Martin Luther King, Jr. National Historical Park); and
- all the national battlefields, monuments, and memorials dedicated to those who

fought for our nation (e.g. Saratoga National Historical Park, Vicksburg National Military Park, World War II Memorial, Vietnam Veterans Memorial).

These are just a few of many such people and associated parks.

The third category of national park heroes and heroines includes all of us who volunteer our support for the national parks by: (i) maintaining trails; (ii) staffing visitor centers; (iii) participating in programs of citizen science by monitoring ecologically and culturally sensitive sites; and (iv) joining friends groups and philanthropic organizations such as the National Park Foundation, the National Parks Conservation Association, and friends groups associated with many individual national parks. We can welcome and encourage visits to the national parks from underrepresented racial and ethnic groups. We can all live in ways that decrease the need for more and more natural resources and consumption of fossil fuels, and consider the welfare of the national parks when voting in local, state, and national elections.

One of the reasons the national parks resonate so powerfully is their foundational democratic character: They're established to ensure access to these special places by all Americans. This in turn suggests that each of us is obligated to contribute to their welfare. As society has become more polarized and divisive, protecting our parks can be the cause that helps combat growing partisanship and incivility. Ultimately, no matter your politics, it's up to those who love national parks to support them (see Conversations 96 and 97 on being a steward and friend of the national parks).

In 1962, Rachel Carson, author of *Silent Spring*, an exposé of the environmental impacts of DDT and other pesticides, wrote that "no carefree love of the planet is now possible" (cited in Manning *et al.*, 2016, p. 275). Her words ring true now more than ever: If we love the national parks, then we must help care for them.

References

Brulliard, N. (2020) These 10 National Parks Wouldn't Exist Without Women. National Parks Conservation Association, March 1. Available at: https://www.npca.org/articles/1478-these-10-national-parks-wo uldn-t-exist-without-women (accessed 14 July 2024).

Manning, R., Diamant, R., Mitchell, N. and Harmon, D. (2016) A national park system for the 21st century. In: Manning, R., Diamant, R., Mitchell, N. and Harmon, D. (eds) *A Thinking Person's Guide to America's National Parks*. Braziller Publishers, New York, pp. 261–278.

National Park Service (2017) American Heroes Celebrated in National Parks. Available at: https://www.np s.gov/orgs/1207/07-28-2017-american-heroes.htm (accessed 17 July 2024).

Public Broadcasting Service (PBS) (2024) A film by Ken Burns *The National Parks: America's Best Idea*. Meet the People. Available at: https://www.pbs.org/kenburns/the-national-parks/meet-the-people (accessed 17 July 2024).

Stoneman Douglas, M. (1947) *The Everglades: River of Grass*. Pineapple Press, Sarasota, Florida.

Bibliography

_____

National Park Service Websites

The following National Park Service websites are listed alphabetically according to the article title so information about a specific aspect can be easily located. All these websites were accessed on July 17 2024.

7 Ways to Safely Watch Wildlife (2020) Available at: www.nps.gov/subjects/watchingwildlife/7ways.htm.

Accessibility (2024) Available at: https://www.nps.gov/aboutus/accessibility.htm.

Advice from a Ranger: Visiting National Parks with Kids (2020) Available at: https://www.nps.gov/articles/visiting-national-parks-with-kids.htm.

Alternative Transportation Program (2020) Available at: https://www.nps.gov/orgs/1548/multimodal-transportation.htm.

America the Beautiful-The National Parks and Federal Recreational Lands Access Pass (2022) Available at: https://www.nps.gov/subjects/accessibility/interagency-access-pass.htm.

American Heroes Celebrated in National Parks (2017) Available at: https://www.nps.gov/orgs/1207/07-28-2017-american-heroes.htm.

American Indian Heritage (2021) Available at: www.nps.gov/subjects/americanindians/index.htm.

America's Wilderness Webisode Series (2023) Available at: https://www.nps.gov/subjects/wilderness/multimedia.htm.

Applying for a Job with the National Park Service (2023) Available at: https://www.nps.gov/aboutus/how-to-apply.htm.

Arrowhead Artwork (2022) Available at: https://www.nps.gov/subjects/hfc/arrowhead-artwork.htm.

Arts in the Parks (2022) Available at: https://www.nps.gov/subjects/arts/index.htm.

Be Prepared for Your Activity in the Park! (2024) Available at: www.nps.gov/subjects/healthandsafety/prepare-for-your-activity.htm.

Become a Junior Ranger (2024) Available at: www.nps.gov/kids/become-a-junior-ranger.htm.

Become a Law Enforcement Ranger (2024) Available at: https://www.nps.gov/aboutus/become-a-law-enforcement-ranger.htm.

Biking (2024) Available at: https://www.nps.gov/subjects/biking/visit.htm.

Civil Rights in America (2024) Available at: https://www.nps.gov/subjects/civilrights/index.htm.

Climate Change and Your National Parks (2023) Available at: https://www.nps.gov/subjects/climatechange/index.htm.

Climate Change in National Parks (2023) Available at: https://www.nps.gov/subjects/climatechange/upload/2023-03-03-UPDATE-CC-Unigrid-compliant.pdf.

Climate Friendly Parks Program (2024) Available at: https://www.nps.gov/subjects/climatechange/cfp-program.htm.

Concessions Accessibility (2023) Available at: https://www.nps.gov/subjects/concessions/access.htm.

Digital Stories (2019) Available at: https://www.nps.gov/subjects/digital/digital-stories.htm.

Educator Resources (2024) Available at: www.nps.gov/teachers/index.htm.

Educators (2024) Available at: www.nps.gov/learn.

Entrance Fees by Park (2024) Available at: https://www.nps.gov/aboutus/entrance-fee-prices.htm.

Entrance Passes (2024) Available at: https://www.nps.gov/planyourvisit/passes.htm.

Fish & Fishing (2022) Available at: https://www.nps.gov/subjects/fishing/fishing-in-parks.htm.

Foundations of Interpretation Curriculum Content Narrative (2007) Available at: https://www.nps.gov/idp/interp/101/foundationscurriculum.pdf.

Full List of Theme Studies (2024) Available at: https://www.nps.gov/subjects/nationalhistoriclandmarks/full-list-of-theme-studies.htm.

Gold Star Family Voucher (n.d.) Available at: https://www.nps.gov/customcf/goldstar/voucher.htm.

Green Parks (2023) Available at: www.nps.gov/subjects/sustainability/green-parks.htm.

Historic Preservation Training Center (2022) Available at: https://www.nps.gov/orgs/1098/index.htm.

Horseback Riding and Stock Use (2023) Available at: www.nps.gov/subjects/stockuse/visit.htm.

Hunting (2023) Available at: https://www.nps.gov/subjects/hunting/visit.htm.

Leave No Trace Seven Principles (2024) Available at: https://www.nps.gov/articles/leave-no-trace-seven-principles.htm.

Multimedia Search (n.d.) Available at: https://www.nps.gov/media/multimedia-search.htm.

Multimedia Search – Webcams (n.d.) Available at: https://www.nps.gov/media/multimedia-search.htm#sort=Date_Last_Modified+desc&fq%5B%5D=Type%3A%22Webcam%22.

Museum Collections (n.d.) Available at: https://museum.nps.gov/ParkIndex.aspx.

Museum Management Program (n.d.) Available at: https://www.nps.gov/museum/index.html.

Museum Management Program (2020) Available at: https://www.nps.gov/orgs/1454/index.htm.

National Park System (2024) Available at: https://www.nps.gov/aboutus/national-park-system.htm.

National Park System Designations (2017) Available at: https://www.nps.gov/articles/nps-designations.htm.

National Parks Protect our Ocean and Coasts (2022) Available at: https://www.nps.gov/subjects/oceans/index.htm.

National Parks with Wilderness (2024) Available at: https://www.nps.gov/subjects/wilderness/wilderness-parks.htm.

NPGallery Digital Asset Management System (n.d.) Available at: https://npgallery.nps.gov.

NPS Data API (2019) Available at: www.nps.gov/subjects/digital/nps-data-api.htm.

NPS Disability History Series (2024) Available at: https://www.nps.gov/articles/disability-history-series-introduction.htm.

NPS Uniform Collection FAQs (2024) Available at: https://www.nps.gov/subjects/hfc/nps-uniform-collection-faqs.htm.

Office of International Affairs (2023) Available at: https://www.nps.gov/orgs/1955/index.htm.

Park Landforms (2019) Available at: https://www.nps.gov/subjects/geology/landforms.htm.

Pets (2023) Available at: www.nps.gov/subjects/pets/index.htm.

Places to Get Interagency Passes (2024) Available at: www.nps.gov/planyourvisit/pickup-pass-locations.htm.

Plan Your Vacation Like a Park Ranger (2024) Available at: https://www.nps.gov/aboutus/news/plan-like-a-park-ranger.htm.

Plan Your Visit (2024) Available at: https://www.nps.gov/planyourvisit/index.htm.

Recreate Responsibly (2024) Available at: https://www.nps.gov/planyourvisit/recreate-responsibly.htm.

Requesting Permission to Use the NPS Arrowhead (2022) Available at: www.nps.gov/subjects/partnerships/arrowhead-requests.htm.

Series: Disability History: an Overview (n.d.) Available at: https://www.nps.gov/articles/series.htm?id=88713887-1DD8-B71B-0B40487E6097176E.

Social Media (2022) Available at: https://www.nps.gov/subjects/digital/social-media.htm.

Sustainability in the National Park Service (2023) Available at: www.nps.gov/sustainability/index.htm.

Telling All Americans' Stories (2022) Available at: https://www.nps.gov/subjects/tellingallamericansstories/index.htm.

Ten Essentials (2024) Available at: www.nps.gov/articles/10essentials.htm.

The Antiquities Act of 1906 (2023) Available at: https://www.nps.gov/subjects/archeology/antiquities-act.htm.

The NPS App (2021) Available at: https://www.nps.gov/subjects/digital/nps-apps.htm.

Theme Studies (2022) Available at: https://www.nps.gov/subjects/nationalhistoriclandmarks/theme-studies.htm.

Transforming the NPS Digital Experience (2020) Available at: https://www.nps.gov/subjects/digital/index.htm.

Trip Planning Guide (2023) Available at: https://www.nps.gov/subjects/healthandsafety/trip-planning-guide.htm.

Unmanned Aircraft in the National Parks (2017) Available at: https://www.nps.gov/articles/unmanned-aircraft-in-the-national-parks.htm.

Urban Agenda (2019) Available at: https://www.nps.gov/subjects/urban/index.htm.

US Biosphere Network (2024) Available at: https://www.nps.gov/subjects/connectedconservation/us-biosphere-network.htm.

Visitation Numbers (2024) Available at: https://www.nps.gov/aboutus/visitation-numbers.htm.

Visitor Use Statistics (2024) Available at: https://irma.nps.gov/Stats/.

Volunteer with Us (2024) Available at: https://www.nps.gov/getinvolved/volunteer.htm.

Volunteer with Us – News & Stories (2024) Available at: https://www.nps.gov/subjects/volunteer/news.htm.

Volunteer with Us – Volunteer Events Calendar (2023) Available at: https://www.nps.gov/subjects/volunteer/vip-events.htm.

Volunteer with Us – Volunteer Programs (2023) Available at: https://www.nps.gov/subjects/volunteer/programs.htm.

Wilderness is for all (2023) Available at: https://www.nps.gov/subjects/wilderness/index.htm.

Additional Resources

Abbey, E. (1990) *Desert Solitaire: A Season in the Wilderness*. Simon & Schuster, New York.

Aldo Leopold Wilderness Research Institute (2024). Available at: https://leopold.wilderness.net/ (accessed 3 July 2024).

America's National Parks (n.d.) Passport to Your National Parks. Available at: https://americasnational-parks.org/passport-to-your-national-parks/ (accessed 5 July 2024).

Arthur Carhart National Wilderness Training Center (2024). Available at: https://carhart.wilderness.net/ (accessed 3 July 2024).

Bremer, T.S. (2021) The Religious and Spiritual Appeal of National Parks. *Sacred Wonderland*, August 29. Available at: https://www.sacredwonderland.us/religious-and-spiritual-appeal-of-national-parks/ (accessed 3 July 2024).

Bremer, T.S. (2023) In America, national parks are more than scenic – they're sacred. But they were created at a cost to Native Americans. *The Conversation*, November 20. Available at: https://the-conversation.com/in-america-national-parks-are-more-than-scenic-theyre-sacred-but-they-were-created-at-a-cost-to-native-americans-215344 (accessed 3 July 2024).

Brulliard, N. (2020) These 10 National Parks Wouldn't Exist Without Women. National Parks Conservation Association, March 1. Available at: https://www.npca.org/articles/1478-these-10-national-parks-wouldn-t-exist-without-women (accessed 14 July 2024).

Brundtland, G. (1987) *Our Common Future*. Report of the World Commission on Environment and Development. United Nations General Assembly document A/42/427. United Nations, New York. Available at: http://www.un-documents.net/ocf-ov.htm (accessed 11 July 2024).

Callaghan, A. (2024) What are Public Lands in the U.S.? Available at: https://www.publiclands.com/blog/a/public-lands-in-the-united-states (accessed 18 July 2024).

Center for Large Landscape Conservation (2022) US Biosphere Regions. Available at: https://largeland-scapes.org/biosphere-regions/ (accessed 5 July 2024).

Congressional Research Service (2013) National Park System: What Do the Different Park Titles Signify? Available at: http://npshistory.com/publications/r41816.pdf (accessed 28 June 2024).

Congressional Research Service (2022) *National Monuments and the Antiquities Act*. Library of Congress, Washington, DC.

Corn, J. (2016) Machines and ingenuity. In: Manning, R., Diamant, R., Mitchell, N. and Harmon, D. (eds) *A Thinking Person's Guide to America's National Parks*. Braziller Publishers, New York, pp. 149–162.

Costanza, R., de Groot, R., Sutton, P., van der Ploeg, S., Anderson, S.J. *et al*. (2014) Changes in the global value of ecosystem services. *Global Environmental Change* 26, 152–158.

Cronon, W. (1996) The trouble with wilderness: Or, getting back to the wrong nature. *Environmental History* 1(1), 7–28.

Dallas, K. (2021) The religious significance of America's national parks. *Deseret News*, September 21. Available at: https://www.deseret.com/faith/2021/9/21/22683320/state-faith-newsletter-us-national-parks-religious-significance-arches-bryce-canyon-rocky-mountain/ (accessed 3 July 2024).

Find Your Park (n.d.) Friends Groups. Available at: https://findyourpark.com/get-involved/friends-groups (accessed 16 July 2024).

Flyr, M. and Koontz, L. (2023) 2022 National Park Visitor Spending Effects: Economic Contributions to Local Communities, States, and the Nation. Natural Resource Report NPS/NRSS/EQD/NRR–2023/2551. Fort Collins, Colorado. Available at: https://www.nps.gov/nature/customcf/NPS_Data_Visualization/docs/NPS_2022_Visitor_Spending_Effects.pdf (accessed 3 July 2024).

Gonzalez, P. (2020) Human-caused climate change in United States national parks and solutions for the future. *Parks Stewardship Forum* 36(2), 188–210.

Google Arts & Culture (n.d.) The Hidden Worlds of the National Parks. Available at: https://artsandculture.google.com/project/national-park-service (accessed 9 July 2024).

Graber, D. (2016) Conserving biodiversity. In: Manning, R., Diamant, R., Mitchell, N. and Harmon, D. (eds) *A Thinking Person's Guide to America's National Parks*. Braziller Publishers, New York, pp. 69–81.

Hammitt, W.E., Cole, D.N. and Monz, C.A. (2015) *Wildland Recreation: Ecology and Management*, 3rd edn. Wiley Blackwell, Hoboken, New Jersey.

Hardin, G. (1968) The tragedy of the commons. *Science* 162(3859), 1243–1248.

Harmon, D. (2012) Beyond the 59th park: Reforming the nomenclature of the US National Park System. *The George Wright Forum* 29(2), 188–196.

Harmon, D., McManamon, F. and Pitcaithley, D. (2006) *The Antiquities Act: A Century of American Archaeology, Historic Preservation, and Nature Conservation*. University of Arizona Press, Tucson, Arizona.

Hudspeth, T., Camp, M., and Cirillo, J. (2016) Lifelong learning. In: Manning, R., Diamant, R., Mitchell, N., and Harmon, D. (eds) *A Thinking Person's Guide to America's National Parks*. Braziller Publishers, New York, pp. 57–68.

Interagency Visitor Use Management Council (2016) *Visitor Use Management Framework: A Guide to Providing Sustainable Outdoor Recreation*. US National Park Service, Denver, Colorado.

Latson, R. (2022) What's With All These Different Park Units, Anyway? *National Parks Traveler*, August 4. Available at: https://www.nationalparkstraveler.org/2022/08/whats-all-these-different-park-units-anyway (accessed 28 June 2024).

Leave No Trace (2024a). Available at: https://lnt.org/ (accessed 10 July 2024).

Leave No Trace (2024b) Training for All. Available at: https://lnt.org/get-involved/training-courses/ (accessed 10 July 2024).

Lee, R.F. (1970) The American Antiquities Act of 1906. National Park Service, Washington, DC. Available at: https://irma.nps.gov/DataStore/DownloadFile/675601 (accessed 18 July 2024).

Legacy, C. (2024) NPS Historic Preservation & Training Center. Available at: https://stewardslegacy.org/hptc (accessed 14 July 2024).

Leopold, A. (2020) *A Sand County Almanac*. Oxford University Press, New York.

Leung, Y., Spenceley, A., Hvenegaard, G. and Buckely, R. (2018) *Tourism and Visitor Management in Protected Areas: Guidelines for Sustainability*, Best Practice Protected Area Guidelines Series No. 27. International Union for Conservation of Nature (IUCN), Gland, Switzerland.

Linenthal, E. (2016) Civic engagement. In: Manning, R., Diamant, R., Mitchell, N. and Harmon, D. (eds) *A Thinking Person's Guide to America's National Parks*. Braziller Publishers, New York, pp. 127–136.

Lower, R. and Watson, R. (2023) How Many National Parks are There? National Park Foundation. Available at: https://www.nationalparks.org/connect/blog/how-many-national-parks-are-there (accessed 28 June 2024).

Manning, R. (2007) *Parks and Carrying Capacity: Commons Without Tragedy*. Island Press, Washington, DC.

Manning, R. (2016) How America's Best Idea Can Be Colleges' Best Opportunity. *The Chronicle of Higher Education*, April 13: https://www.chronicle.com/article/how-americas-best-idea-can-be-colleges-best-opportunity/2024June2

Manning, R. (2022) *America's National Heritage Areas: A Guide to the Nation's New Kind of National Park*. Globe Pequot Press, Guilford, Connecticut.

Manning, R. (2024) *A Guide to U.S. World Heritage Sites: The Heritage of Humanity*. Globe Pequot Press, Guilford, Connecticut.

Manning, R. and Manning, M. (2020) *Walks of a Lifetime in America's National Parks*. Falcon, Guilford, Connecticut.

Manning, R., Lawson, S., Newman, P., Hallo, J., Monz, C. *et al.* (2014) *Sustainable Transportation in the National Parks: From Acadia to Zion*. University Press of New England, Lebanon, New Hampshire.

Manning, R., Diamant, R., Mitchell, N. and Harmon, D. (eds). (2016a) *A Thinking Person's Guide to America's National Parks*. Braziller Publishers, New York, pp. 117–126.

Manning, R., Diamant, R., Mitchell, N. and Harmon, D. (2016b) A national park system for the 21st century. In: Manning, R., Diamant, R., Mitchell, N. and Harmon, D. (eds) *A Thinking Person's Guide to America's National Parks*. Braziller Publishers, New York, pp. 261–278.

Manning, R., Anderson, A. and Pettengill, P. (2017) *Managing Outdoor Recreation: Case Studies in the National Parks*, 2nd edn. CAB International, Boston, Massachusetts.

Manning, R., Newman, P., Barber, J., Monz, C., Hallo, J. *et al.* (2018) *Natural Quiet and Natural Darkness: the "New" Resources of the National Parks*. University Press of New England, Lebanon, New Hampshire.

Manning, R.E., Budruk, M., Goonan, K., Hallo, J., Laven, D., Lawson, S., McCown, R., Minteer, B., Newman, P., Perry, E., Pettengill, P., Reigner, N., Valliere, W., van Riper, C. and Xiao, X. (2022) *Studies in Outdoor Recreation: Search and Research for Satisfaction*, 4th edn. Oregon State University Press, Corvallis, Oregon.

Maounis, J. (2016) Treasures of the nation. In: Manning, R., Diamant, R., Mitchell, N. and Harmon, D. (eds) *A Thinking Person's Guide to America's National Parks*. Braziller Publishers, New York, pp. 175–184.

Miles, J. (2020) Essay: Revisiting mountains without handrails. *National Parks Traveler*, May 31. Available at: https://www.nationalparkstraveler.org/2020/05/essay-revisiting-mountains-without-handrails (accessed 16 July 2024).

Millennium Ecosystem Assessment (2005) *Ecosystems and Human Well-being: Synthesis*. Island Press, Washington, DC. Available at: https://www.millenniumassessment.org/documents/document.356.aspx.pdf (accessed 4 July 2024).

Minteer, B.A. and Manning, R.E. (2003) *Reconstructing Conservation: Finding Common Ground*. Island Press, Washington, DC.

Minteer, B. and Manning, R. (2016) Wilderness preserves. In: Manning, R., Diamant, R., Mitchell, N. and Harmon, D. (eds) *A Thinking Person's Guide to America's National Parks*. Braziller Publishers, New York, pp. 105–116.

Mitchell, N. (2016) Storied landscapes. In: Manning, R., Diamant, R., Mitchell, N. and Harmon, D. (eds) *A Thinking Person'sGuide to America's National Parks*. Braziller Publishers, New York, pp. 163–174.

Nash, R. (2001) *Wilderness and the American Mind*, 4th edn. Yale University Press, New Haven, Connecticut.

National Park Foundation (2024). Available at: www.nationalparks.org (accessed 16 July 2024).

National Park Service (2016) *The National Parks: Index 2012-2016*. National Park Service, Washington, DC. Available at: https://www.nps.gov/aboutus/upload/npindex2012-2016.pdf (accessed 18 July 2024).

Public Broadcasting Service (PBS) (2024) A film by Ken Burns *The National Parks: America's Best Idea*. Meet the People. Available at: https://www.pbs.org/kenburns/the-national-parks/meet-the-people (accessed 17 July 2024).

Recreate Responsibly (2022) To Recreate Responsibly is to care for one another and the places we play. Available at: www.recreateresponsibly.org/ (accessed 10 July 2024).

Repanshek, K. (2024) Traveler's View: Should International National Park Visitors Be Charged More? Available at: https://www.nationalparkstraveler.org/2024/01/travelers-view-should-international-national-park-visitors-be-charged-more (accessed 16 July 2024).

Reynolds, J. and Diamant, R. (2016) Practicing sustainability. In: Manning, R., Diamant, R., Mitchell, N. and Harmon, D. (eds) *A Thinking Person's Guide to America's National Parks*. Braziller Publishers, New York, pp. 241–250.

Sax, J. (1980) *Mountains Without Handrails: Reflections on the National Parks*. University of Michigan Press, Ann Arbor, Michigan.

Spence, M.D. (1999) *Dispossessing the Wilderness*. Oxford University Press, Oxford.

Stoneman Douglas, M. (1947) *The Everglades: River of Grass*. Pineapple Press, Sarasota, Florida.

Sutton, P.C., Duncan, S.L. and Anderson, S.J. (2019) Valuing our national parks: An ecological economics perspective. *Land* 8(4), 54.

The Wilderness Society (2024) The Wilderness Act. Available at: https://www.wilderness.org/articles/article/wilderness-act (accessed 3 July 2024).

Thompson, J. and Houseal, A. (2020) *America's Largest Classroom: What We Learn from Our National Parks*. University of California Press, Berkeley, California.

Tilden, F. (2008) *Interpreting Our Heritage*, 4th edn. University of North Carolina Press, Chapel Hill, North Carolina.

Treuer, D. (2021) Return the national parks to the tribes. *The Atlantic*, May.

Tweed, W. (2016) Dynamic nature. In: Manning, R., Diamant, R., Mitchell, N. and Harmon, D. (eds) *A Thinking Person's Guide to America's National Parks*. Braziller Publishers, New York, pp. 81–92.

UNESCO World Heritage Convention (2024) World Heritage List. United Nations Educational, Scientific and Cultural Organization (UNESCO). Available at: https://whc.unesco.org/en/list/ (accessed 5 July 2024).

United States Government (n.d.) Every Kid Outdoors. Available at: https://everykidoutdoors.gov/index.htm (accessed 10 July 2024).

United States Government (2019) National Park Service Organic Act. An Act to establish a National Park Service, and for other purposes. Public Law (United States) 64–235, H.R. 15522, 39 Statute 535, enacted August 25, 1916. Available at: https://www.govinfo.gov/content/pkg/COMPS-1725/pdf/COMPS-1725.pdf (accessed 18 July 2024).

US Department of the Interior (2005) NPS Organic Act. Available at: https://www.doi.gov/ocl/nps-organic-act (accessed 1 July 2024).

US Department of the Interior (2023) America's Public Lands Explained. Available at: https://www.doi.gov/blog/americas-public-lands-explained (accessed 1 July 2024).

USAJobs (2024) National Park Service Open Positions. Available at: https://www.usajobs.gov/Search?a=IN10 (accessed 17 July 2024).

USGS Store (n.d. a) Annual Pass. Available at: https://store.usgs.gov/pass (accessed 11 July 2024).

USGS Store (n.d. b) America the Beautiful National Parks & Federal Recreational Lands Passes. Available at: https://store.usgs.gov/recreational-passes (accessed 11 July 2024).

USGS Store (n.d. c) Military Pass. Available at: https://store.usgs.gov/MilitaryPass (accessed 11 July 2024).

Volunteer.gov (2024) Federal Volunteer Opportunities. Available at: https://www.volunteer.gov (accessed 16 July 2024).

Watkins, T. (2023) How overseas visitors can help steward our national parks. *PERC*, December 21. Available at: https://www.perc.org/2023/12/21/how-international-visitors-can-help-steward-our-national-parks/ (accessed 16 July 2024).

Watson, R. (2024) Take a virtual visit to a national park. *National Park Foundation*. Available at: www.nationalparks.org/connect/blog/take-virtual-visit-national-park (accessed 8 July 2024).

Weichec, N. and Muth, C. (n.d.) National parks: places of wonder, history, spiritual refuge. *National Catholic Reporter*. Available at: https://www.ncronline.org/blogs/eco-catholic/national-parks-places-wonder-history-culture-spiritual-refuge (accessed 3 July 2024).

Wikipedia (2024) List of the United States National Park System Official Units. Available at: https://en.wikipedia.org/wiki/List_of_the_United_States_National_Park_System_official_units (accessed 1 July 2024).

Wilderness Connect (n.d.) The Wilderness Act. An Act to establish a National Wilderness Preservation System for the permanent good of the whole people, and for other purposes. Public Law 88-577 (16 U.S.C. 1131-1136). 88th Congress, Second Session, September 3, 1964. Available at: https://wilderness.net/learn-about-wilderness/key-laws/wilderness-act/ (accessed 16 July 2024).

Workman, R.B. (2024) National Park Service Uniforms. Available at: http://npshistory.com/publications/nps-uniforms/index.htm (accessed 1 July 2024).

Photograph Attributions

_____

The following attributions relate to images used on the front and back covers of the book and in the Introduction. Attributions for the photographs used in the conversations are provided with the images.

Front cover
Yosemite National Park—Wikimedia Commons/King of Hearts
Statue of Liberty National Monument—Wikimedia Commons/William Warby

Back cover
Glacier Bay National Park and Preserve—National Park Service (NPS)
San Antonio Missions National Historical Park—Wikimedia Commons/Riis2602
Bryce Canyon National Park—Robert Manning

Introduction to the Book
World-famous Old Faithful Geyser erupts in Yellowstone National Park—NPS/Jacob W. Frank
Grand Canyon National Park—Tuxyso/Wikimedia Commons/CC BY-SA 3.0
Acadia National Park — NPS/Kent Miller
Monument at the Gettysburg National Military Park—NPS/Mary O'Neill
Alligator protects its nest in Everglades National Park—NPS/Lori Oberhofer
Golden Gate National Recreation Area—Wikimedia Commons/Carol M. Highsmith
Women's Right National Historical Park—NPS
Denali National Park and Preserve includes the highest peak in North America—NPS
Assembly Room of Independence Hall (part of Independence National Historical Park)—NPS

Index

www.ingramcontent.com/pod-product-compliance
Lightning Source LLC
Chambersburg PA
CBHW041427270326
41932CB00026B/3404